Co-op & Condo Ownership

The Complete Guide for Apartment Buyers, Owners and Boards

Preface By Donald M. Halperin

Introduction By Vicki Chesler and Matt Kovner

Edited By Vicki Chesler

from the publishers of

The New York
COOPERATOR
The Co-Op and Condo Monthly

Published by The New York Cooperator
301 East 45th Street, Suite 5C
New York, New York 10017
(212) 697-1318 Fax: (212) 682-7369

This publication is designed to provide accurate and authoritative information in regard to the subject matter covered. It is sold with the understanding that the publisher is not engaged in rendering legal, accounting or other professional services. If legal advice or other expert assistance is required, the services of a competent professional person should be sought.

First Edition, Second Printing
Printed in Canada
Library of Congress Catalog Card Number: 95-69416
ISBN: 0-9646542-0-2

To Matt, whose support and encouragement keep me going. To Melissa and Kelsey, who bring joy and meaning to my life. To my sister, Lynn, who has always looked out for me. To my mother, whom I couldn't live without. And to the memory of my father, whose obsession with the English language probably led me to where I am today.

Vicki Chesler

To my mother, without whom there would be no words, and to Vicki, Melissa and Kelsey, without whom words would have no meaning.

Matt Kovner

A C K N O W L E D G M E N T S

There are a number of people whose hard work and dedication made this book possible, people who deserve to be recognized for their contribution to this ambitious project. First, for her tireless efforts—at all hours—I would like to thank Carol Hanisch, who put together the manuscript, from the original articles that appeared in *The New York Cooperator* to their final design as a book. Next I would like to thank Pat Sims, whose discerning eye caught every typographical and grammatical error and kept our content consistent.

I would also like to thank David Goldbeck and Kate Norment for their invaluable advice, and Genell Subak-Sharpe, who brought me into the publishing world in the first place and whose advice and encouragement have continued to inspire me to undertake ever more ambitious endeavors in my chosen field.

Of course, without the skillful writing of our authors, the book would not have been possible, and I thank them—all 55 of them—for sharing their expertise and writing abilities with our readers. Thanks are also due to those who took the time to read the manuscript prior to publication and share with us their valuable insights: Mary Ann Rothman of the Council of New York Cooperatives and Charlie Rappaport of the Federation of New York Housing Cooperatives along with many others.

I must also thank my entire family—both Cheslers and Kovners—for putting up with the long hours, extra time and mood swings involved in the preparation of this book.

Finally, I would like to thank the entire staff of *The New York Cooperator*, both past and present, for all the hard work they have put in over the years to bring straightforward, timely and practical information about co-op and condo ownership to our readers, and for their contribution in making *The New York Cooperator* a growing, successful company.

Vicki Chesler
Executive Editor

C O N T E N T S

Preface

Introduction

Chapter 1: How Co-ops and Condos Work
1 Apartment Ownership: What Does It Mean?

Chapter 2: Buying and Selling An Apartment
9 Look Before You Leap: How to Evaluate an Apartment
13 Do Your Research First: Preparation Can Help Your Purchase
16 From Patios to Pools: Putting a Dollar Value on Amenities
20 Do's & Don'ts for Sellers: Enhance the Saleability of Your Home
22 Tribulations of Selling: It Ain't Over 'Til It's Over

Chapter 3: Board Operations
25 What Board Members Do: Defining Roles Makes the Job Easier
28 The Voting Process: Holding Successful Board Elections
31 Electing Board Members: Good Candidates Are Needed
33 Board Power: Crossing the Line Between Director and Despot
36 Successful Board Meetings: Planning and Delegation Are Key
39 Board Member Psyche 101: Improving Communications

Chapter 4: Successful Building Management
43 Matchmaking in Management: Finding Your Dream Firm
45 Choosing a Managing Agent: Know What to Ask
48 From RAM to CPM: Who Certifies Building Managers?
50 Self-Management: A Hard-Working Board Has Much to Gain
53 Protect Your Building: Bribery and Kickbacks Can Be Avoided

Chapter 5: Your Building's Financial Health

57 Understanding Corporate Finance: Run Your Building Efficiently
59 Understanding Cooperative Finances: A Review of the Basics
62 Reading Financial Reports: Boards Must Know How
65 Budget Plans and Projections: Look at the Bottom Line
67 Co-op Income: Maintenance and Late Fees
70 Budget and Reserve Planning: Anticipate Spending
72 Preserve the Reserve: Investments That Work
78 Is Your Building Fiscally Fit? Detecting Early Warning Signs
80 Consider a Credit Line: Ready Money at Lower Cost
82 CIRA Guidelines: Long-Term Financial Audits
84 Responding to CIRA: Should Buildings File or Not?

Chapter 6: Underlying Co-op Mortgages

87 Building Refinancing: Restructure Mortgages With Care
88 Underlying Mortgages: A Practical Guide to Refinancing
92 Long-Term Financing: Lock in Rates, Budget in Costs
93 A Risk Worth Taking: Floating Rates Can Mean Big Savings
95 If You're Refinancing, Be Sure the Building's in Top Shape
97 Removing Obstacles to Financing: The Banking Industry Eases Up
100 Finding Willing Lenders: Boards Can Help Shareholders Sell

Chapter 7: Keeping Your Building in Top Shape

103 Annual Maintenance: Assume the Worst and Be Prepared
105 Checklists: A Preventive Maintenance System That Really Works
108 Servicing Equipment: What Should Contracts Cover?
111 Maintaining Your Boiler: Water Treatment Stops Corrosion
113 Off-Season Overhaul: Get the Heating System in Order
116 Heat System Upgrade: Proper Maintenance Reduces Fuel Costs
118 Spring Cleaning Time: Do Heating System Maintenance Now
119 Reduce Your Fuel Usage: Heat Computers Offer Sure Savings
122 Keep Cool: Maintain and Update Your Air-Conditioning System
123 Elevator Maintenance: The Importance of Ironclad Contracts
125 Raise the Comfort Level: Make Sure Windows Are Up to Par
127 Water Costs on the Rise: Meters Lead to Conservation Efforts

Chapter 8: Major Contracting Projects

131 Avoid Construction Chaos: Establish and Follow Standard Procedures
133 Capital Improvements: Trust the Pro's to Do It Right
135 Professional Advice: Need an Architect or Engineer?
138 Solving Contract Disputes: Put It in Writing at the Outset
139 Alternative Funding Sources: Financing Capital Improvements

Chapter 9: Facing Sponsor Default

143 A Growing Problem: The State of Sponsor Default
146 A New Trend: Co-ops Declare Bankruptcy to Prevent Foreclosure
149 Keeping an Eye on Sponsors: The Law Mandates Disclosure
151 White Knight to the Rescue: Investor Plays Hero to Co-op in Distress

Chapter 10: Law and Governance

155 Shareholders' Rights: How Far Can House Rules Go?
158 Effective Rule-Making: Do It Right to Avoid Lawsuits
162 Not Written in Stone: Changing Governing Documents
164 Examining Books and Records: When Do Owners Have the Right?
168 Gaining Legal Entry: Co-op Owners Must Allow Board In
169 "Owning" Outdoor Space: Board Control of Terraces and Roofs
172 Fundamentals of Subletting: A Reasonable Policy Gets Best Results
175 Mediation Alternative: "Wave of the Future" for Avoiding Lawsuits
178 Keeping Co-ops and Condos Healthy: A Legislative Agenda
181 New York's New Lead Law: Defining and Treating the Hazards

Chapter 11: Taxation Issues

187 A Deluge of Taxes for Owners: Take Action to Reduce Burden
190 Stop Your Taxes From Going Up: Class II Owners Must Act Now
191 Real Estate Tax Reform: Moving in the Right Direction
195 Reduce Your Tax Bite: Challenge Assessments Annually
198 Save on Estate Taxes: Set Up a Personal Residence Trust

Chapter 12: Building-Wide Insurance

201 Buying Insurance: How Much Is Right for Your Building?
203 Comparative Shopping: Reduce Premiums and Increase Coverage
206 Avoid Insurance Lawsuits: Hold Adequate Personal Coverage
208 Directors' and Officers' Insurance: Be Sure Your Co-op Carries It
210 Insure Against Pollutants: Toxic Contamination Is a Building Risk

Appendices

213 Appendix A : About the Authors
219 Appendix B: Glossary of Terms
225 Appendix C: Industry Resources and Reference Guide

Index 235

P R E F A C E

Over the course of twenty-four years, during which I was a public official, I saw a fascinating socioeconomic change take place. A new form of housing proliferated: cooperative and condominium ownership.

From three different vantage points in my career—as a state senator, as an attorney and as New York State's housing director—I have seen the mix of home owners, renters and co-op and condo owners change drastically. Traditionally, New York had been a town divided, where with few exceptions, you were either well off enough to afford a single-family home, or you rented an apartment.

I remember a speech I gave as a state senator, in the early 1980s, which discussed the fact that New York City had the highest percentage of rental units of any major metropolitan center in the United States. Converting to co-op and condo ownership has changed that mix, I think, for the better. The main reason is choice. Thousands upon thousands of New Yorkers have a choice where none existed before.

I believe that New York benefits from having as many different forms of home ownership as possible. Apartment ownership has been good for this city and this state. The wave of converting rental property to individual co-op and condo apartments that began in New York has now swept across the country, reaching all the way to the West Coast.

As a state senator, I was involved in numerous co-op conversions in my district, mostly from the viewpoint of the tenants and prospective buyers. I saw offering plans that were fair to the tenants and the prospective purchasers, and those that were not. Constituents came into my office wondering what to do about the conversion of their buildings: Was it a good idea to buy? Would they be allowed to stay on as renters? If they negotiated with the sponsor could they get a better deal? My staff and I helped constituents with these issues and more. I am proud that we were able to offer assistance to many who were making the most important decisions of their adult lives.

In the mid-eighties, I gained another viewpoint on the issue when I joined a law firm that prepared hundreds of co-op and condo plans. I was then able to observe the process from the perspective of the sponsor.

For several reasons, housing in New York is expensive. In the past, many families were priced out of the market, unable to save enough for a down payment on a home and unable to break free from a lifetime of renting. With the conversion of rental property to co-ops and condos, more and more New York families could buy a piece of the American Dream of owning their own home. First-time real estate buyers now also had the opportunity to obtain a substantial asset that could be passed on to their children. While it is essential to maintain renting as an available option in New York, it is also important to have ownership alternatives. Co-op and condo ownership brings with it a greater sense of community, of responsibility to neighbors and of permanence. This all adds up to a healthier New York.

While home ownership may be healthy for our sense of community, it may not always be such a happy state for the owners. In fact, new co-op and condo owners found out that there was an enormous amount of work and many things to learn as home owners. As New York State director of housing, I observed how first-time owners had to learn to manage their own real estate affairs. Many sat back in their chairs after working on their building budgets and thought about their former landlords with a new level of respect. Had he or she really balanced all of these expenses, from real estate taxes to oil deliveries to building maintenance? Maybe the landlord hadn't been such a "bad guy" after all.

For those looking to navigate the unknown seas of co-op and condo ownership, *The New York Cooperator* offers this handy compass. *Co-op & Condo Ownership: The Complete Guide for Apartment Buyers, Owners and Boards* is a useful reference tool for those who are considering buying a co-op or condo, and an invaluable guide for current owners feeling their way through the maze of information that relates to apartment ownership.

I applaud the publishers of *The New York Cooperator* for again offering a valuable service to New Yorkers. For over fifteen years, they have provided their magazine free of charge to co-op and condo owners. With the publication of this important guide, *The New York Cooperator* has firmly secured its place as a leading source of information and guidance to thousands of New Yorkers. I know there will be many grateful current and prospective cooperators who benefit from this publication.

Donald M. Halperin
Former New York State director of housing and former commissioner
of the New York State Division of Housing and Community Renewal

INTRODUCTION

What you hold in your hands is the culmination of years of work. We founded *The New York Cooperator* in 1980 and our first issue rolled off the presses in 1981. But it has been at least six years since we first began to discuss publishing a book about cooperative and condominium ownership. We had an excellent body of information and hundreds of requests. The only thing holding us back was time.

Even once we made the decision to go ahead with the book, it took months of preparation before we actually started to roll with production. We started by looking back over the last few years of *The Cooperator* and compiling all the articles we had run. Next, we read them all and picked out the best ones—from 1992 to 1994—that would comprehensively cover all the topics we felt were of central importance to anyone considering buying an apartment or already living in one.

Because we founded *The Cooperator* at the very beginning of the co-op boom in New York, we remember well how little most people knew about apartment ownership at the time. Even today, while the words "co-op" and "condo" have become commonplace, and nearly everyone knows basically what these entities are, many people find that once they have immersed themselves in the co-op and condo market, there is an awful lot to learn.

Whether you are a first-time buyer, a new owner or a veteran board member, you will find this book to be an invaluable reference tool that you will refer to over and over again. Be it during the buying process or in the midst of a heated board meeting, you will find the answers to your questions in these pages.

We look forward to bringing more books to the public in the future, to update and enhance the information herein. And we welcome the response of our readers whose needs we continue to strive to meet, through our monthly magazine, *The New York Cooperator;* our annual trade show and educational event, the Co-op & Condo Expo; our ongoing seminars and educational programs; and now, our books.

We thank you for purchasing this book, and congratulate you on your efforts to learn as much as you can about this venture you have embarked upon: navigating the waters of co-op and condo ownership. We hope we have provided a guide to help you find patches of blue sky and smooth sailing.

Vicki Chesler and Matt Kovner
Editor and Publisher of The New York Cooperator

How Co-ops and Condos Work

• *A brief history of co-ops and condos*
• *How co-ops and condos operate*
• *Differences between co-ops and condos*

Apartment Ownership: What Does It Mean?

By Vicki Chesler

Ever since single-family homes became affordable to the middle class in the wake of World War II, home ownership has been part of the American Dream. Nevertheless, it took another few decades for the concept of home ownership to take root in some of our nation's cities, especially in New York where apartment houses are the predominant form of housing, and renting was always the norm. Although a small number of cooperative housing ventures existed as far back as the 1800s, apartment ownership did not become mainstream in New York City until the 1980s. In the nation at large, condominium ownership was not even introduced until the 1960s, and that, too, caught on in a big way in the '80s.

Since that time, more and more Americans have joined the ranks of apartment owners, from Florida's Gulf Coast to Manhattan's Upper West Side. But although this type of ownership allows individuals to share the maintenance duties—and in some cases abdicate them entirely to professional managers—it also obligates each owner to see to it that his investment is properly maintained. Because in any communal living situation, each resident's actions can have an impact on everyone else in the community. If one shareholder in a ten-unit co-op fails to pay his or her maintenance, the corporation loses 10 percent of its income, and that money is needed to pay vendors, taxes, maintenance and other expenses.

With the introduction of co-op and condo ownership into our cities and suburbs, Americans were offered, for the first time, the opportunity to own their homes while still opting for apartment or garden complex living. Instead of spending thousands of dollars a year (or even a month, in some of New York's toniest locations) on rent, with no equity to show for it, apartment owners could buy into their buildings, making their monthly payments count as a permanent investment. Since everyone has to live somewhere, there is no better way to build personal (and family) wealth than to put that monthly living expense into real estate ownership. And with the risk of "losing the lease" no longer a concern, apartment owners could invest in their living spaces, taking down walls, combining apartments, installing permanent fixtures and built-in furniture without the risk of losing their investment when the time came to move on.

In the 1980s, New Yorkers couldn't buy apartments fast enough. Insider prices gave many renters the chance to buy their units at well below market value. Conversion sponsors and real estate speculators made a fortune in sales and apartment "flips," and many individual buyers made enormous profits by buying as insiders and selling to outsiders as apartment values rose. After the Gold Rush died down and following the stock market crash of 1987 and the subsequent recession, apartment values dropped considerably from the inflated prices of the market boom. Today, those living in the New York metropolitan area can buy a two-bedroom co-op with balcony, swimming pool and parking in Fort Lee, New Jersey, for $65,000. Or a one-bedroom on a high floor with marble bath in a prime Manhattan neighborhood for under $200,000. Such prices were unheard of during the 1980s when studios were selling for $250,000. Today's market offers the buyer looking for a place to live many reasonable choices. And as a long-term investment, a co-op or condo in a nice building in a good location will withstand the test of time.

In addition to being a good investment, co-op and condo ownership offers buyers the opportunity to share the responsibilities of running the property with a community of owners. In a high-rise, these responsibilities include everything from collecting maintenance fees to making sure the elevators are running and the boiler is operating efficiently. In a garden complex, these duties include everything from mowing the lawn to pruning the trees to repaving the driveway and maintaining the roofs. With a whole building full of people pitching in, financially if not physically, the job becomes less of a burden, and owners have more free time to pursue other activities, whether they are climbing the corporate ladder or rock-climbing at their weekend homes.

The more you, as an apartment buyer, know about the operations of your building, the better off you will be, and the better off the building as a whole will be. And the more you know, the better equipped you will be to join the board and take an active role in maintaining the quality of life and the efficient operation of your building.

Across the nation, condominiums have become the predominant form of apartment ownership, but in New York co-ops have historically been more prevalent. This could change with time, however, since nearly all new residential apartment units for sale in New York City are condos. Cooperatives and condominiums are set up essentially the same way throughout the country, although specific laws and regulations may vary from state to state. Thus, the state regulations referred to in this book are those enacted in New York State. If you live in another state, check with your attorney to see what, if any, variations exist.

The Cooperative Corporation

Cooperative housing is a unique form of ownership with a set of legal regulations all its own. From taxation to financing to individual rights of ownership, the rules that govern co-ops are different from those governing other types of real estate ownership.

The fundamental difference between owning a co-op and owning a house or a condo is that co-op owners do not actually own their apartments. What they own are shares of stock in the corporation that owns the building in which the apartment is situated. The corporation, in turn, leases each shareholder an apartment. The number of shares owned corresponds to the size and relative merits (height of floor, terrace rights, views and so on) of the unit leased. Likewise, the voting power of each shareholder corresponds to the number of shares he or she owns.

A cooperative housing corporation functions in much the same way as a business corporation: Management and financial decisions are made by an elected board of directors; financial statements are distributed annually to all shareholders; a shareholders' meeting is held each year to disseminate information and to hold board elections. Co-op corporations are even governed by the same law as business corporations: the state Business Corporation Law, which holds co-op directors to the same standards as corporate boards throughout the state.

There are, of course, some very significant differences between the operations within a housing co-op and those of a business organization. The most obvious difference is the fact that the shareholders and the board all live in the building. Not only do they all have a vested interest in the building as an investment, but they also have a personal interest in it as a residence that reflects and provides a certain quality of life. Add to this the fact that each shareholder is part landlord (a co-owner of the building) and part tenant (leasing from the corporation), and it is clear that the board-shareholder relationship can sometimes get quite complicated.

Governing Documents

The rights and responsibilities of the board and the shareholders are outlined in several important documents: the Business Corporation Law, as mentioned above; the original offering plan and amendments of the co-op, legally referred to as the prospectus; the building's by-laws, which govern the rights of shareholders vis-à-vis the corporation; the proprietary lease that goes along with each unit, which governs the rights of each shareholder as a tenant, and the house rules. Co-op residents should be familiar with all of these documents, and should know what each one says. They should also know whether it is possible to amend them, and if so, how to do so.

The Business Corporation Law is the realm of state lawmakers. Amendments to that law, as to any law, must be made by elected officials. The prospectus, which must be filed with the state's attorney general before any shares can be sold, may be amended numerous times throughout the conversion process and beyond. Once the closing is complete, the sponsor (or other holders of unsold shares) is required to amend the prospectus annually regarding the current financial status of the sponsor and the building. The amendment information as well as all other material changes and each secondary offering of shares by the sponsor must be forwarded to each shareholder as well. The by-laws of the building can be amended by a two-thirds majority vote of all shareholders, in most cases, and the house rules can be changed by a simple majority vote of the board of directors. It is possible, however, for the shareholders to curtail the board's power to enact house rules without shareholder approval. This can be done by amending the by-laws to state that shareholder approval is required to enact or amend house rules.

The proprietary lease can be amended by shareholders only, at the annual shareholders' meeting, at a special meeting called for that purpose (a petition by holders of 25 percent of the shares is required to call such a meeting) or by the solicitation of proxies without a meeting. In any case, advance notice of a proposed amendment vote is required. Changing the proprietary lease usually requires a two-thirds majority of voting shares, although some buildings may require as much as a three-quarters majority. Note that the percentage requirement to pass a vote is based on actual *shares* voted, not share*holders*. This demonstrates how some shareholders have more voting power than others. For example, the owner of the three-bedroom penthouse unit may have twice the number of shares as the owner of the ground floor one-bedroom. Ms. Penthouse's vote thus carries twice the impact of Mr. One-Bedroom's vote.

Board Elections

The co-op board is nearly always made up of an odd number of people, usually between five and nine, to avoid deadlock votes. Board terms generally last from one to three years, depending on the building's by-laws, and are often staggered to avoid a complete changeover of the board in any one year. Board elections are held at the annual shareholders' meeting, which usually takes place in the spring. However, if the shareholders perceive a problem with the board, they can call a special meeting by petition of holders of 25 percent of the shares to discuss holding interim elections. (For more on board operations, see Chapter 3.)

Taxation

When it comes to taxation, co-ops are considered to be unique by the Internal Revenue Service. Most co-op buildings have an underlying mortgage that is paid monthly as part of each shareholder's maintenance fee. Each shareholder may deduct the interest portion of his share of the mortgage payment, just as a single-family homeowner does. However, IRS Code Section 216 stipulates that, if more than 20 percent of the co-op corporation's income in any given year comes from sources other than shareholders, every shareholder in the corporation will lose his homeowner's status for that tax year. This provision is known as the 80/20 rule, and co-op boards must be careful to avoid falling into this predicament.

For example, if a one hundred–unit building collects $500 per month from each unit, for a total of $600,000 in shareholder income per year, and has a commercial tenant in the building that pays $7,000 per month, for a total of $84,000, then the total annual income for the corporation would be $684,000. "Outside" income in this co-op represents 12.28 percent of the total annual income, so the shareholders' tax deductions are safe. If the commercial rent went up to $13,000 per month, or $156,000 per year, outside income would represent 20.63 percent of the corporation's total income of $756,000 for the year—causing every shareholder to lose his or her mortgage-interest and real estate tax deductions for that year.

There are other significant differences between the way co-ops are taxed and the way other forms of residential real estate are taxed. The building's real estate taxes are divided up among shareholders and are included in the monthly maintenance fee. In New York City, co-op buildings have been taxed at a higher rate than single-family homes, and efforts are being made to reform the real estate tax system to make it more equitable. Other tax issues are also being challenged, including the IRS's right to tax the income generated by a co-op's reserve fund investments. (For more on taxes, see Chapter 11.)

Financing

A mortgage on a co-op unit is somewhat different from a mortgage for a condo or single-family home. In the latter, the real estate becomes collateral for the loan, allowing the bank to foreclose and repossess the property in the event of a default. In the case of a co-op apartment, the bank can end up holding corporate shares, not real property, if the buyer defaults. In addition, the co-op board has lien priority over the bank in that the co-op corporation can claim the shares, terminate the lease and evict the defaulting tenant. The co-op can then sell the unit and use the proceeds to pay off any unpaid maintenance charges as well as legal fees incurred in the foreclosure. Any money left over goes to the bank. Thus, co-op loans are considered by banks to be riskier than single-family home and condo mortgages, and accordingly, they come with higher interest rates. Nevertheless, many banks are eager to make co-op loans, and they are not particularly difficult to obtain. (For more on mortgages, see Chapter 6.)

Co-op and Condo Management

Another major difference between a housing corporation and a business corporation is that in a business, the board of directors is usually paid, sometimes rather handsomely. In a co-op, however, board members are volunteers—building residents who are willing to put in the time and energy to attend meetings, make decisions, do research and make numerous telephone calls, all in the name of "the common good."

Because boards of both co-ops and condos are made up of volunteers, most of whom have full-time jobs and other time demands outside the building, it is common practice for boards to hire professional management firms to help with the day-to-day operations and oversee the building's finances. While many small buildings are able to do all of these things themselves, and even some very large buildings have been successful at self-management, the vast majority of both co-op and condo buildings hire managing agents.

Management contracts, which usually run between one and three years, generally cover all back-office operations—from monthly billing and maintenance collection to daily bank deposits and bill-paying—as well as management of building staff, handling of sublets, maintenance of building systems and attendance of board meetings. The management firm may handle other situations as well, as they arise, such as refinancing and major capital improvement projects. A good managing agent can make life much easier for the board and all the building's residents. Likewise, an agent that does not live up to the board's expectations can cause countless hours of extra work for board members, and can cost the building large sums of money in late fees, fines and unnecessarily high contracting costs.

Condominium Ownership

The main difference between a cooperative and a condominium is that a condo owner actually buys a piece of real estate—an apartment—not shares in a corporation. The common space and fixtures of the building are jointly owned by the unit owners according to the size and value of their apartments as each owner's "common interest allocation." Because the total value of the building is divided up among the unit owners, there is no underlying mortgage on the building, and the building cannot be used as collateral on a capital improvement loan or any other type of financing, without approval of 100 percent of the unit owners.

Each owner may take out a mortgage to buy an individual unit, however, and his or her mortgage interest is fully tax deductible. Each unit owner receives his own real estate tax bills and pays them personally. Thus, the monthly maintenance fee in a condo is considerably lower than in a co-op, because the taxes are paid separately by the owner, and there is no building mortgage to be paid off. At the same time, the purchase price of a condo is generally higher than that of a comparable co-op, for basically the same reason. Taking all things into account, the ownership costs are approximately the same.

While condos are also run by elected boards, the board of a condo has less absolute power than that of a co-op. While a co-op board can refuse to allow a resident to sell his or her unit to a particular buyer "for any reason or no reason," as long as their decision is not based on illegal discrimination, a condo board has only one recourse if it does not like a buyer: the "right of first refusal." In the event that the board wants to deny a unit owner the right to sell to a particular buyer, it can do so only if the condo intends to buy the unit itself. Since it is rare for a condo to exercise its right of first refusal, most buyers have no problem making a condo purchase, since there is no actual "board approval" process.

In addition, condo boards have less control over who sublets their apartments than do co-op boards. While subletting can be completely banned in a co-op, or very strict rules applied, it is generally allowed with a small bit of paperwork required and perhaps a small administrative fee in a condo building. Most condos will also allow units to be used for commercial purposes, such as professional offices.

Condos and co-ops have similar governing documents, although the board of a condo is not subject to the rules of the Business Corporation Law, since the entity is not a corporation. Instead, condominiums were established as a legal form of real estate ownership in 1961 by federal law. Since then, all fifty states have enacted their own regulations to govern condo operations. Other than that, the rules regarding the governing documents—the prospectus, the by-laws and the house rules—are the same in a condo as in a co-op.

One important distinction is that in the event of a foreclosure in a condo, the bank has lien priority, meaning that it gets first dibs on the proceeds of the apartment sale. After paying off the balance due on the mortgage, any leftover money goes to the condo. If there is a rental tenant in the unit during the pendency of the foreclosure (which can take years), the condo can apply to the courts for receivership, which, if approved by the judge, would allow them to collect the rent directly from the tenant and use the money to offset past due or current common charges.

Understanding the workings of your building will allow you to make the best possible apartment purchase, the best sale when the time comes and to be an active and knowledgeable member of your building community. It will also help you avoid conflicts within the building and help prevent the building and its residents from becoming embroiled in unnecessary legal entanglements, a worthwhile consideration in today's litigious society.

Buying and Selling An Apartment

- *Identifying a good buy*
- *Putting value on amenities*
- *Selling your apartment*

Look Before You Leap: How to Evaluate an Apartment

By Ed Serken

If you've been apartment shopping, you may think you know everything there is to know about the unit you've got your eye on. The price is right, the space is in excellent shape and there's room to spare. Generally, you get a good feeling every time you step through the door. But hold on before signing that contract; a good feeling is not enough. There are a number of factors you should consider before committing yourself to the purchase of a co-op or condo. Buying an apartment is not the same as buying a home. An apartment is more than just a place to live; it is part of a community. Everything is integrated in a co-op or condo, from the building's finances to its physical condition. Thus, the more you know about both, as well as the type of people who inhabit the building, the better off you'll be when it comes to making the right decision on which apartment to buy.

Ask the Right Questions

"The only way to begin the process of looking for a co-op or condo is to ask the right questions," says Chris Thomas, vice-president of the Brooklyn offices of William B. May, a real estate brokerage firm. "When you have the answers, you can home in on any trouble spots." Before you allow yourself to fall in love with the views or the prewar details, take a look at the basics.

"If the apartment has a higher asking price than others in the same line, find out why," says Marilyn Harra Kaye, president of The Prudential LBKaye International Realty. "It may have a brand new kitchen or a fantastic view." Find out if any major renovations are planned, look over the building's current financial statement, meet building residents and find out how they like living there.

"If you are concerned about resale value, take a hard look at the building's location, finances and services," advises Joyce West, executive vice-president and director of

Greenthal Residential Sales.

When Stephanie Kovner, a first-time buyer, started looking at apartments, she gradually got a feel for the market and what questions she should ask. Although she didn't meet with any sellers, she did see a lot of listing agents to whom she addressed her inquiries. "I would ask them what they knew about the building in terms of stability," she explains. "Were they selling a lot of apartments in the building? What about renovations? Anything coming up or planned for the future? I wanted to know the philosophy of the building on a number of different things, including assessments and maintenance charges."

Once she had narrowed it down to one favorite, she began to delve deeper. "The listing agent provided me with all the information I needed, like the financial statements and prospectus for the building. He was very helpful," says Kovner. In addition, the managing agent was prompt in answering all her questions and gave detailed information on the stability of the building.

It was an altogether different story for a woman researching an East 70s co-op. "The broker I was dealing with wasn't forthcoming and I found out that there were a number of things he wasn't telling me," she explains. For example, one of the things she was concerned about was noise pollution and construction going on in the neighborhood. When she asked the broker, he assured her there was none, but she discovered otherwise when she hired Bold Property Information Systems to do a property risk report for her on the building. Bold, a five-year-old company that works with banks, attorneys and prospective buyers in researching all aspects of a building, can help buyers do their research.

When Gail Fernandez was looking to buy, she had to contend with a listing agent who didn't seem to care if she bought or not. "The agent wasn't very helpful at all," she says. "He wasn't very encouraging in his description of the place over the phone. I almost didn't go look at the apartment and when I did, he didn't have a floorplan for me. He didn't answer any of my questions. He didn't even seem to care if I liked the apartment or not." In a case like this, buyers need to reach out to other sources for the information they need.

Ferreting Out Financials

Reading over the financial statements is vital to discovering the building's financial stability. According to Jody LaMonte, a residential broker and vice-president with The Corcoran Group, "Looking over the statements for the past three years will give the buyer an idea how monies are being spent for the building, the status of the reserve fund, the salary of the building's employees and any ongoing maintenance expenses." In a co-op, she adds, "It will also tell you about the underlying mortgage: when it's due, what the rate is and the amount." If you're not sure that the information you're getting is correct, there are ways to check the building's underlying mortgage on your own. Your local business library has on microfiche every recorded mortgage. By going there and telling the front desk what address you're interested in, you can locate the REDI reference books or microfiche (published by TRW/REDI Property Data) that contains the real estate data you need.

It is very important to look at the percentage of sponsor-owned units in a co-op building. Erich Gonchar, an attorney with Hall, Dickler, Kent, Kent, Friedman and Wood, cautions, "Lenders generally will not provide a loan to purchasers if there are numerous sponsor-owned apartments. The reason behind this is that many sponsors who owned apartments have defaulted on payment in their maintenance expenses, causing these additional expenses to be passed on to the shareholders in the building." Ask the managing agent to provide this information.

The financial statement will also show any arrearages, indicating whether there are any "bad seed" shareholders who are routinely behind on their maintenance payments, says Joyce West. And ask your broker to find out if there have been any foreclosures in the building, she suggests. "If a bank forecloses on a co-op unit, they will sell it off at a below-market price just to cover the outstanding mortgage," West points out, a practice that can bring prices down throughout the building.

When looking at the maintenance charges, find out if there are any tax abatements in place and when they expire. An expiring J-51 tax abatement, for example, can mean a significant increase in maintenance.

"It doesn't mean buyers should shy away, but they should make an offer that reflects the fact that the exemptions will be over soon," says Chris Thomas. Find out through the seller or managing agent what the building's general policy toward assessments is, he advises. "Most sellers will be aware of assessments and will have to come clean if asked directly. Your attorney could also work language into the purchasing agreement that states there will be no assessments within twelve months of the sale," he adds.

Also be sure to investigate the state of the reserve fund. Stephen Beer, a certified public accountant with Czarnowski & Beer, says, "You might think a high reserve fund is enough, say $100,000 in reserve. If there have been electrical and other maintenance upgrades in recent years, then yes, it might be enough. If that type of work has not been done, however, the board might have special assessments coming up, borrow against the building to pay for them and then raise the maintenance to cover it."

Thomas suggests that buyers ask the seller straight out if there are any forms of pending litigation against the building or its units. "It's difficult to research this part if no judgments were rendered, but cover yourself by asking the seller and make it a condition of sale that nothing is pending," says Thomas.

Give the Building a Physical

Another way to do some research is to ask to see the prospectus. Within this important document you'll find the engineer's report, which many brokers agree is very helpful in determining the physical condition of the building. The engineer's report is usually based on a thorough examination of all maintenance aspects of the building, from boiler to windows. The owner of the co-op should have one, but even if he doesn't, it should be on file with the attorney general's office, and can be obtained through your broker.

Dennis Greenstein, a partner with the law firm of Haas, Greenstein, Cohen,

Gerstein & Starr, P.C., emphasizes the importance of reviewing the minutes of several board meetings. "They can tell you a lot: Are there going to be any renovations done soon? Are there any problems with the building now? All of this can be revealed in the way the board meets and talks. Are they saying that physical problems are being resolved or do they keep coming up? You want to know this." Anita Perrone, vice-president and director of advertising for The Corcoran Group, agrees: "If anything's coming up, like multimillion dollar renovations, it'll be in the board's minutes."

Check Out the Neighborhood

"Buyers should be sure to see enough apartments in the area they're interested in so they can make their own judgment as to value," says Marilyn Harra Kaye. "Their broker should educate them, but they should also educate themselves by reading the paper and shopping around." Kaye says that thirty to forty apartments is not that much to see if you are looking for a three-room apartment.

Loss of light and major alterations to the area surrounding the property are also considerations affecting an apartment's value. "Many buyers are interested in finding out if anything is going up next to the building they're looking at," says J. Henry Haggerty, former director of operations for Bold. "They can lose a lot of light if a bigger building goes up across from theirs. That's why we keep track of empty lots and any construction going on." Bold's researchers travel to over one hundred city, state and federal agencies, such as the New York City Department of Buildings, gathering facts. In addition, over fifty types of newspapers are reviewed for any pertinent statements relating to real estate, such as empty lots or proposed new construction projects. All of this information is transferred to a computer data base and when someone orders a report, it's a matter of punching the address in and collecting the data.

"People are very surprised to find out they thought they knew everything and didn't," adds Haggerty. "There are some things you just can't know about an apartment. You might have seen the building in the daytime, or at night…but not at four in the morning, which is when the all-night disco down the block starts up!" The property risk report includes such things as noise pollution and any potential problems the buyer might encounter from the neighborhood, such as an all-night club or a high crime ratio.

Meet the Neighbors

The managing agent can usually arrange a meeting for the buyer with the board members. That is what Gail Fernandez did when she got nowhere with her real estate broker. Through the managing agent, she got phone numbers of board members and contacted them. "Meeting with the board members helped me make my decision," she asserts. Another way to get an idea of the residents is simply to come half an hour early the next time you visit the apartment, sit in the lobby and watch the people who come and go. Jody LaMonte says that looking over the lobby can also give the prospective purchaser a way to see what the building is like. "If the condition of the lobby is not up to par, it can mean one of two things," she says.

"One, they haven't gotten around to upgrading it, or two, the building has a lack of funds."

Talking to neighbors is also a plus. Ask them how they like living in the apartment. Anita Perrone of The Corcoran Group sees "trade ups" as a good sign for the building. "If residents tell you that people in the building instead of moving out are purchasing bigger apartments because they love living there, then you know something is right," she explains.

Stephanie Kovner decided to find out who her potential neighbors would be by contacting someone on her building's board. "She raved about how great the building was," she recalls. Kovner also talked to the doorman to get a feel for the place.

Knowledgeable Professionals

Be sure to consult with an attorney and an accountant familiar with co-ops and condos before signing any deals. Aaron Danzig, an attorney with the firm Baer Marks and Upham, warns, "You want to make sure it's in the contract what is staying with the apartment after it's been sold. If not, you could walk in on the day of closing and find the chandeliers ripped out and the washing machine and dryers you saw before now gone!"

Your accountant can be helpful in assessing not only the financial condition of the building but what kind of impact ownership will have on your personal finances. If there are any questions about the physical condition of the building, you may also want to consult an engineer and/or an architect to review the building engineer's report.

The best approach when looking to buy is to rely on a broad range of trained professionals—from a real estate broker to the managing agents of the various buildings you look at to an accountant and attorney and other independent consultants. Such precautions will protect your interests and help you find an apartment that not only suits your taste, but will also turn out to be a peach instead of a lemon.

Do Your Research First: Preparation Can Help Your Purchase

By Roberta Faulstick Benzilio

If you have recently been looking to buy a co-op or condo, you have already realized what a daunting task it can be, especially for first-time buyers. No matter how difficult it may seem, before entering into any sale, make sure you have prepared yourself accordingly and know what you want and how to get it.

What Can You Afford?

Before you bid on any property, make sure you have a clear idea of what you can afford. The traditional formula dictates that your housing costs total no more than a quarter of your household income. In New York, however, with its high housing costs, a third of your earnings is more the rule of thumb.

It helps to know how to work out your total monthly costs. Let's assume you are buying a $100,000 co-op with a maintenance of $750 per month. You have decided to put down 20 percent, or $20,000. Therefore, you're financing $80,000. Assuming a fixed rate of 9 percent, your calculation should be: $80,000 multiplied by .09, then divided by 12, which will give you a $600 monthly mortgage payment. This plus the $750 maintenance fee will result in a monthly expense of $1,350.

A co-op's monthly maintenance includes real estate taxes. Therefore, in the case of a co-op purchase, you don't need to consider additional monies for taxes. However, in a condominium, the monthly common charges (the condo's equivalent of maintenance fees) do not include real estate taxes. Thus, you have to figure in real estate taxes separately. Take, for example, a $100,000 condo with a common charge of $350 per month and monthly real estate taxes of $240. With that same $20,000 downpayment, your numbers should resemble this: $600 for your monthly mortgage payment plus the $350 common charge and $240 for real estate taxes, which adds up to $1,190 in total monthly housing costs.

Don't forget that whether you are buying a co-op or condo, the interest portion of your mortgage is fully tax deductible. By speaking to your accountant, you will be better able to understand the savings this represents. Briefly explained, however, it means that you can afford to spend more per month on a mortgage than on rent, because of the tax savings. This deductibility extends to the underlying mortgage and property tax of a co-op building. Therefore, in most cases, a portion of the maintenance, often as much as 50 percent, is also tax deductible.

Be Realistic

Now that you know what you can afford, start thinking realistically about what your money will be able to buy. Anywhere you go, the better the location, the higher the price. This also goes for amenities and apartment size. Make a wish list of your requirements, including preferred neighborhoods, unit size, number of bedrooms and baths, amenities (such as fireplaces, balconies, laundry rooms), building type (such as doorman, walk-up, prewar, postwar, brownstone) and state of renovation. Start the list with the "Must Haves" and work your way down to the "Nice Ifs."

Although it's nice to think you can always get what you want, this is often not the case. What you should be looking for is a halfway point: what you'd like and can afford, in your chosen neighborhood. If you are on a budget, it's fair to assume you won't be able to get everything on your wish list. However, being tied to a budget will keep you focused on what's most important to you.

Be Informed

Getting to know the state of the market for your preferred property type will give you the confidence to make an offer that's not too high or too low. Start off by reviewing newspaper ads to see what comparably sized properties are being listed at. But since asking price and closing price can be quite different, it's also a good idea to become familiar with the "recent sales" columns in *The New York Times* and *Newsday*. You can add to this knowledge by asking your broker to show you recent sales figures for similar units. Compare these numbers to the prices of units you are currently viewing. When looking, take into account the state of renovation, condition of appliances, floor (high/low), views, building amenities and such apartment amenities as balconies and fireplaces.

Next, be informed ahead of time about your borrowing power. Have your mortgage broker qualify you or prequalify yourself. Obtain your own credit record and review it. If your report is not 100 percent clean, be prepared with answers about any outstanding items.

Another thing to research carefully is the building's financial condition. Remember that the building also has to qualify with the bank. Some examples of what a bank might ask you about the building are: How many units are owner occupied (as opposed to being investor owned and rented out)? What percentage of the units are sponsor held (unsold)? What is the building's underlying mortgage? An underlying mortgage that is disproportionately high compared to the building's assessed value is a danger sign. It means the building is overleveraged, and this will no doubt translate into a very high monthly maintenance. Make sure that there isn't an assessment currently being charged or likely to be charged in the near future. Reasons for such assessments would be large capital improvements, lawsuits against the building and so on. Such an additional fee can put a strain on your budget and also make the co-op more difficult to sell in the future.

Because of the nature of co-op financing, unpaid maintenance on the building's other units could put your investment in jeopardy. Make sure the sponsor can afford the maintenance on any unsold units. If several units fail to pay, the building's underlying mortgage could fall into arrears and the entire building could be repossessed by the bank. You would lose your downpayment, you'd still be liable for your own mortgage for the co-op shares you purchased and the real estate itself would have reverted to the bank.

Board Approval

As a buyer, you must also be knowledgeable about the co-op's by-laws and requirements for board approval. Financial qualifications form the bulk of most board requirements. Another consideration is how much of the purchase price you are financing. Most co-ops require at least 25 percent down. Others will ask for 50 percent down. With many exclusive co-ops, boards will require that the unit be purchased outright in cash. Many boards also want you to have a net worth that represents a multiple of the unit's purchase price.

It's also valuable to realize that if you buy a co-op, the sale process is tied to board requirements; therefore, you will need board approval when it comes time to sell your unit as well.

A final word on board requirements: If you have pets, mention this to the board as early as possible. It would be a waste of time to get through all the other hurdles of buying a co-op only to find the building doesn't allow them.

Have important credentials ready, such as tax returns, proof of employment and bank statements. Be sure that the downpayment is liquid or easily accessible. After all your market research, you should be ready to make an offer for an apartment that fits the bill. If your offer is accepted, be ready to act and close the deal.

Some Facts About Bidding

Begin the bidding process by making an offer based on your understanding of the market. Don't make an unrealistically low initial bid. If you want to be taken seriously, start close to what you want to pay. Again, be realistic about the increments by which you raise your offer. It helps to realize that an extra $5,000 amortized over the life of the loan translates into about $37.50 a month. Compare this to what it would mean to lose the deal.

Be fair. Don't expect the seller to come all the way down to your price. Be willing to meet him halfway. Try to put yourself in the shoes of the seller, which you may, in fact, be several years down the road!

Before you start bidding on a co-op or condo, you should feel you are going into the process educated and ready. You should be left with the feeling that even if you lose the apartment, you gave it your best shot. And if you were realistic, informed and ready to enter the fray, you will certainly succeed in the next round.

From Patios to Pools: Putting a Dollar Value on Amenities

By Peter R. Marra

Anyone who has looked through housing listings in New York has encountered the abbreviated sub-language of the real estate world in such designations as WBF, W/D, D/W and hi ceils. In realtor parlance, these add up to A-M-E-N-I-T-I-E-S. Amenities can add tens of thousands of dollars to the value of an apartment, and can make the difference when a buyer is choosing between two similar apartments. Apart from that old adage about location, location and location, amenities constitute the most attractive selling points of any property.

Architectural Amenities

Amenities fall roughly into three categories: architectural, functional and lifestyle. Architectural amenities can be ornamental—such designations as "arch. detail" and "orig. moldings" come to mind—or structural—"hi ceils," "sunken LR," balconies, terraces and so forth. Real estate appraiser Dominick Pompeo, a partner at Brooklyn-based Pompeo and Mulle, says architectural detail can command great value in landmark areas or areas in which the market reflects a desire for craftsmanship. Brooklyn Heights, Park Slope and Greenwich Village all fit this bill. Some architectural niceties have a purely visceral appeal, such as a fantastically ornamental iron gate in front of a West Village townhouse or a wood-burning fireplace (WBF), which is hardly a necessity in an overheated Upper West Side apartment. Other architectural amenities, like skylights, actually serve a necessary function.

Functional Amenities

Functional amenities, as distinct from architectural amenities that serve a function (for example, a working fireplace), can be illustrated by major appliances that make the resident's life easier. Washer-dryers (W/D) or laundry rooms (LR), dishwashers (D/W) and air conditioning (A/C) fall into this subset. New windows may not seem like something many people would value enough to pay extra for, but if you've lived in an apartment with leaky windows, you know that cold winds aren't the only thing windows keep out: Street noise and the grimy dust of the city also make their way in through old, cracked, loose windows. Gourmet kitchens, or kitchens with restaurant-grade appliances, such as Garland stoves and Sub-Zero refrigerators, are one rung up on the ladder of functional amenities: These are in the homes of owners who will do a lot of entertaining.

Lifestyle Amenities

Jacuzzis and steam rooms sometimes denote owners for whom bathing is one of the more important rituals of life. Those amenities that have to do with the broader qualities of a property are called lifestyle amenities. If there is a health club in the building in which you're buying an apartment, it may or may not add value to the apartment—it depends. Expert appraiser Pompeo feels that if there's a club in the building, and membership is restricted to residents, it could have significant value. But if the club allows outsiders, or if the cost of membership is excessive, any value added is offset by the cost of joining. The only benefit then is having it in the building—a nominal value at best, considering how proliferative well-equipped health clubs have become in all parts of the city. Likewise, Pompeo says, a pool might even be detrimental to an apartment's value. Increased insurance, attraction of nuisance, cost of maintenance and—heaven forbid—risk of leakage all paint a gloomy long-term picture for top-of-high-rise pools. In several buildings, high-floor apartments have experienced damage as a result of flooding from a rooftop pool.

Lifestyle amenities are less directly connected with the apartment itself; they have to do with the apartment's surroundings, services and neighborhood. Some buyers might think a tree-lined street is important; others might put more of a premium on having good shopping and restaurants nearby. A doorman is a lifestyle amenity, adding an element of security and convenience—expect to pay higher maintenance or common charges as a result. Similarly, a parking garage in the building is an extra that costs an additional amount per month, but for which many are prepared to pay.

How Amenities Are Valued

Which brings us to the issue at hand—namely, how should a buyer, seller or broker value amenities? And specifically, do some amenities actually break down into a dollar value?

Pompeo comments that the values are rather subjectively based on the view of experienced appraisers, and they tend to come in right on the mark. There will always be an individual for whom an amenity—let's say a fireplace—has no meaning. Then there are others for whom parking is an absolute necessity, and for which they will pay extra. The appraiser's job is to forecast what the average purchaser will pay in the current market, and that figure is derived based on comparable sales, experience and other mitigating factors.

In terms of appraisals, some amenities objectively add to the value of a property. Others add value subjectively, but still in real dollar amounts; these are the extras that might not figure in a professional appraiser's assessment of an apartment, but for which some buyers are nonetheless willing to pay extra. To demystify this idea of "objective" and "subjective" value, let's say that some amenities have purely emotional value, whereas others can be expected to add a certain amount to the price of an apartment.

WBFs (Wood-Burning Fireplaces)

A fireplace can add $2,500 to $7,500 to a property's value, according to Pompeo, depending on the type of structure, where it is in the room, how well it is finished and what it adds to a room's ambiance. A fireplace can add very little, or a lot of value, depending on its context. In some cases, fireplaces may even be detrimental, in terms of heat loss. In a typical Brooklyn brownstone, a "plain" (not ornate) fireplace might be valued at $2,500; a very ornate fireplace (in working condition, of course) at $7,500.

Christopher Thomas, sales manager for William B. May's Brooklyn offices, explains: "Because most of our apartments are in historic buildings, fireplaces— working or not—are more or less an expectation. Therefore, in 'Brownstone Brooklyn,' fireplaces are valued less than elsewhere in the city."

Parking

Parking can be extremely significant to a property's value or have no effect at all, depending on the location and the buyer. Pompeo cites the case of a Murray Hill townhouse whose owners made a driveway and garage out of the front half of the "English basement" floor. This added about $100,000 to its value, mostly due to scarcity of parking in that area. The nearest parking was several blocks away, and even there, parking would have cost some $600 a month. As for the lost space inside the house, the appraiser did not deduct much value for the loss of the room— since the front room was below grade, it was considered ancillary space anyway. Even better, the back of the house, which lets onto a garden, was preserved as kitchen space and maid's quarters. But this is a rare example. Both Pompeo and Thomas agree that it's the unusual buyer who will value parking enough to pay extra for it. Says Thomas, "Few people expect parking, so when they contemplate buying a place, they don't value it in terms of the price that a parking spot would add to it."

Outdoor Space

Thomas reports that, in Brooklyn, gardens are the most desirable form of outdoor space. A garden can increase an apartment's value by $25,000 to $50,000, depending on its overall value to begin with.

In Manhattan, gardens are extremely rare, and outdoor space more frequently takes the form of terraces and roof gardens. Pompeo assigns a decked rooftop with no direct access from the apartment an approximate value of $1,000 to $2,500. A terrace—that is, a private space with access from the apartment—can add significant value. Some of the factors Pompeo takes into consideration in valuing a terrace are its views and exposures, whether or not comfortable entertainment would be possible there and, of course, the type of unit to which it attaches. A terrace to a penthouse might add $25,000 to $50,000, while a mid-range terrace just big enough for a table and four chairs might add $5,000 to $10,000.

A tenth-floor apartment with a balcony is assessed at a higher value than a similar apartment with a balcony on the third floor. Why? On the tenth floor you'll have more light, less traffic noise, less city grime—in short, there is more removal from the grit of city living as you get higher up. And the views are better. In short, the balcony that's up higher is a more pleasant place to be…and this may translate to a higher value than the same unit seven flights down.

Views

Do views add value? Thomas gives this example comparing similar apartments with and without views: Two apartments in prime Brooklyn Heights are comparable in every way except for the views. The apartment on Columbia Heights, with sterling views of downtown Manhattan, just sold for $345,000. A counterpart on nearby Monroe Place, without views, was purchased for $315,000. Adds Pompeo, "Depending on what view it is, values go up. A panoramic view of the city can add $25,000. A water view can add $50,000. A run-of-the-mill view may add $5,000 to $10,000."

Kitchens and Baths

In prewar apartments, renovated bathrooms and kitchens are considered amenities. An up-to-date, functional bathroom, which includes clean new tile work, lighting and fixtures, might initially cost $15,000 to $40,000 to put in. Later, the asking price for the unit might reflect this investment, at a premium. Says Thomas, "There can be a lot of variations on the main theme, but well-designed kitchens and baths, with all the bells and whistles, can add more to the value of an apartment than the sum of all their parts." How much such kitchens and baths add, however, depends on the category of the apartment itself. Thomas continues, "The scale has to be right. In a small apartment where the kitchen is small and dark and old, a brand-new kitchen might not add that much to the price. However, a small dark kitchen in a major apartment would be a big drawback, and would take value away from its sale price, whereas a well-lit, well-functioning kitchen in such an apartment could enhance its value by $30,000 to $40,000."

New Windows

Pompeo says that new windows add value if you add storm windows, or if you change them to Thermopane. Because new windows are easier to open, clean and maintain, and because they save in fuel bills, they will add value to what it cost you to put them in. However, if you already had functional windows, and replaced them with windows styled primarily for aesthetics, you might only get 25 to 50 percent return on the dollar.

Postwar Versus Prewar

What influence does building type have on the dollar value of an amenity? Is there a difference in price between a prewar co-op with a terrace on Fifth Avenue and the postwar co-op with a terrace on the same floor next door? The prewar terrace would most likely add more value to the apartment, for a number of reasons. First, terraces are more common in postwar buildings; therefore, the market rule of scarcity driving up price comes into play. Also, terraces in prewar buildings are generally more ample, or wrap-around, often being created by building setbacks on higher floors. Finally, the architectural facets of this amenity must be considered. In general, the level of detail to be found in prewar buildings is much greater than in their postwar counterparts. A prewar terrace might feature carved balustrades, ornamental ironwork, gargoyles and slate paving stones, whereas the little postwar terrace across the way would likely sport concrete slab flooring and simple steel railings. It is the uniqueness and limited number of prewar buildings, and the fact that they are irreplaceable, which finally accounts for their greater value.

The Most Sought-After Amenities

While some amenities are considered "frills" and do not figure heavily in a buyer's decision, there are others that are consistently sought after. However desirable a fireplace or terrace might seem, you may be surprised to find that light is the single most important amenity. Thomas says that good light can make a difference of 10 to 20 percent in the value of an apartment that's otherwise identical to one without. Buyers most frequently ask for good light, views and outdoor space. A sense of connection to the outdoors while maintaining privacy is probably the ne plus ultra for the New York apartment owner.

Things that function well, such as new windows, new bathroom fixtures and kitchen appliances, also add to the value of an apartment. In the long run, updated and/or smoothly functioning essentials will add more to an apartment's value than frills like a Jacuzzi or steam room, which might not be everyone's first choice.

Do's & Don'ts for Sellers: Enhance the Saleability of Your Home

By Barbara S. Fox and Marilyn L. Herskovitz

Is there a more important time to lavish care on your home than when you're ready to move in? Yes—when you're ready to move out. Well-cared-for homes—even those needing renovation—sell more quickly and at better prices. Attention to detail not only presents a welcoming image, but also a reassuring one, suggesting that you have cared for what is unseen—such as plumbing, electrical and general maintenance—as well as the visible decor.

Ten Do's

When you introduce your home to a prospective buyer, you want it to make a good first impression. To accomplish this, we've outlined ten easy steps to make your home more attractive—and more saleable:

1. Do a thorough top-to-bottom cleanup of every inch of your home.

2. Repair and repaint any water damage, mildew or other obvious damage or deterioration, especially where paint is chipping or peeling.

3. Replace existing light bulbs with higher wattage.

4. Keep the kitchen spotlessly clean with all dishes, pots and pans put into neatly arranged cabinets. Repair any broken cabinets, hardware and appliances.

5. Keep bathrooms spotless. Regrout wall tiles and clean tile grout. Repair any broken cabinetry, hardware or mirrors. Replace old shower curtains. Keep towels neatly folded.

6. Straighten all closets and remove excess clothing. The less crowded a closet, the larger it appears. Straighten shoes and clear off closet floors. Make sure closet lights are working.

7. Be sure your home is free of odors such as cat litter boxes, cigarette smells and cooking odors. Use potpourri, scented candles and/or room spray when needed.

8. Keep fresh flowers or plants in abundance to give your home a warm, "homey" feeling.

9. Keep your apartment as "neutral" as possible so potential purchasers can project their furnishings and personal taste into the space.

10. Pull black-out shades, curtains or blinds up to their highest point, or remove them completely.

Ten Don'ts

On the other hand, there are things a seller can do that may actually hinder the sale of his or her property. Here follows a list of ten things not to do when putting your apartment on the market:

1. Don't assume that people see only raw potential and won't notice a dingy, untidy space. It isn't necessary to spring for an expensive renovation, but a new paint job and/or a thorough cleaning can make the difference between an interested buyer and another walk-out.

2. Don't make it difficult to show the property. Admittedly, scheduling can be a problem, but make the effort and show the property at the customer's request. Sellers often make the mistake of being aggressively present and talkative during the showing. Instead, leave the talking to an experienced broker who is trained to spotlight your property to its best advantage.

3. Don't wait around for the "right" buyer. There is a misconception that foreign investors are out there paying top dollar in the American market. The truth is that foreign investors make up a small percentage of the market today, and they are much more canny about market prices than rumor would have it.

4. Don't overprice your property. A common mistake is to set an unrealistically high selling price, sometimes at 20 percent or more than is feasible. An attractive asking price is crucial: A property might be extremely alluring at $500,000, but at $650,000, it will be shown in another, higher competitive level of properties and be judged as a poor second. Work with an experienced brokerage firm to set a

viable price and gauge how much fluctuation there will be within that range.

5. Don't refuse to reduce your price even though your property has been on the market for two years or longer. Some properties are not selling now for what they were able to command at one time. The seller has to be pragmatic about today's market.

6. Don't ignore your broker's advice. The experienced broker is committed to selling your property at the highest viable price in the shortest amount of time.

7. Don't forget about timing. Putting a nine-room apartment on the market in mid-August is a disadvantage. It should be listed for sale in mid-September, after private schools reopen, to achieve the best results.

8. Don't fail to do your homework. Know your closing costs, including various fees and taxes, as well as "flip tax," the fee charged by many co-ops when a unit changes hands, and assessments, in advance. You will then be prepared to go to contract quickly with a local lawyer.

9. Don't be rigid. Be as flexible as possible with closing dates. More sales fall through than people imagine because a seller would not accommodate a buyer's desired closing date.

10. Don't fall prey to distrust. Trust your broker and the other professionals you hire to make the sale a success.

Tribulations of Selling: It Ain't Over 'Til It's Over

By Stuart M. Saft, Esq.

Most sellers believe that once they have identified a purchaser, the hardest part of selling their apartment is over. Unfortunately, that is frequently not the case. If the seller wants to make certain that the sale is actually consummated, he or she must be ever vigilant. There is a big difference between finding a purchaser and closing a sale.

To bridge that gap, the seller has to be certain that a) the purchaser does not become seized with "buyer's remorse," b) the contract is actually executed, c) the purchaser can and will obtain financing, if the contract is conditioned on financing and, most important, d) the board of directors approves the purchaser. After all, the apartment is not sold until the closing has occurred.

The Contract Process

The most dangerous time for a seller is the period between the time the parties shake hands on the terms and the execution of a binding formal contract of sale. Until the contract is executed, the purchaser is not bound to acquire the apartment regardless of how honorable the potential purchaser seemed when the parties agreed to the terms. Many purchasers fall victim to a disease called "buyer's remorse," which strikes even the hardiest individual when he or she realizes that the search for the ideal property has been completed and now it is time to actually make a choice and, worse still, pay for it. Signing the contract is the moment of truth; does the purchaser really want and can the purchaser really afford what he or she always thought he or she wanted?

Executing the contract is not as easy as it seems since the parties will frequently have to face a clash of egos. A seller could spend months (or even years) trying to sell an apartment and, when he has finally found a buyer, decide that, out of principle, he must have a certain light fixture from the apartment, leading to a fight with the buyer over whether or not it is included in the sale. Similarly, the purchaser might be spending $500,000 for an apartment but decide that he or she might not want to go through with the transaction because a $500 refrigerator has a scratch. There is no end of stories of how minor problems killed major deals. Problems may also arise when one or both of the attorneys want to use the contract negotiation as an opportunity to improve the business deal or demonstrate how good he or she is at negotiations.

Another possible hitch during contract negotiations is that the two parties may realize that there was no prior meeting of the minds on the terms of the sale. Sometimes the parties have been supplied with slightly different information by their brokers. The confusion can get even more complicated if there are several brokers involved. Nevertheless, assuming that the parties make it through the contract process, they are not yet home free.

Specific Caveats

Most people believe that it is the purchaser who should be concerned that the contract contain representations and warranties to protect him or her. However, there are representations and warranties that the seller should also make certain are contained in the contract. The seller's execution of the contract and taking the apartment off the market require a certain leap of faith: the assumption that the purchaser can and will actually close. If the purchaser does not have the intention or wherewithal to close, then the seller has lost several months and possibly the entire selling season—potentially a year. For this reason, the seller should insist that the contract contain a representation by the purchaser that the purchaser has the cash available to pay the nonfinanced portion of the purchase price. In addition, since the seller will be relying on the purchaser's obtaining financing and passing board review, the contract should also contain a representation as to the purchaser's income and net worth. It does not have to be a precise number, but just a minimum (for example, the purchaser earns more than $40,000 a year and has a net worth over $150,000) or whatever the seller believes the board is looking for in purchasers. The seller should also request that the purchaser disclose in the contract what modifications to the apartment the purchaser will be telling the board it intends to make to the apartment. A number of purchasers have been rejected over the years because boards felt the existing shareholders would be adversely affected by protracted alterations to apartments. These issues will provide the seller with an understanding as to whether the purchaser is a good risk. There is no reason to sell the apartment to someone who is going to be turned down for financing or not approved by the board.

The seller should also insist that he or she be kept advised of the purchaser's progress in obtaining financing and in applying to the board for approval. The seller must make certain that the purchaser is meeting the deadlines for filing the various documents as required by the contract. The earlier the seller realizes that there is a problem with the purchaser, the sooner he can begin to consider alternative courses of action.

Board Approval

There are certain actions a seller can take to help the buyer pass co-op board inspection and obtain financing. The purchaser's lender will need information regarding the building and the corporation and will want the apartment appraised. For this reason, the seller should have available a copy of the corporation's most recent financial statement and should be available for the appraisal in order to answer questions regarding the building and the neighborhood. Even if it means having to take a morning off from work, it will be time well spent if it helps the purchaser obtain financing.

The main reason the approval process is delayed or results in an unsatisfactory conclusion is inadequacy or delay in the purchaser's submission of its application. Most boards will not even look at an application unless it is complete. Once the buyer has completed the application, the broker can speed the process by reviewing the application package, making certain it is complete and then providing each board member with a copy.

There is one more aspect of the transfer that the seller cannot lose sight of: luck. The seller needs luck in finding a purchaser who is ready, willing and able to purchase the apartment. If a minor issue arises prior to or during the closing that is important to the purchaser, then the seller should try to cooperate in order to make certain that the sale goes through.

Board Operations

- *The role of the board of directors*
- *Obligations, responsibilities and limitations*
- *Running a successful board*

What Board Members Do: Defining Roles Makes the Job Easier

By Laura Rowley

The way two different boards operate can vary as dramatically as the lifestyles of a Californian and a New Yorker. The entire board is responsible for its building's financial well-being, operating and capital budget, insurance, security and interior and exterior maintenance. The board has to hire the right professionals, approve buyers and sublettors, enforce house rules and work harmoniously with the managing agent and residents in running the building. In short, an impossible job. Understanding who is responsible for what can make the job a lot more manageable.

According to New York attorney Bruce D. Friedberg, "The roles of the board members are defined in the by-laws, and their powers are set out in the Business Corporation Law (BCL)." Both the by-laws and the BCL are necessarily vague about specific duties, so that each board is able to "mold its own management team," as Friedberg puts it. "Each board dictates what its own management strategy will be."

The Board President

In general, the by-laws and BCL state that the president presides over all meetings of the board and shareholders, has the power to create committees and appoint committee heads and set the agenda for the board. But the style of the president's administration is purely a matter of personal taste. While some co-ops are headed by benevolent despots who are personally unpopular but get the job done, others are ruled by noble conciliators who receive laurels from the masses but are slow to accomplish anything. The best board president is a mixture of the two.

The president must have the ability to delegate the day-to-day tasks and still make sure that both short- and long-term goals are attained. For example, while the president should be consulting with the managing agent about how to handle a reported heating problem, he or she should not be taking individual complaints from the shareholders.

"The board president is like the father of the building," says John Osnato, Jr., president of a Brooklyn co-op. "It should really be someone who is available, even during the day, because it's helpful when situations arise." On one occasion a shareholder was moving out and had gotten an elevator key from someone filling in for the super; the shareholder was locking the elevator when loading and unloading, so no one could go up or down. "We almost had a riot here," says Osnato, who was on hand to confiscate the key when he found out.

The president should work toward building a consensus on the board about financial and maintenance issues and gaining the trust of the other members so that some decisions can be made individually to avoid getting the board bogged down in minutiae. The president should prepare an agenda for board meetings in advance, including ongoing projects and new proposals, with an indication of how much time should be spent on each. For some presidents, the most difficult area is the management of board discussion on a particular issue, so that while everyone has an opportunity to speak, the conversation does not become a long-winded war of egos, and finally culminates in a vote.

It is up to the board president to establish committees to oversee such areas as finance and maintenance, and he or she should work to get shareholders more involved in running the building by encouraging them to head committees on security, house rules, communications or beautification. This approach helps avoid an "us versus them" attitude and enhances the universal commitment to the co-op's quality of life. In addition, the committees can often become a developing ground for new board members.

The Treasurer

According to the BCL, the treasurer has care and custody of the corporation's funds, and this role is the most specific of any on the board. "You don't have to be an accountant or a financial planner, but you have to know numbers and have an appreciation for a spreadsheet," says Dr. Mitchel Levine, who handles a $6 million annual budget as treasurer of a self-managed co-op on Riverside Drive.

The treasurer is chairman of the finance committee, and holds primary responsibility for the budget. "You have to keep on top of spending on a monthly basis so you can cut back or add funds to make sure you don't come up short at the end of the year," says Levine. The treasurer should also ensure that proper checks and balances are implemented within the co-op, such as purchase orders, work orders and time cards.

Paperwork is a large part of this job: Every month the treasurer should be asking the managing agent for copies of paid bills, bank reconciliations and bank statements. The managing agent's statements should be reviewed with the board's accountant, comparing them to the actual bank statements. The treasurer should ask for explanations of any large withdrawals and deposits of a similar amount within a short period of time. If something appears suspicious, the treasurer must report it immediately to the board's attorney and its insurance agent. If it is not reported, the co-op's ability to be reimbursed by the bonding company may be jeopardized. Make sure the management firm is bonded for more money than it is handling and call the bonding company to see that the managing agent is up to date in its coverage.

The treasurer should also approve payment of all bills by the managing agent; before approval, the supplies or work covered by the check should be examined to make sure the items were delivered in full or the job accomplished satisfactorily. The treasurer should also make sure that all checks are backed up with an invoice or voucher approved by at least two authorized board members.

On the income side, the treasurer has to ensure that the building's income is collected accurately and on time from shareholders and other debtors, such as the laundry room servicer and commercial tenants. The first time a shareholder misses a payment, the treasurer should ask the board's attorney to start default proceedings. The treasurer also has to protect the co-op's income once he or she gets it in house.

Levine says he divides funds among a liquid account and investments of six months, two years, three years and so on to get the highest rate of return. "You also have to look into ways of earning money that conform with the philosophy of the board," he says. "For example, I know this board would be uncomfortable investing in other real estate. You have to be a good listener and hear what the board is saying so that you don't plan a budget that is acrimoniously received."

The Secretary

As one of the directors, the secretary votes on issues before the board and collaborates in all board decisions. But the secretary's primary role is to keep proper minutes of all board meetings, which constitute the official record, required by law, of what took place. They are the defense the board may have to rely upon to explain its actions in the case of a lawsuit, and a history of the building that can help potential buyers see how the co-op operates.

However, this doesn't mean the minutes should be a novel-size blow-by-blow account of every meeting. A lengthy diatribe by one member about the slamming elevator doors can be noted by saying, "The condition of the elevators was discussed." In fact, detail is often to be avoided in case of a suit; a joke told in poor taste during an approval process might become the basis for a discrimination action. But accuracy is key, and the secretary should always present a draft of the minutes to the rest of the board for review before the next meeting, when they should be approved as the first order of business. Because the wording of minutes is crucial, the secretary should also consult with the board's attorney regarding proper phrasing. The secretary may want to delegate the job to a professional outsider so that he or she has more time to participate in board discussion, but the board should require a confidentiality agreement from the person taking the minutes. Reports from the committees and managing agent should be attached to the minutes.

The Vice-President

The BCL and by-laws say very little about this office; the vice-president's specific role is to take the place of the president when that person is absent or unable to perform in the role. As a director, the vice-president has the same fiduciary responsibility as the other members of the board, but less of the direct burden for seeing projects through. The vice-president usually heads up a major committee such as the maintenance committee, which works with the managing agent to determine the short- and long-term needs of the building and how to budget for these items, or the approval committee, interviewing potential buyers and sublettors.

Many buildings don't have the roles so neatly defined. At Levine's Riverside Drive building, for example, every board member heads a committee that captures his or her personal interest, whether it is the children's playroom, the fitness center or the newsletter. "We make everyone who has a specific interest take responsibility for it," says Levine. "Everyone has a special area of interest that they give a lot of time and research to, but we also stay focused and coherent as a group so we can get things accomplished."

The Voting Process: Holding Successful Board Elections

By Laura Rowley

Cooperative and condominium elections generally garner about as much attention as New York City Council elections. Especially in buildings where things are running relatively well, most shareholders are too busy or disinterested to sign and send in proxies, much less attend an annual meeting. But consider this: The board is the single greatest influence on how well the building's value holds up during the recession. And if your lobby looks shabby, if the elevators snap shut on residents and your maintenance is steadily rising, it's time to vote or even consider running for the board.

Elections in co-ops and condos are governed by the by-laws that appear in the building's prospectus, the initial offering plan that all co-ops and condos must give to new buyers. The by-laws require an annual meeting of the shareholders, and most elections take place in May or June, according to Alvin I. Apfelberg, a co-op attorney. Most offering plans require that residents be informed about the annual meeting no less than ten days and no more than forty days in advance. Officers— president, vice-president, secretary and treasurer—are elected internally by the directors. Board terms can run for a year or multiple years, and some buildings will stagger terms to maintain continuity on the board.

There are basically two styles of voting—"straight" and "cumulative." Assume an election is being held in which six people are vying for three seats. In straight voting, you vote the number of shares you own for each candidate: If you own one hundred shares, you can vote one hundred votes each for your preferred candidate A, B and C. Cumulative voting, on the other hand, is the number of shares you own multiplied by the number of seats open. In our mythical election, your one hundred shares, multiplied by three open seats, give you three hundred votes to be distributed among the candidates in any fashion. Thus you can throw all three hundred votes to your neighbor Mrs. Smith, because you know she's dedicated to solving the slamming-door elevator problem. (To have legal cumulative voting, the process must be prescribed in the certificate of incorporation.)

Participation

Unfortunately, in many buildings you won't find six candidates vying for three seats. "In the majority of buildings you can't scrounge up a candidate to save your life—people don't want a second job that's unpaid," says Marcie Waterman, an attorney with Deutsch Tane Waterman & Wurtzel. "Inevitably, the night before the election, existing directors find themselves pleading with shareholders to run."

Some managing agents will help the board with the process of recruiting candidates. "My favorite technique is to invite people who call up to complain to serve on the board," says Martin Kera, an attorney and president of Bren Management. "I've never had any takers."

Even if the current board members are able to encourage some residents to participate, they may run into a problem when they get to the annual meeting: The quorum, commonly defined as 50 percent plus one, is not always easy to attain. Waterman describes one building in Queens that held five separate "annual" meetings before finally getting a quorum. For buildings that face such extreme voter apathy, Business Corporation Law Section 603 allows a board to hold an election without a quorum. According to Waterman, if within a certain period of time there has not been an election, or there has been an election in which no quorum was obtained, the holders of 10 percent of the shares can sign a petition calling a special meeting. Whoever shows up at this meeting is deemed to be a quorum for the purpose of electing directors.

But to avoid this problem, the board should work closely with the managing agent to make sure the pre-election process goes smoothly. "The managing agent's job is to help with coordination—notifying shareholders about the meeting, sending proxies, setting dates and times—but not to get involved in the election itself," notes Robert Freedman, president of Maxwell-Kates, a management company.

In many buildings, getting proxies returned is also a laborious task. Kera says he often gets only 10 percent of the proxies back, and subsequently has to phone all of the shareholders to remind them. On the night before the meeting, several board members should canvas the building, asking residents to either attend or hand in their proxies at that time.

Contentious Boards

There are a few buildings in which elections are fraught with contention, but the fight for board seats is usually related to something going on in the building: missing funds, skyrocketing maintenance, questionable special assessments, serious physical plant problems, bad contractors, poor security and so on. "The more people have to reach into their pockets to pay maintenance increases or special assessments, the more you will see opposition to the board," says Marc Luxemburg, a partner in the law firm of Snow Becker Krauss and president of the Council of New York

Cooperatives.

Phyllis Weisberg, a partner with Kurzman, Karelsen and Frank, agrees. "I've seen some elections that were so hotly contested they ended up in litigation," she says, adding that aside from maintenance increases, "lobby renovation seems to be an explosive issue." Where the elections are a potential bloodbath, Weisberg recommends spending a little more to get an independent observer to run the election, such as the Honest Ballot Association (HBA). The Queens-based HBA, a nonprofit group founded by President Theodore Roosevelt in 1909 to oversee governmental elections, handles about 150 board elections every year, a number that is "climbing steadily," according to Maralin Falik, HBA's director.

"You can't imagine what's out there," says Falik. "I've had elections where we've needed guards." If all parties agree, HBA will run the entire election according to the building's by-laws, from printing and distributing proxies to collecting them, validating signatures and tabulating the vote. Cost starts at about $800. "Everyone is happier when the managing agent and the building's attorney are not involved in the tabulation of the vote," she says.

Other instances of contested elections are those in which the sponsor is no longer in control, but still owns the majority of shares. Often, Luxemburg notes, two parties will form: one that favors cooperation with the sponsor and one that is antagonistic to him. Recently, the New York Appellate Court, First Division, ruled that the sponsor in a Rego Park complex could vote his shares as well as appoint directors, a process that gave him de facto control of the board, in spite of the fact that he no longer formally controls it. "Unfortunately, the courts have uniformly allowed the sponsor to choose between [friendly and unfriendly] slates," says Luxemburg.

There is also the rare renegade board, which breaks all the rules and never even bothers to hold an annual meeting or elections. Shareholders in this situation do have recourse: They should first send a letter to the board inquiring about the situation. If there is no response, they need to get 25 percent of the shareholders to sign a petition calling for a special meeting to elect a board of directors. If the board ignores this effort, the shareholders can hold the meeting and the election themselves. At this point, it's a good idea to call your own attorney.

Luxemburg says in general he finds the election process is much more congenial than it was ten years ago. For example, in some of his buildings, if there are eight candidates for seven seats, the least experienced person is made an advisor to the board, taking part in meetings but not voting. If someone drops out over the course of the year, the eighth person is appointed to fill the seat. "This concept seems to be taking hold," he says. "Boards are trying to reduce the image of us versus them."

Electing Board Members: Good Candidates Are Needed

By Anne Gaddis-Marcus

The arrival of spring heralds board election time for many co-ops and condos. Held during the annual shareholders' meeting—often in April, May or June—board elections are eagerly awaited by some, dreaded by others and completely ignored by a surprisingly large number of residents.

"The meeting is the one time shareholders have a voice to comment on the direction of existing board policies," says Jay Zinns, an attorney with Jacobs, Zinns, Schneyer & Braff, P.C., who provides counsel to a number of co-ops. But surprisingly enough, he adds, the shareholders' voice often ends up never being heard. In fact, he says, one of the biggest obstacles that faces an election is getting a quorum (usually 50 percent of the shareholders plus one).

Andrea Scheff, president of NRK Management, says that while a low turnout is a shame, she encourages her building boards to look on the bright side and take it as an indication that there are no serious problems in the building. "I have boards who say, 'No one's going to show up this year,' and I tell them, 'That means they're happy with you,'" she says. "The biggest turnout is when there's anger with a sponsor."

Stuart Fish, an attorney with Cutler & Fish, which provides legal counsel to about twenty-five building boards, says that while he has witnessed plenty of elections at which the turnout was small and the atmosphere funereal, he has also been in packed rooms in which hostile scenes have erupted between board members and lobbying groups trying to oust them from power. He recalls one election in particular, at which a woman stood up screaming about how the running of the building was worse than her experience as a Holocaust survivor.

"Some elections last just eleven minutes with not a single question asked or any expression of discontent," Fish says. "But at the same time I've seen plenty of finger-pointing and yelling. I'm always surprised by all the anger that can come out at these things."

Generating Interest

In an attempt to drum up interest in the election and get people to attend the meeting, announcements, including information on the candidates and the financial records for the year, are usually sent out at least ten days and no more than fifty days before the election, based on whatever is specified in the by-laws. Managing agents often participate in this planning process by notifying each of the shareholders in advance about the election and then following up with a reminder letter. It should also be the agent's responsibility to prepare the proxies and ballots, find a convenient location for the meeting—it could be the building's lobby, a community space or even a nearby school, church or synagogue—and make sure in advance that there is a quorum.

Managing agents also typically make sure that the microphone, chairs and podium are set up at the meeting site in advance, and make themselves available at the meeting to take attendance, give a brief management report and count the votes. It is usually the board's responsibility to contact people to submit proxies (giving the right for someone else to vote for them in their absence.)

Seeking Help

In some instances, an outside company will be brought in to help with the election process. One such firm, the Co-op Election Company, has been asked to handle everything from getting the vote out and guaranteeing a quorum to conducting ballot and proxy tabulations to helping a co-op or condo avoid costly court fights or other problems resulting from disputed election results.

"The result of all of our attention is an election free of disputes, feelings of partiality or controversy," says Co-op Election Company president Joyce Miller. "Since so many elections can get caught up in problems, it is no wonder that many residential buildings are seeking outside help to facilitate the process."

The Candidates

During the planning process, information on potential candidates is gathered and distributed, usually by mail. Some buildings will post résumés of potential candidates; others may host a "meet the candidates night" during which shareholders can be introduced to those running for office.

But very often there simply aren't enough people interested in running for any of the posts. Bruce Cholst, of Rosen & Livingston, a law firm specializing in co-ops and condos, attributes this not only to the fact that serving on a board is done on a volunteer basis, but also to the fear of being sued that keeps some potential board members from running for office. Cholst points out that the problem has been addressed through a 1987 ruling stating that shareholders can vote to amend the certificate of incorporation to excuse board members from ever being sued for making bad business judgments provided they were not made in bad faith.

Miller, who has been treasurer of her own building board since 1989, says board members should always be "on the lookout" for potential candidates. "It's the responsibility of the board to get to know people," she says, adding that those shareholders with professional experience, such as architects, lawyers, engineers and even decorators, can greatly enrich a board, and make the process of negotiating building projects a lot smoother. If candidates happen to be scarce, Miller advises the president to get on the phone with other board members to see if they know anyone who might be interested.

"You should create a farm system for budding board members by forming board subcommittees that are open to shareholders, such as a lobby committee, a capital improvements committee, a legal committee and a financial committee," says Cholst. "You're inspiring interest in community affairs by reaching out to people to give of themselves in areas in which they are interested and have knowledge. And it's also a way to try them out."

Andrea Scheff says she considers it a wise idea to stagger elections, so that "you don't have all new blood at once and you always have people who are familiar with the running of the building." Though usually one year, the length of the term for board members can vary from building to building.

Strategic Campaigning

Assuming that there are some shareholders willing to make a run for a position on the board, on the night of the election, after the minutes are read and the various committees give their reports, the candidates and incumbents usually stand up to make two- to three- minute speeches. "The best way to campaign is to get up there and appeal to what people need," says Helene Hartig, a real estate lawyer and longtime board member, "whether it's for a leniency in subletting or pet policies. Also, if you give the idea that you are a team player, you have a better chance."

Cholst stresses that it never hurts for candidates to introduce themselves to people in the building in advance of the meeting, to get a reading on the concerns of shareholders before they are addressed from the podium. "And people tend to vote for names they recognize," he says.

Fish says he has seen situations in which the better-qualified candidates managed to blow their chances by getting up and saying all the wrong things. "They came off as very self-congratulatory and ended up alienating groups in the co-op," he says. Meanwhile, he has also seen candidates with fewer credentials just as easily swing the votes their way by strongly attacking the way things were run in their buildings "with some very scandalous statements."

Albert Gordon, who is president of his co-op board, encourages shareholders to get involved. No matter the pitfalls, everyone at one time or another should serve on a board, he says. "Service on a board is of great importance to all the tenant owners," says Gordon. "To enhance the attractiveness of living in a co-op, one should cooperate!"

Board Power: Crossing the Line Between Director and Despot

By Sam Adler

For a variety of reasons, an us-versus-them attitude between shareholders and boards continues to thrive in many buildings. In some cases, shareholders have to go to court to oust a sponsor from the board, and even after his control expires, board members may continue to identify with his interests. Shareholder apathy often makes it difficult to achieve a quorum, a prerequisite to holding an election and voting out the board. But even democratically elected boards may put their own interests before those of the shareholders.

Dissident groups arise most often "when boards have repeatedly failed to give complete information to shareholders on major expenditures or acted in an imperious manner," notes Morton H. Rosen, a partner with the law firm of Rosen & Livingston.

As a result of *Levandusky vs. One Fifth Avenue Corp.*, a 1991 case in which the state's highest court gave boards wide discretion to run the affairs of the co-op corporation, shareholder suits have been sharply reduced. However, *Levandusky* does not prohibit litigation against self-dealing boards or those who fail to act in the best interests of the building.

"Many shareholders seem to feel their home is their castle, notwithstanding what the by-laws and proprietary lease say. That's where the Levandusky case fits in," says Marc Luxemburg, a partner with the law firm Snow Becker Kraus and president of the Council of New York Cooperatives. So while shareholders today may have little recourse when their boards veto alterations, they can still go to court to compel a board to provide a shareholder list or financial records, or to challenge a sweetheart contract the board made with the sponsor.

Potholes and Sweetheart Deals

While a war-zone atmosphere can't be much fun to live with, things can be worse when the board's decisions directly affect owners' pocketbooks, along with the quality of life. At a 375-unit co-op in Port Jefferson, Long Island, the maintenance has increased about 26 percent over the past three years to an average of $608 a month. Meanwhile, hallways need painting, carpets are filthy, mailboxes are falling off the wall and the parking lot is riddled with potholes, says one board member, who believes he was only allowed onto the board because he had been making a lot of noise about the fact that there hadn't been a board election in four years.

Because of apathy, the last few elections had failed to draw a quorum. But when maintenance hikes drew a healthy—albeit angry—response at the last annual meeting, the entrenched board resorted to dirty tricks. According to one board member, the sponsor and his allies waited in another room while the managing agent, who was running the annual meeting, went through the proxies. When it became apparent that the shareholders were within striking distance of a quorum, the managing agent notified the sponsor and his allies that they should go home and take their voting shares with them. He then cancelled the meeting for lack of a quorum.

Shareholders should be aware that such self-dealing violates federal law, according to Martin Kera, a partner with the law firm Kera & Graubard. Under the federal Co-op and Condo Abuse Relief Act, sponsor-controlled boards may not enter into long-term contracts or sweetheart deals with the sponsor.

In addition, the Port Jefferson shareholders mentioned above had to hire their own accountant, who found that the board vice-president was not charged late fees when she paid maintenance late and that the management company was cutting checks without a board member's signature. When these improprieties were brought to light, the managing agent's contract was terminated, and the vice-president resigned and moved.

The shareholders have since petitioned the board for a special meeting to elect a new slate of directors. Although the petition was signed by 19 percent of the shares—9 percent more than is required by the Business Corporation Law—the board refused to recognize it, claiming that the by-laws require signatures from 25 percent of the shares. The shareholders are now in court trying to force the board to hold a special election.

Carried Away With Power

With such opposition, why wouldn't a board step down? "Sometimes people on boards get carried away with the power," Kera explains. "They do whatever is good for them but don't think about the rest of the building. If a problem in the building bothers someone on the board, he or she may do something about it. If it doesn't, they may not."

This kind of self-interest was another board's motivating factor in a controversy at a sixty-unit condo on the Upper West Side. "Half the board lives in the penthouse, and they used $20,000 in building funds to pay for a problem affecting only the penthouse," says one unit owner.

When the owner smelled a rat, he consulted the board's attorney, who agreed that the penthouse owners had wrongly called an individual apartment repair a structural problem, and that they should have shelled out their own money. The unit owner is in the process of gathering signatures on a petition to call a special meeting on the matter.

"It's not easy because there are so many absentee owners," he says. The meeting is slated for January and the angry owner still isn't sure what redress he is seeking. Nobody wants to get involved in litigation, though. "We're going to have to settle somehow," says the owner. "I don't agree with one board member who says to let it go and warn the guilty directors that it won't be tolerated next time. We want our money back."

"One of the least used, but most effective weapons for shareholders who are unhappy is to call a special meeting," says attorney Alvin Apfelberg. The shareholder should have 25 percent of the shareholders sign a petition "to discuss the following items—then list them. This meeting gives you the chance to have it out before you get into litigation."

For example, Apfelberg had a case in a 175-unit building on the East Side, where a number of shareholders were angry about the board's decision to install fancy, expensive windows. They gathered the signatures, called the meeting and resolved the issue before any blood or money was spilled. "Litigation should be the last resort, and you should know you're on solid ground, because if you lose, you may have to pay attorney's fees to the board," Apfelberg points out.

Seven-Year Litigation

Waste of funds is just one contention of Karen de Kleinman, a real estate broker and unit owner who is suing the board of managers at her Fifth Avenue condo for refusing to comply with a court order to furnish her with a mailing list of owners and access to all of the building's books and records. De Kleinman, who has been in litigation with the board for the last seven years, brings to mind the crank shareholders who have nothing better to do than make the lives of the board members miserable. The difference is that she has won enough victories along the way to be taken seriously.

Among her grievances are a sweetheart deal the board entered into with a health club operator that included providing him with a $25,000 grant and a $25,000 interest-free loan. The operator didn't pay a single installment on the loan, and the board wound up subsidizing him at the rate of $1,000 a month.

De Kleinman says the board refused her a list of condo owners, depriving her of the chance to present her election case to them. When she previously tried to run for the board, she says, the board passed an amendment prohibiting real estate brokers from sitting on the board because of conflict of interest. De Kleinman took the matter to court and the judge found the board had acted improperly in imposing the restriction.

Phyllis Weisberg, a partner with Kurzman, Karelsen and Frank, the board's attorney, refused to comment on De Kleinman's claims, citing pending litigation. She notes, however, that De Kleinman is in bankruptcy and two of her units have been foreclosed upon, and that the courts voided a sale of one of her units when she sold it in violation of the board's right of first refusal.

Boards confronted with angry shareholders have to maintain communication and openness, stresses Stuart Saft, a partner with the law firm Wolf Haldenstein Adler Freeman & Herz, LLP and chairman of the board of the Council of New York Cooperatives. "Boards should keep in mind that flexibility is key in this market," he says. This may include approving sublets for longer periods, easing up on buyer applications to some degree and being more flexible concerning renovations, especially for couples with children who can't sell their units. Most important, notes attorney Mort Rosen, "boards shouldn't forget that they are working for their neighbors, and are not landed gentry."

Successful Board Meetings: Planning and Delegation Are Key

By Alex Ladd

Days, and sometimes weeks, before co-op and condo board members gather for their monthly meetings, board presidents and managing agents pore through documents and letters from shareholders, scribble down notes for an agenda and anticipate and settle any problems they foresee in the hope that their meetings will run smoothly. By getting the bulk of work out of the way before meeting time, they save themselves from rounds of lengthy discussions that go nowhere, arguments that veer away from the issues at hand and late-night bickering that can leave board members feeling sour and exhausted.

At co-op and condo board meetings, usually held one evening a month, board members review and vote on a wide range of building-related items, including capital improvement projects, financial reports, maintenance fees and budgets.

Where, When and How Long

Deciding when and where to have meetings can have a lot to do with how well they are run. "An effective meeting can be run by setting up a calendar in advance so that all board members can be there, and so things of importance are voted on by everyone," says one managing agent at Century Operating Corp.

Depending on a board's preference, meetings may be held in a board member's apartment, a common room in the building, a local restaurant or the managing agent's office. A former vice-president of management at Lawrence Properties, who used to attend over five board meetings a month, suggests that meetings be held in a conference room or at the agent's office, rather than inside someone's apartment, where, as he says, "it tends to get overly chatty and comfortable." The advantage to holding meetings in a manager's office is that all the necessary documents are at his or her fingertips, and the meetings tend to run faster.

Board president Edward Henry favors meeting in a conference room in his large East 86th Street co-op, because "the meetings are more businesslike and tend to start on time." And Robert Wesner, board president of the Corniche, a co-op on East 87th Street, says that because his building does not have a conference room, meetings take place at the board attorney's office.

Some professionals say a well-run meeting should last no more than an hour; Wesner says an hour and a half long should do the trick. "If it goes beyond that," Wesner says, "it means that things are being argued and tabled instead of solved before the meeting starts."

According to Henry, his board typically meets for about three hours. "We have a big building and a very active board," he says. "To meet once a month for two and a half or three hours to discuss the management of a $4.5 million corporation does not seem unreasonable."

How do you make a meeting run smoothly? By being prepared, say professional managers. The key to success, says Glenn Kuffel, president of Pride Property Management, is to "remain focused on the agenda." A properly prepared agenda should be written up by the manager based on discussions with the board, and handed out "at least seven days in advance," says Kuffel.

Mazie LaGoff, who recently completed a four-year term as board president at Pratt Towers, a co-op on Lafayette Street in downtown Brooklyn, advocates a pre-set meeting length. "Before I became president, sometimes meetings that began at 8 P.M. would end at 1 or 2 in the morning," she says. "We said the meeting will end at 11 P.M. and that's it. If there was still something to talk about after that, we would set aside an extra half hour, or have a special meeting on another day."

Pre-Meeting Preparation

According to LaGoff, pre-meeting legwork should include providing all board members with pertinent information days before a meeting is actually held. This has the dual function of saving important meeting time and assuring that board members make informed decisions, she says.

To assure that all board members are up to date on the latest developments, LaGoff says she would review all building-related letters and documents that came in between meetings and then pass them on to each of the eight board members prior to the meeting.

Before each meeting, Century provides board members with a summary of what has taken place since the previous meeting, a status report on pending matters and a monthly financial statement. "From the management's point of view, well-planned communication with board members helps a meeting be more informative and move expeditiously," Century's director of management adds.

Wesner tries to get a feeling in advance as to how board members will vote on a particular issue, in order to anticipate problems that might crop up during a meeting and to avoid futile arguments. "Instead of having [the board members] debate this stuff as a group and lose control, know how they will vote beforehand," he advises. "If you can't do that, then postpone the meeting."

Setting the Agenda

The agenda may be prepared by the board president or the managing agent, but in any case, the planning of an agenda should involve input from both parties. Although it is the board president's job to actually run the meeting and help keep it moving along, "Both the president and the agent should lead the board in the right direction and help them stay on track with the issues," says Carole Ferrara, president of Carole Ferrara Associates, a management firm that specializes in co-ops of under seventy-five units.

How the agenda is organized differs among managing agents and board presidents. Some like to see the weightier items, such as budgets, addressed early on at board meetings, before energy levels have begun to flag. Henry disagrees, saying that in his board's case, if agenda items are prioritized, meetings often languish toward the end, with board members losing interest in the topics. "We try to have an agenda that deals with issues in a logical framework, and not go from a shareholder policy to boardroom policy and then back to a shareholder policy," he says.

As board president, Wesner makes it his job to keep the items on a meeting agenda moving swiftly along, otherwise "you can lose the focus of a meeting easily," he says. Managing agents, too, can help keep board members from digressing from the issues on the table. "The agent needs to say, 'Let's stick to the business at hand,'" says one agent at Lawrence Properties.

While presiding over meetings as board president, LaGoff would jump in to summarize the different points of view, and then call for a vote whenever conversations veered away from issues. "Meetings can get very hot at times," she says. "You have to learn to be tactful and not get caught up in the emotions. Many times people want an argument."

Delegation and Decision-Making

Along with carefully organizing the agenda and keeping the meetings focused on the important issues, board presidents and managing agents emphasize that it is important to delegate responsibility. Both Wesner and Henry agree that since their board members are a very competent group of people, they learn to do a lot of listening, instead of criticizing.

"Everybody who gets involved has a certain amount of energy that they want to use," says Henry. "If you channel that energy properly, it's to everybody's benefit. If everybody has something to do, it avoids the problem of the director who always sits back and criticizes."

Henry tries to keep meeting time strictly for reviewing and setting policies, rather than for telling the officers assigned to particular tasks how to actually carry them out. "We confine meetings as much as possible to policy and leave the execution of that policy to the officers, each of whom has an assigned set of responsibilities," he says. And by doing this, he says he avoids unnecessary, time-consuming arguments among his members. "Typically, boards will fight over $3.50 or $5 polish when the real issue is how shiny they want the building," he says. "It's important to focus discussions on policy-level matters and to stop petty debates."

Board Member Psyche 101: Improving Communications

By Marc Broxmeyer

Have you ever noticed that when certain board members speak you find yourself getting sleepy and when others speak you have difficulty in understanding them? Much research has been done over the years to prove that we all have patterns in the way we communicate. We also create beliefs that influence our present-day decision making, even though they were established by events that may have occurred many years ago and are no longer relevant.

We all have the ability to communicate in many ways but we tend to lean toward certain ways more than others, just as we have full use of both hands but tend to favor one over the other. There are many different communication patterns that exist and an endless number of beliefs that we create. As you begin to understand some of the more common patterns and belief systems, you can start to immediately observe them not only in yourself but in others as well.

You may be wondering how change can be created by simply observing communication. By having awareness of your own communication patterns and the patterns of other board members you will have a better understanding of how you and your board members interact. This will allow you freedom of choice in your communication rather than automatic responses.

The first communication pattern that we will explore can be easily identified and is best described as general/specific. The person who tends to speak in general terms would describe things in terms of "the big picture." He or she might describe a problem regarding a roof repair as follows:

"We have leaks again and we have three bids. We have chosen the least expensive contractor who says he can start very soon."

A board member who is very specific may feel that there is information that is being left out and may even have trust issues arise because he feels that information is being intentionally withheld.

Such a board member might describe the same situation by saying: "The roof is leaking again for the second time this year. The first time in February the water was coming from over Apartment 6B and the contractor, Fix a Leak, Inc., repaired it at a cost of $1,500 but would only guarantee it for sixty days. We now have constant leaks over 6C that might be coming from the same place as the old one came from. The new estimate is for $2,000 but we can get a ninety-day guarantee. I spoke to the contractor and he thinks he can start Wednesday."

A board member who tends to process information more easily when it is in general terms has by now probably fallen asleep, eaten two more cookies or has started to slowly crawl out of his skin.

If you have identified yourself as someone who is overly specific you may notice that some people become distracted when you are speaking. You might therefore reflect on the degree of detail you are going into. On the other hand, if you find that many people seem to be dissatisfied with your report and are asking too many questions, you might wonder whether you have glossed over the details, leaving too much unanswered.

The next communication pattern is everyone's favorite: saying black when others say white and white when others say black. This pattern is called the polarity response. The board member who is blessed with this type of responsive behavior can often be annoying or even seem confrontational. Sometimes the disagreements caused by a polarity response can waste precious time and cause anxiety for other board members. In this situation, the board president should limit the discussion and move the meeting along. It is important to remember that this type of pattern does have its usefulness. A polarity response is very helpful when all areas in making a decision need to be explored. You can be sure that if there is another way to do it, this board member will find it and be sure to let you know.

The opposite of the polarity response is a pattern called the pleaser. This board member will go to great lengths to avoid disciplining or firing an employee regardless of how justified it might be. He or she will have difficulty dealing with contractors or managing agents who are not doing their job and will shy away from confronting that home owner who consistently violates house rules. This is not the board member to head up the housekeeping committee.

Self/other is the name of the next set of patterns. The board member who is self-oriented will tend to look at things only from the perspective of his own world. This board member, who sees the world only through his own eyes, might lose the ability to judge how certain decisions may be reacted to by the rest of the residents in the building.

The board member who is other-oriented concerns him or herself primarily with what everyone is going to think rather than considering whether the decision is a sound one for the building. The exaggerated concern over what everyone else is going to think can so paralyze the decision-making process that nothing can ever seem to be decided on.

It is important to remember that in all patterns, what makes them desirable or undesirable is the context in which they are used. In fact, we all exhibit these behaviors at one time or another. The problem arises when these patterns are excessive or board members are improperly given responsibilities that don't match their strengths.

An experienced property manager may not know the names of these patterns but should definitely have had enough experience in dealing with boards and building matters to guide the board president in selecting the best person for each job. It may also be helpful when interviewing managing agents for your building to choose the one who exhibits good communication awareness and patterns that seem congruent with those of your board.

Successful Building Management

- *Choosing a management firm*
- *Self-management*
- *Checks and balances*

Matchmaking in Management: Finding Your Dream Firm

By Duke Ratliff

The union between a co-op board and its management firm can be likened to marriage. Making the right match involves finding someone with integrity, similar interests and the ability to make a commitment. In the words of Smokey Robinson, "you better shop around." Of course the perfect management-board relationship may prove as elusive as the perfect marriage. Promises are often made to be broken.

"Personalized service" is undoubtedly the catchphrase of the management industry, promised by every firm, no matter what its size or type of back-office support. The only way for a board to determine how much truth lies behind this sales slogan is through careful research. Start by asking how many buildings or units each account executive handles, and go for a limit of six or seven one hundred–unit buildings per agent. On the other hand, one agent handling two buildings can be prone to errors if he's also doing the accounting and legal work. Look at what resources the firm has at its disposal; these can range from an in-house lawyer and an accounting department to purchasing, engineering and capital improvement units. It's important to weigh an agent's fee according to what these systems can save the building in the long run.

Establish Priorities

The board should establish its priorities, whether it is correcting accounting problems or planning major capital improvements, and then seek a firm with that specialty. "Each building that we manage has a specific concern," says Mark Moskowitz, president of the Argo Corporation. "Older buildings might have plumbing problems. Someone contemplating lobby renovations might want to ask questions regarding a firm's expertise in construction."

Some board members say they have chosen a new firm specifically for its small size. Andy Squire, board president for a small Upper West Side co-op, says one reason it chose J. C. Klein was because the firm "had one managing agent with two principals. The principals were involved in the managing tasks. Now they're a little bigger, but if I want to talk to Joe Cusenza [the company's president] I can call him up. It's more than personalized service; he's an owner."

But boards who have chosen a firm for its moderate client list may find that in six months the secret is out and the firm's growth is exploding. Earlier accounts can be lost in the paper shuffle. Part of the interview should discuss where the firm is headed, what its goals are and the cap on the number of accounts it will accept.

Just as important as where it's headed is where the firm has been. Timothy J. Fine, executive vice-president and managing director of the Greenthal Group, suggests asking how the company performed at other buildings. "There is a checklist that comes with the business," Fine says. "How do they supervise construction projects? How do they get competitive prices from qualified providers? You don't want a great deal from a lousy company. You should hear about aggressive competitive bidding."

Speak to Other Clients

Boards can benefit from gauging the technical abilities of the firm, according to Fine. "Ask questions about capital improvements, mention current problems and find out how they can solve them," he says. One managing agent provided a prospective client with a list of every one of its accounts, with the board presidents' names and numbers. It is a good idea to ask for more than ten references.

The most common problem during the management search, according to Fine, is when the board is impressed with one particular agent, but knows little about the whole firm. "When you overemphasize an individual, you leave yourself vulnerable to a company that can't back up the agent," Fine explains. "For instance, unless the firm has experience dealing with legal problems, the guy can't help you. Or eventually he might leave the company and you're faced with whether or not to stay with the firm."

This was an issue for Hedvah Shuchman, a recently resigned longtime board president of a thirty-five–unit West Village condominium, which had gone through five management firms since 1982. "After several changes, we were looking for stability and regular attention to our problems, but being so small we do not command the attention of a larger building," she explains. The co-op board sought an agent who lived in the neighborhood, and felt fortunate to find one associated with a firm in the building's price range. "Within four months that agent left the firm," Shuchman says despondently.

Of utmost importance, according to Fine, is a firm's honesty. Tales of sweetheart deals, kickbacks and double-billing are enough to make any shareholder paranoid. "Look for integrity," says Fine. "There's no substitute for a partner who you can trust to manage your assets." Ed Falk, the board president at an Upper East Side co-op, agrees. Suspicious accounting errors in routine billing by a former managing agent led to a change in firms and a sideline business for Falk auditing co-op and condo books.

"Most agents specify bills under a certain amount will be paid without being sent to the treasurer. All too often routine bills are handled routinely," Falk says. He recommends that buildings set as low a minimum as possible, adding that $250 is a good standard.

What Does the Fee Cover?

When the co-op began the search for a replacement firm, Falk says the board put a lot of emphasis on the fee, something he might not do today. "We were just so disgusted," he says. "We knew the old firm had taken us so we were not willing to give another company a large fee. In retrospect, price would still be a factor, but if a firm wants more money, look to see what you're getting for that money."

Services rendered are of primary concern during the current economic crisis. Tendencies to slash costs may tempt some boards to choose a bargain-basement firm, but most board presidents and managing agents agree that this would be a mistake. "After a management firm is chosen, the building will normally live with that company for a few years," says Moskowitz of Argo. "The building should feel comfortable with the fee and the company. It's equally important that the results be considered."

The recession might change the basis for evaluating those results. "The worsening economy has resulted in more maintenance delinquencies," Moskowitz says. "Potential clients should want to know how a firm goes about collecting the delinquencies." To avoid the disappointment of misplaced trust, demand that potential firms put on paper what their services are. "You really want an agreement that is as specific as possible with respect to the service to be rendered," says Michael Salberg, an attorney with Graubard Mollen Horowitz Pomeranz and Shapiro, who works with many co-op boards. "There should be a dialogue on what the role is. It should be an agreement that is understandable. Managing agents tend to put in language like 'supervise the daily operation.' If it means the manager will make site visits two or three times a week, the agreement should specify that number."

Boards should prepare for the worst even before hiring a firm, according to Salberg. "If the relationship is not a good one, you want to get out of it quickly," he says. "I always discourage terms for more than a year unless it can be terminated within thirty to sixty days' notice."

Choosing a Managing Agent: Know What to Ask

By Anne Gaddis-Marcus

There's no question about it—choosing a managing agent can be among the most difficult challenges a co-op or condo board faces. One company may give a terrific presentation, but then follow it up with less-than-terrific service; or the service may be great, but new projects are handled poorly. Once new boards are elected, personalities may clash, or the new board may simply want to start over with a clean slate upon taking office. Whatever it is, finding a managing agent that fits a particular bill on a time-tested basis can be difficult indeed.

Judy Holton, board president of her Staten Island co-op, recently found herself shopping for her building's third managing agent in seven years, before settling on Marvin Gold Management Co. "We weren't sure how much longer our other company was going to exist," she says, explaining that stability became a criterion in their search for a new agent. "And we wanted a company that was pro-active; who could take the ball and run with it."

In order to find that perfect match, various managing agents and real estate professionals suggest that boards make an extremely careful and extensive search that involves talking to other boards, conducting interviews in which all the important questions and expectation are laid on the table and evaluating a firm's qualifications in terms of the building's specific needs.

Beginning to Shop

Richard Barry, CEO of Century Operating Corp., advises that when a building first sets off on a search for a managing agent, it begin by asking other boards for recommendations. He also suggests boards consult with professional organizations like the Council of New York Cooperatives and the Federation of New York Housing Cooperatives.

Federation president Charles Rappaport won't recommend one particular managing agent over another, but he will send out a list of the twenty-five to thirty firms who have been approved as associate members of his organization, along with a few tips. "And then it's up to the board to evaluate them in terms of what it wants for its building," he says.

For starters, Rappaport suggests that board members make the rounds to different co-ops to see how their buildings are being maintained and talk to board presidents to get the rundown on how their management companies' back offices operate. "And then once you're satisfied, make a trip to the company's main office," he says. "Hardly anyone ever sees what's in the back office and yet that's where 85 to 90 percent of the building's services take place." He cautions boards not be overly concerned with the location of the firm's main office, because "the fact that you're in the Bronx and they're in Brooklyn has no significance whatsoever. The telephones always work, and there's a site manager who will visit your building."

As part of the interview process, Rappaport strongly urges boards to sit down with the site manager who will be assigned to their building, and ask questions such as what his or her action would be in a given emergency situation. Neil Davidowitz, vice-president of Orsid Realty, advises boards to ask prospective firms how long they've been in business and to get a list of all the buildings they manage, how long they've been with the firm, and the name of the agent handling each building. "Get detailed information on bookkeeping procedures, with special emphasis on the bill approval process," he adds. "Check their systems and controls on vendor pricing and purchasing." He also advises boards to ask about the "quantitative and qualitative nature of visits to the building."

Barry points out that every building has different needs when it comes to management. And Rappaport reminds boards that "the person might be the best managing agent in the world, but if the chemistry isn't right, there's no point in going forward."

Barry suggests that board members come to the interview prepared with a list of questions to help steer the management principals away from lengthy presentations and toward the building's particular needs. "The boards who make the most intelligent decisions are the ones that have a list of prepared questions and ask the same questions to each management company," he says, "whether it be about capital improvements, budgeting or whatever else."

Checking Credentials

Hillary Becker, past president of the Institute of Real Estate Management (IREM), suggests that boards find out whether the companies they are considering have a certified property manager (CPM) designation, are accredited management organizations (AMO) or are part of an organization like IREM, which promotes building professionalism and ethical standards.

The New York Association of Realty Managers (NYARM) recommends that boards call the organization when checking out a firm. "We have a job bank where we can tell you generally who's available, what their level of skill is and whether they have the background, the education and the training credentials you are looking for," says a NYARM past president. "You want somebody who understands all of the administrative aspects, who has a really good working knowledge of the physical plant and has some computer and accounting skills. They should also have good employee relation skills and some psychological and sociological skills as well."

Jeffrey Gold, vice-president of Marvin Gold Management, says that one of the key questions board members should ask a managing agent is how good the support services are. "Anybody can come to the building once or twice a week," he says. "But when there's a problem, do they have the resources and know-how to deal with it?" In-house CPAs, controllers and other experts are all a plus, he says.

What Services to Expect

Gold says that realistic expectations of what managing agents should do once you have hired them can vary according to what was actually agreed upon in the firm's initial proposal to the building, but he adds that there are some services that every manager should provide, no matter what their individual expertise. They include collecting carrying charges, maintaining an appropriate list of income and expenses, giving concise, accurate monthly financial reports and inspecting the property on a regular basis.

Leslie Kaminoff, president of AKAM Associates, agrees, adding that boards should also check the purchasing policies of a company. "To protect the integrity of the management process, a managing agent should not be allowed to bid for capital improvements," he says. "Sealed bids should have to go either to the board members or the engineer."

Kaminoff also strongly recommends that boards look for a company that does only management because "management is a business unto itself." He points out that there are a lot of companies who, along with managing buildings, own property, or are associated with sponsors or developers, or are in the brokerage business and do management "to fill in time or to get other business."

Jerome Belson, president of Associated Builders and Owners of Greater New York (ABO), says that managers should not only be capable of interaction with the board members at a moment's notice, but should also take calls from individual tenants when questions or problems arise. "Since most people work during the day, there should be one night a week when management is available for direct tenant discussion," he says.

According to Bill Carter, board president of his ninety-four–unit co-op on East 12th Street, whether your building gets a management company's undivided attention depends mostly on the individual agent servicing your building. "Do they actually take care of the building or do you end up having to see that everything gets done yourself?" Carter recommends people ask around well in advance. He advises that all board members conduct an extensive, careful search "because once you're in with a managing agent, you're kind of stuck."

If, after researching, interviewing and checking references, a board still has some reservations, Gold encourages it to make sure the contract has a built-in way out. "We include a thirty-day cancellation clause in our contracts," he says, "because we find that once the marriage is over, the marriage is over."

From RAM to CPM: Who Certifies Building Managers?

By Vicki Chesler

While many board members take heart in the fact that their managing agents are "certified," they are often unsure of exactly what that signifies. Your agent may sign his or her name with an impressive series of letters following it, but what is a RAM, CPM, ARM or AMO? Although there is currently no state licensing of building managers, there are three major trade organizations in the New York area that conduct certification programs for professional building managers.

Registered Apartment Manager

The oldest of the three is Associated Builders and Owners of Greater New York (ABO), the local chapter of the Washington-based National Association of Homebuilders (NAHB). According to executive director Herb Warshavsky, ABO has offered registered apartment manager (RAM) certification for about ten years. He estimates that there are approximately five hundred RAM-certified managers in New York today.

Developed by NAHB and approved by the Department of Housing and Urban Development (HUD), the RAM certification program is a two-semester course offered at New York University's Real Estate Institute. Warshavsky says the course is also offered on Long Island and in the Bronx. The NYU course consists of two eleven-week sessions, with one evening course per week. The cost is $360, and recertification is required every three years by attending approved meetings, seminars and courses. A minimum of two years' experience in management is required in order to take the RAM course. There is also a senior RAM designation, which requires additional courses. At the end of the course, tests are taken, which are sent to Washington, D.C., for grading. "Certification is a way of upgrading the profession," says Warshavsky.

Certified Property Manager

The Institute of Real Estate Management (IREM) was founded in Chicago in 1933, according to Otis Jones, president-elect of the Greater New York Chapter. IREM offers three different certification programs: certified property manager (CPM), for professional managing agents; accredited residential manager (ARM), for on-site building staff and accredited management organization (AMO), for management firms.

The CPM designation has the most rigorous requirements of the various management certification programs, and generally takes five years to complete, says Jones. Candidates for CPM designation must meet certain eligibility requirements, including five years of management experience, membership on a local realty board and membership in IREM. There are currently approximately 162 CPMs in the New York chapter of IREM, says Jones, all of whom have completed the required three course levels, passed the tests and prepared an approved management plan. Some of the courses are offered at NYU's Real Estate Institute, but advanced courses are generally offered in other cities.

"We are a professional group of people," says Jones. "We think that all managers should be certified. It benefits the entire profession."

IREM is affiliated with the National Association of Realtors, and its certification programs are recognized by the New York State Division of Housing and Community Renewal (DHCR) and the city's Department of Housing Preservation and Development (HPD) and Housing and Urban Development (HUD).

Accredited Realty Manager

The New York Association of Realty Managers (NYARM), founded in 1958, offers New York Accredited Realty Manager certification, also at NYU's Real Estate Institute. Certification requires completion of five courses plus a written report. Most managers take one to two years to complete the program, but it can be done in under a year if a more intensive course load is undertaken. NYARM also offers some credit courses at its annual trade show.

The organization is an advocate of state licensing of building managers, and has lobbied heavily for the passage of a licensing bill. State Senator Donald Halperin (D-Brooklyn) introduced such a bill in 1992, but it was not approved and has been reintroduced this year. NYARM's stance is that one of the main advantages to licensing is that it would require some uniformity in the level of professionalism among managers, if they are renewed through continuing education and testing at least every five years.

Self-Management: A Hard-Working Board Has Much to Gain

By Angelina Esposito

The desire to control their own property and finances combined with dissatisfaction with their present managing agent is pushing more and more boards toward self-management. Board members are taking the first steps into uncharted territory with fingers crossed, exploring the different avenues of self-management from creating an in-house back-office operation to hiring an on-site or resident manager to working with companies geared toward successfully directing self-managed buildings.

"Self-management is not for everyone," says Ben Braunstein, president of Realty Resources, a firm that provides training and services for self-managed buildings. But for those boards who are willing to take a hands-on approach and get involved in the day-to-day operations of the building, self-management is an alternative worth considering. "After all," says Harold Wolf, president of the Back Office, another service organization, "who is going to manage your property better than someone who has a vested interest in it?"

Who Is Doing It?

A number of buildings, mostly very small or very large, are successfully managing their own operations. "If the board has the know-how, is willing to contribute a great deal of attention and knowledge toward running the building, and is capable of approaching the situation with an open mind, then self-management is possible," says Albert J. Poppiti, board president of 1874 Pelham Parkway, a ninety-five–unit co-op in the Bronx. According to Poppiti, the benefits of self-management outweigh the convenience of using any managing agent. Control over finances, cost efficiency at all levels, a hands-on approach regarding long-term and day-to-day planning and the elimination of the middle man are just some of the advantages he cites.

Poppiti's building decided to switch to self-management eight years ago because the board was not pleased with the managing agent. "They were raking us over the coals," says Poppiti. "Our interests were not being enhanced and our money was being mismanaged; they did not care what kind of financial ruin they put us in. We wished we had switched sooner."

Since the switch, the co-op has paid off its underlying mortgage, has not raised the maintenance in twelve years and has $100,000 in the reserve fund. "The savings cannot be measured," says Poppiti. "Our quality of life has improved, and that is important."

Mitchel Levine, treasurer of Schwab House, a 640-unit co-op on Riverside Drive in Manhattan, agrees heartily: "No matter how effective a managing agent is," he believes, a professionally managed building "will never be as productive as a well-run self-managed building."

Ten years ago, when they made the switch, the greatest concern among board members at Schwab House was insuring fiscal security. "We were not satisfied with our managing agent. They lost bills, sat on bills and never had the payroll information. We wanted accurate and timely information to ensure the availability of sufficient funds at all times. Since we have been self-managed we have what we want," says Levine. Over the last ten years, Schwab House has experienced a savings of between $30,000 and $40,000 in management fees and has had only a 15 percent maintenance increase.

Today the building is financially sound with a reserve fund of $1.4 million, a stabilized savings of 25 percent to 30 percent and a healthy budget of $6.8 million. "I do not think any of this would have happened with a managing agent no matter how good they were. They do not have the level of interest we have; they are too removed to be where we want them to be," says Levine.

Schwab House has an in-house back office, set up by Levine, with a full-service bookkeeper, a full-time receptionist, an executive manager and an on-site manager. The building's maintenance staff of fifty-five employees has a more positive outlook on how the building is being maintained since switching to self-management. "The name signing the check makes a difference," says Levine. "There is a sense of loyalty when a board member signs your paycheck."

Knolls Co-op Section 1 in Riverdale has had similar results with self-management. "We were unsatisfied with the level of service provided by our managing agent. They were impersonal and would not listen to our problems. We decided to take matters into our own hands," says board president Robert Davidow. After more than forty years of self-management, this 240-unit co-op has saved over $1 million.

Knolls Co-op has an in-house back office, engineer and bookkeeper, has not increased the maintenance in ten years and has burned the mortgage. "If the board is capable and willing to self-manage, like we were, then go for it," advises Davidow. "The results are amazing."

According to James Heller, chief operating officer at Plaza 400, a 628-unit co-op on East 56th Street, "Self-management creates an improved quality of life. There is someone here every day. The building is carefully monitored at all times as opposed to having a roving managing agent." During the building's conversion in 1981, the board of directors felt that they could give more attention to the building if they ran it themselves. They have no regrets. With everything in-house and a staff of forty-five, "Everything is immediately attended to and the doors are always open to the management office," says Heller.

Considering Self-Management

For those considering self-management, the questions are endless: Do I use a back-office service? Do I need an on-site manager? How do I begin to organize? Most boards advise that it is a decision that takes much thought, consideration and exploration. The board president of a large Park Avenue co-op has been considering such a switch. Though currently there are two managing agents—one for the building and one for the co-op's on-site health club—he feels that the building could get better mileage from its management dollars if the board hired one resident manager. "Greater control over the maintenance of the building and enhancement of the quality of life are my biggest concerns," he says.

At this point, his board is exploring options and trying to decide what it takes to self-manage. "Our biggest problem concerns how much time the board is willing to spend," says the board president. "Our focus is on how to organize and maintain all systems that are currently in place, without disturbing the building." Some of the questions the board has encountered are: Does it make sense to have an on-site manager and how much will it cost? Can we use our managing agent more productively? Do we need a back office and, if so, what makes it run efficiently? The board will be looking into various companies that offer services to self-managed buildings.

Support Services

There are a number of companies directed toward serving and educating boards of self-managed buildings. The Back Office has been servicing self-managed buildings for two years now, working directly with the board members. The firm will provide bookkeeping and accounting services, pay vendors and contractors, keep track of inventory and invoices, issue late notices, plan and update budgets and guide boards in the selection of contractors. They will also provide monthly reports. The cost for all these services is $5 per unit per month for the first two hundred units. Company president Harold Wolf works with smaller buildings, with a minimum charge of $100.

According to Wolf, a board can experience savings of 65 to 75 percent of the managing agent's fee. But "it is not just the money side," Wolf says. "It is how much better your home will be when someone with a stake in the property is running the show."

Another company that works with self-managed buildings is Escrow Services of New York. This company will hold your tax money until it is time for the property tax to be paid, allowing the money to earn interest the entire time. The tax money will be protected up to $1 million. As a registered agent the company can even pick up the tax bill for you. Escrow Services will also do the billing, payables, disbursements and provide monthly reports. The cost for these services is $4.25 per unit per month. "Using the services of an outside agency allows the board to keep an eye on what is going on," says president William Voss.

Besides offering back-office services such as billing and collecting maintenance, providing complete expense and income reports and working with outstanding payables, Realty Resources also offers a training course for buildings switching to self-management. According to president Ben Braunstein, the course provides information on the basic regulations that buildings must follow, what is expected of boards, what they need to do to get started, how to organize and much more. The goal of the course is to "teach boards everything about self-management so there is no confusion from day one," says Braunstein.

The initial set-up fee starts at $395, depending on the number of units, and includes entering the necessary data into Realty Resources' computer system and complete training on how to self-manage. There is also a twenty-four–hour hotline. "We offer ongoing support and comprehensive assistance," Braunstein says.

B. J. Murray installs turnkey real estate computer systems in both self-managed buildings and buildings using a professional managing agent. The system offers financial statements, payroll, late fees, work orders, inventory and all other accounts receivable and accounts payable. The cost for the system runs anywhere from $7,500 to $150,000, depending on the complexity of the setup. The payroll, purchase order and inventory software can be purchased separately for between $75 and $100.

Who Should Self-Manage?

According to Glenn P. Murray of B. J. Murray, "You need a commitment from everyone in order to make a successfully well-managed building." The board has to consider who the vendors will be, how they will keep track of on-site inventory, whether there are facilities available for an office and whether the board is willing to deal with the tenants one on one.

If a board is emotionally involved in the maintenance of the building, has the time to devote and the energy and ability to self-manage, they should consider switching, says William Voss of Escrow Services. "When the board is involved, it is the best of all situations. The quality of service is better than the best managing agent," he says.

Braunstein advises self-management for buildings smaller than fifty units and larger than three hundred units. It can be too expensive for a small building to hire a managing agent, he points out, with fees as high as $400 to $500 per unit per year. At the other end of the spectrum, large buildings have the resources to hire an on-site manager, and their boards are usually very involved in building operations, he says.

Protect Your Building: Bribery and Kickbacks Can Be Avoided

By Robert B. Anesi, Esq. and Joseph V. Clabby

Recent newspaper reports have taught a sad lesson to the owners of cooperative and condominium apartments in New York City. Unless the boards of these buildings exercise proper care, corrupt vendors and managing agents can add dramatically to operating costs.

In June, 1994 the Manhattan district attorney's office filed criminal indictments against dozens of professional co-op and condo managers doing business at some of the largest building management companies in New York City. The accusations claim that many of those providing management services to cooperative and condominium apartment buildings have stolen from these buildings by accepting bribes or kickbacks from vendors of goods and services to the buildings.

Vendors give bribes or kickbacks to managing agents to ensure that the managing agents select them for a particular project at a building or to assure that they get business from the building in the future. Bribes or kickbacks take the form of direct cash payments by vendors to building managers, lavish gifts during the holiday season or gratuities such as a vendor remodeling the kitchen in the home of a building manager.

Co-op and condo boards must protect their buildings and neighbors from this depredation. Unless they do so, the cost of this corruption gets passed directly to apartment owners in the form of higher maintenance or common charges, and higher assessments.

What Can Boards Do?

Boards that relinquish too much authority to their managing agents to select vendors risk exposing their buildings to corruption. Board members must exercise closer oversight of all aspects of contracting with outside vendors for goods and services. Doing so will sharply reduce the ability of managing agents to demand bribes or kickbacks.

The following are some methods to limit the opportunity for this type of corruption:

1. Always get a minimum of three sealed bids for any significant project. Do not rely on the managing agent to recommend or select the vendors to participate in such bidding. Contact boards of other buildings, with different managing agents, for references. Board members must make themselves somewhat familiar with the reputable vendors available for any project contemplated.

2. Investigate vendors considered for a project. Do not expose your building to a vendor with a history of problems. Check for complaints filed with various consumer protection agencies, such as the New York City Department of Consumer Affairs. Inquire with the Better Business Bureau and the local chamber of commerce about the vendor. Contact the New York State attorney general as to whether the firm has ever been the subject of complaints or enforcement litigation.

3. Insist on getting the names of a vendor's principals. Check for judgments, tax liens and criminal convictions against both the vendor and its principals. Obtain a Dun & Bradstreet report on the vendor. Require a vendor, as a condition of awarding a contract, to authorize a credit check with one of the major credit reporting agencies in the United States.

4. Do the obvious: Get references and pursue them. For example, visit buildings where the contractor has worked earlier. Ask to see the work performed and speak directly with those in the building who had contact with the vendor. Remember, reputable companies will be proud of their work and only too happy to have potential new clients inspect it.

5. Boards should consider retaining a professional to complete these tasks. Professionals will be familiar with the resources available to investigate the reputation of a vendor and will complete the task much more quickly than an individual

board member. Budgeting for a professional to investigate will always be less expensive than the unknown cost of corruption.

6. For any major project, retain a professional to conduct a project audit before awarding a contract. For example, a building considering bids for a new roof should retain a roofing consultant to review the bids to determine if any excessive or unnecessary costs exist that could be used to pay a kickback. Reliable experts can be located by compiling a list, getting references and talking to their past clients. Most will conduct audits for reasonable fees. Never let the managing agent select a consultant for this purpose.

7. Consider having the consultant return to the project at various stages of completion to review what has been done, especially if the vendor demands more money for unanticipated extra work.

Vendors providing regular or continuing goods or services to buildings, such as fuel companies, exterminators and cleaning services, should be subject to audits as well. On-site audits, which actually monitor the work being done or the goods being delivered, will produce information to compare against invoices. Demand invoices that provide sufficient detail to describe the precise nature of goods or services rendered.

Never permit a managing agent to have complete control over the receipt of goods and services and payment for those items. Doing so invites invoices for items never delivered and the kickbacks that follow.

Check Policy on Gratuities

Demand disclosure statements from both managing agents and the management companies as to whether either accepts seasonal gratuities from vendors. Ask whether your management company has a published policy on managing agents' accepting such gratuities. Inquire whether a management company will commit to such a policy to get or keep your business. Ask if vendors will make the same pledge as a condition of getting work from your building.

Board members must be actively involved in the details of running their buildings. Only then will cooperatives and condominiums get the upper hand in combatting costly corruption.

Your Building's Financial Health

- *Understanding financial reports*
- *Planning long-term and short-term budgets*
- *Investments and income generation*

Understanding Corporate Finance: Run Your Building Efficiently

By Leslie Kaminoff and Jill Smith

Insuring the financial viability of your building is probably the single most important aspect of good management. Yet many boards remain surprisingly ignorant of the fundamentals of corporate finance and accounting. Whether your field of expertise is medicine or graphic design, you can learn the basics needed to keep your building on solid footing if you are properly instructed.

Every month, your board should review certain financial reports to be sure that the building's budget is being followed, that maintenance fees are being collected on time and that the reserve fund is secure and growing. Just knowing what reports to read and how to read them can make a big difference in the ability of the board to operate effectively.

Assessing Your Manager's Back Office

Your financial reports should be generated on a timely basis and delivered to you by your managing agent. Therefore, it is imperative that your management firm be capable and communicative in this area. Take a look at the qualifications of the people doing the financials at your management firm. How is the department structured? Be sure to have one contact person in the finance department at the management firm. In addition, your agent should be familiar with and understand your building's finances.

The department should include bookkeepers, accountants and a back-office staff that understands finance. It should be split up to ensure that there are checks and balances to protect you from fraud or theft. You don't want the bank reconciliation to be done by the same person who does the bookkeeping; it should be done by an independent person who can detect any abnormalities and keep you informed. Be sure that there is no commingling of funds with other clients. Some firms pool accounts, combining monies from more than one building. This is a formula for disaster. Money for payables should come directly out of the building's operating account. And income should be deposited directly into a lock box at the bank with immediate availability.

High-Quality Reports Are Essential

When it comes to getting the reports you need, flexibility and quality are essential. Your managing agent should be able to customize reports to provide you with the information you need to run your building. The information in the reports must be timely, or their value is diminished. You should have monthly reports no later than the middle of the following month.

In order to protect your building from embezzlement, your management firm should be insured with a fidelity bond of $1 million to $2 million, depending on the size of the account. Be sure the firm has errors and omissions insurance to protect you from professional mistakes. Look at how long the management firm has worked with its insurance company. Check the dates of policies with annual renewals and be sure they are with the same carrier. Ask for ninety days' notice if a change in coverage or carrier should occur.

Analyzing Monthly Statements

Each month, your managing agent should distribute a statement of receipts and disbursements for the previous month. This statement should include a supporting schedule showing who was paid when and how much, and where the income came from (maintenance, transfers, sublet fees, commercial rent and so on). It should show the status of each unit, including any arrears, late charges or transfers of ownership. The accounts payable report should include the date of each invoice received and the date it was entered on the management firm's computer system. There should also be a cash flow report, showing actual bank balances, monies paid out and monies deposited.

Compare unpaid bills month to month to see if payables are rising and to see if you are on budget. Check the credibility of everything on the accounts payable list as soon as it's entered on the report, before the time comes to pay. If there's an error, it should be removed as soon as possible in order to keep the financials clean.

The list of all transfers can be used to compare to the unit payment list to be sure that all transfer fees are current and there are no arrearages. Date of payment must be listed and the late fee policy must be enforced. In order to do this, late fees must be billed immediately and the managing agent should have authority to act on arrearages. This helps avoid making the issue a personal one among shareholders.

You will find that some of your building's reports are done on a cash basis, reflecting actual cash flow—deposits made, checks disbursed. Others are prepared on an accrual basis—reflecting bills received, both paid and unpaid, and income due, whether received or not. The cash-based reports are crucial to following your building's cash flow and knowing the current cash status. The accrual-based reports will help with budget planning, indicating how much money will be due when and how much will be received when. But it is important to have both types of reports in order to really be on top of your corporation's financial picture.

Budget Planning

At the beginning of each year, the operating budget must be reviewed. Look at the monthly expenses in each category and compare them to the budget you have set. Statements should clearly separate operating and nonoperating expenditures—for example, checking account versus reserve fund. You should establish a budget for every category and go over it every month. In addition, the building should attempt to budget in savings, putting aside a certain amount each month to add to the reserve fund. Nonoperating transactions, such as loan proceeds, savings and borrowing from the reserve, should be on a separate line from standard operating accounts.

An annual certified financial report is usually required by each building's by-laws. Independent verification of management records should also be done. The balance sheet, showing the building's assets and liabilities and the stockholders' equity must be included, along with supporting schedules showing a breakdown of disbursements, income, savings and so on.

Understanding Cooperative Finances: A Review of the Basics

By Mark B. Shernicoff, CPA

Every shareholder in a cooperative should have some understanding of the basic financial aspects of operating the building. This includes an understanding of the purpose and uses of the co-op's financial statements, an awareness of the components of the budget, a familiarity with taxation of cooperatives and knowledge of how co-ops raise funds.

Financial Statements

The co-op's financial statements, when audited by a CPA, provide an independent verification of the finances of the co-op. They are usually required in connection with mortgage financings—both the building's underlying mortgage and the share loans of the co-op's tenant shareholders. They will tell the reader how well, or poorly, the co-op did in the year reported on. The statements will include a balance sheet (assets, liabilities and equity), statement of income, expenses and deficit, statement of cash flows and footnotes that will describe the co-op and disclose other pertinent financial data required for a fair presentation of the co-op's financial status.

The auditor's report, which is on the auditor's letterhead, will typically include four paragraphs. The first describes what was audited—for example, the balance sheet of the co-op as of the last day of the co-op's fiscal year and the related statements of income, expenses and deficit and cash flows for the year then ended. The second, sometimes referred to as the "scope" paragraph, describes the scope of the audit and sets forth any limitations that may have been placed on it, either by the client or by the inability to obtain information. The third, or "opinion" paragraph, sets forth the auditor's conclusions concerning the financial statements. The proverbial "clean" opinion will read, "In our opinion, the financial statements referred to above present fairly, in all material respects, the financial position of the co-op as of December 31, 199X, and the results of its operations and cash flows for the year then ended in conformity with generally accepted accounting principles." The fourth paragraph may report the status of the disclosures required by the American Institute of Certified Public Accountants (AICPA) regarding the estimated life expectancy and replacement costs of the building's major systems and components. Most co-ops choose not to make the disclosure and the paragraph will indicate this. Other paragraphs, which may either precede or follow this paragraph, may refer to additional supplemental information, uncertainties concerning the collectibility of disputed amounts, sponsor defaults, litigation and so on.

The Operating and Capital Budgets

The co-op's budget is its financial plan. It includes estimates of the co-op's expenses for the year and the sources of funding. Co-ops should have an operating budget that outlines the co-op's plans for day-to-day operations and a capital budget that outlines the plans for the long-term repair, maintenance and replacement of the co-op's physical plant, including the building's major systems and components.

In the operating budget, the board estimates the expenses for the coming year, such as mortgage payments, real estate tax, labor costs, heating, gas, electric and other utilities, repairs and maintenance, insurance and professional fees. The board will then estimate the revenues from sources other than maintenance, such as laundry room, store rents, garage rents and late charges, which can be used to offset operating expenses. The balance will have to come from the tenant shareholders in the form of maintenance. Other income items, such as interest, transfer fees, sublet fees and the like, are usually used to supplement reserve funds and are not usually used to reduce the maintenance charges to the shareholders.

The capital budget is similar, except that it takes a longer view than a year. The board, together with the agent, engineer or architect and others will review the condition of the building's systems and components and plan for their repair, upgrading or replacement. The required funds can come from existing reserves, additional borrowing, assessments when needed or advance assessments used to build up the reserves. The board can decide to use any or all of these sources to finance the capital budget. Many boards use a mix.

Taxation

The taxation of cooperatives covers many different areas and includes federal, state and city taxes. The most important tax provision concerning co-ops does not result in the taxation of co-ops, yet without it most co-ops would not have been created. This is Section 216 of the Internal Revenue Code. This code section defines a "qualified cooperative housing corporation" for the purpose of allowing its tenant stockholders to get the same tax benefits as homeowners, which include the deduction of the tenant shareholders' mortgage interest and their proportionate share of the co-op's interest and real estate tax deductions, as well as certain tax deferrals and forgiveness available on the sale of a principal residence.

In terms of tax payments, the largest is the real estate tax, which is an ad valorem (based on value) tax and typically represents 25 to 35 percent of a co-op's operating budget. In New York City, where real estate is divided into four classes, co-ops are in Class II, along with all other multiple dwellings. For the city's 1994–1995 tax year, the tax rate will average approximately $10.55 per $100 of assessed value. For this purpose, co-ops are assessed at 45 percent of their value as rental buildings, taking into account the nature of the rentals that might occur in the building if it were not a co-op. In addition, any increases in assessed values may be phased in so that the full impact is not felt immediately. The tax is paid on whichever is lower— the actual assessed value or an amount known as the transitional assessed value, which is the average of the current year's actual assessed value and the previous four years' actual assessed values.

A tentative value for each parcel of real estate in New York City is published every January and the taxpayer has until the following March 1 to file a protest. Most co-ops file utilizing the services of attorneys who specialize in this work. These attorneys, called certiorari attorneys, handle these protests on a contingency basis, charging between 15 and 25 percent of the aggregate savings achieved, taking into account the future savings resulting from the transitional assessment process described above. Every co-op should file a protest as the costs to file are low and the potential savings are great.

Another way to reduce the real estate tax is to participate in the city's J-51 Program. This is a program of abatements and, to a limited extent, exemptions available to owners of multiple dwellings to encourage the upkeep and maintenance of the city's housing stock. Co-ops and condos are eligible for work completed during the first three years after conversion. In addition, benefits may be available after that if buildings meet certain criteria. Currently these are: (1) an assessed value of less than an average of $40,000 per dwelling unit and (2) an average selling price per room for the three years prior to commencement of the work of less than 35 percent of the Fannie Mae (Federal National Mortgage Association) maximum mortgage amount for a single family home, which is currently about $70,000. (If less than 10 percent of the units in the building were sold, only the assessed value test is used.)

For most co-ops, there is no regular federal income tax liability. However, the Internal Revenue Service takes the position that Section 277 of the IRC, which was designed to tax social clubs and other membership organizations, is applicable to co-ops. A number of audits have been done by the IRS and they have assessed tax on income from nonmembers (that is, other than tenant shareholders), primarily interest on reserves, but in a number of cases such things as commercial rents and laundry income. While those co-ops with small assessments have paid the tax subject to the right to claim a refund should it be held that Section 277 is not applicable to co-ops, a few have brought suit in tax court. These cases, which were heard in 1988 and 1989, had not yet been decided at this writing. In addition, there has been an active movement, led by the National Association of Housing Cooperatives and actively supported by the Council of New York Cooperatives, the Federation of New York Housing Cooperatives and the Coordinating Council of Cooperatives, to have Congress clarify that Section 277 is not applicable to housing cooperatives.

The New York State franchise tax and the New York City general corporation tax are similar in calculation and rate. As in the case of the federal income tax, there is usually no tax based on income. However, for both the state and city, there is an alternative tax based on capital. The rate, for both the state and city, is four-tenths of 1 percent of the net assets of the co-op. The value of the assets is based on the fair market value of the property, which, for the city, is approximately 2.2 times the assessed value. However, the state will not always accept that value and frequently searches for alternative values, such as the insured value or the price paid to the sponsor, either of which may be higher than 2.2 times the assessed value. In addition, the state currently adds surcharges that amount to about 30 percent. The minimum state tax, with the surcharges, is $429 and the city minimum is $300.

Raising Funds

The primary source of funds for any co-op is the tenant shareholders. By law, in order to qualify for the federal tax benefits previously mentioned, at least 80 percent of the co-op's gross income must come from its tenant shareholders. Most of this is in the form of maintenance. Other sources include parking fees, electric submetering charges, sublet fees, storage fees and late charges. Funds for capital purposes, however, although frequently raised by assessment, more often come from borrowing. The most common method of procuring funds for capital projects in co-ops is to increase the amount of the underlying mortgage on the property when the mortgage comes due or is refinanced. The next most frequent way is to place a second mortgage on the property, either in the form of a credit line or a fixed amount. Occasionally lenders will lend on an unsecured basis to allow financing of improvements and, in a number of cases, contractors have been financing work on favorable terms as an inducement to obtain the contract. Contractor financing can be very advantageous to the co-op as the rates are frequently lower than those of an institutional lender, and the costs, which can approach 4 percent of the total amount of a mortgage, are much lower.

Understanding a co-op's finances is an important task for the tenant shareholder as well as board members and officers. It is, therefore, incumbent upon all cooperators to keep themselves informed about their buildings' finances.

Reading Financial Reports: Boards Must Know How

By Andrew Essex

Imagine there's a board member somewhere in New York City with this month's financial report spread out before him on the kitchen table. His eyes have already begun to glaze over. He knows that understanding these reports is crucial to the financial solvency of his co-op, but after just a few pages, he feels a terrible urge to nap. Though some of us may sympathize with this poignant figure, most of us accept the painful truth that a co-op is a business and must be run as such. It requires a certain fortitude in the face of often overwhelming and unexpected problems.

To help the board keep abreast of the building's financial condition, certain reports should be received periodically from the managing agent and an independent accountant. So what exactly are these reports that arrive every month to baffle and elude you? Why are they so impenetrable? Are you really expected to understand what you're reading or should you just count on your treasurer to decipher them while you go rent a movie? If you are willing to stay on top of the building's financial and budgeting issues, there are ways to make the monthly report process palatable.

Understanding your monthly reports is a necessity. According to Robert Harwood, corporate treasurer and CPA with Century Operating Corp., a New York–based management firm with over twenty years' experience, "Some board members read and some don't. They expect the managing agent to do everything. Management takes a primary role, but this is a business. It's important that board members read these things and thoroughly digest the information." Andrew Cursio, board treasurer for Savannah Owners Corp., a 144-unit luxury co-op on West 89th Street, agrees: "The treasurer should review each individual bill, get involved with budgeting and help develop investment strategies for the reserve fund."

Michael A. Walter of Michael A. Walter, CPA, adds, "The board must understand exactly where they stand today and where they're going tomorrow. It's a mistake to get caught up in minutiae and completely miss the big picture. Missing the big picture can cost you thousands of dollars."

So how can a board member most efficiently utilize these reports and at the same time actually understand what he or she is reading? It may seem paradoxical but the best monthly reports convey complex facts with true simplicity and concision. For example, computer graphics may be utilized to enhance and illustrate information visually. According to Walter, "You're not on top of your game if this process takes more than fifteen minutes."

One measure of a report's effectiveness is how well it reads—whether the services of your managing agent and accountant and their evaluation of your building's resources have been successfully translated into layperson's terms. "If it pleases the eye, it's easier to sit and bear with," says Harwood. To a large extent, the accountant and managing agent must responsibly educate board members, but all co-op owners would do well to take an active interest in these reports and demand that they be prepared in a discernible fashion.

Century Operating Corp.'s monthly reports contain four important subreports. First, a cash flow statement to monitor all incoming funds, as well as how and why any money was disbursed. This should include a year-to-date report that highlights variations in the budget and functions as a barometer for the co-op. "This often raises sticky questions like Why are we spending so much? What's gone up? Where are we going to get the money?" says Harwood.

Second, a good management report should contain an analysis of charges and collections, which is a detailed report of each shareholder's status, a rent roll (who was billed and who hasn't paid) and any other additional charges. Third, expect to see a shareholders' arrears report. This is used to monitor tenants with balances that are overdue, indicating why these tenants are delinquent and whether any legal recourse is required or under way. And fourth, an open accounts payable report, which charts bills currently unpaid that will have to be paid in the future. This is an important way of keeping abreast of upcoming capital requirements.

Jill Smith, CPA with AKAM Associates, a firm specializing in co-op and condo management, has a slightly different way of preparing monthly reports for co-op boards. On the tenth of every month, AKAM issues a financial management report that encompasses cash-based and accrual-type reports. It also includes a year-to-date budget, as well as variance from actual expenditures receivable and disbursement figures, receipts and an all-encompassing statement regarding the building's finances. This report also includes a summary of all checkbook activity, "which is very important, because the board must know how its money is being spent," says Smith.

Boards should not be intimidated by technical terms. AKAM often customizes its reports in such a way as to make a board comfortable, providing information in a more readable format. Boards are encouraged to contact their managing agents at any time to request additional backup to solve any potential discrepancies. According to Smith, "I don't think this info is particularly difficult to read. It's important that we gear these statements toward the average user." However, pressed further, she confesses that most people count on their board treasurers to do the heavy reading.

Every co-op should also receive an annual audit report from its own accountant. These reports are crucial because they will be examined by banks and potential buyers. According to Michael Walter, "A co-op should have a strategy not unlike that of corporate America for funding repairs and replacements—which increases the sales point of your co-op." A good CPA will include in his report surveys and audits comparing your co-op's expenses to similar-sized co-ops. "Don't hesitate to invite your accountant to every monthly meeting," says Walter. "He brings to the table survey data and unbiased expertise to keep your costs in line."

Your accountant should work closely with the board, summarize the annual audit report every six months and answer any questions board members may have. Monthly reports prepared by an accountant should contain much of the same information as the management report, as well as a seasonalized budget anticipating future bills, insurance matters and the tax implications of any new developments. According to Walter, "The interpretation process is crucial; your CPA must know what he's talking about." In addition, the CPA should work with the board and managing agent to develop a policy for funding future repairs and maintenance. Says Walter, "Things have changed. The rule of the '80s was, we'll just borrow it.

The rule of the '90s is, I wonder if there's a bank that will lend us the money."

Though it's true that treasurers are expected to keep on top of a building's finances, it's obviously in the best interest of the entire board to know exactly what's going on. So demand of your accountant and managing agent easy-to-read reports, stay in touch with your treasurer, avoid stale information and expect a new report every month.

Budget Plans and Projections: Look at the Bottom Line

By William Brangham

Each fall, co-op and condo boards begin the vital process of drawing up their budgets for the coming year and beyond. According to the experts, the budget should include spending and income projections for the coming year as well as projections of monetary needs for the next five years. A well-planned, closely monitored budget can protect owners from unexpected fiscal crunches.

The responsibility for drawing up the actual budget usually falls upon the managing agent. The agent will meet with the board president and treasurer, go over their accountant's records and then map out the building's basic costs compared to its revenues. Because most yearly financial projections begin on January 1, the planning process usually begins in the fall.

"In the '80s, it was cosmetic improvements that were big-ticket additions to a budget," says Ronni Arougheti, executive vice-president and general counsel for Heron Management, a firm that manages over forty buildings in New York. "Now it's these big maintenance improvements that must be considered," she says. Arougheti points out that almost all of the buildings built in New York during the 1970s are now maturing at the same time and most need major internal and external maintenance work. "Back in the '80s, all the engineers were saying, 'These things will need fixing in five to ten years.' Well, five to ten years are upon us and budgets need to reflect that."

What's In a Budget

In addition to major capital improvements, a building's budget must also factor in an array of variables such as individual and/or sponsor defaults and arrears, variable union contracts, rising real estate taxes and a series of new laws and regulations regarding recycling, disabled access, lead abatement and Common Interest Realty Associations (CIRA). "Budgets need to be very detailed these days," says Arougheti. "Buildings are running tightly now and each item in a budget must be examined very, very carefully."

"We focus on the elements that we have some control over," says a representative of Walter & Samuels, a management firm that represents over eighty buildings in New York. "Around 85 percent of the budget is made up of big items that we have little control over," he says. However, like Arougheti, he emphasizes the importance of close scrutiny of all available options. "For instance, a building's payroll costs are usually dictated by union contracts, but we can certainly organize the different work schedules to minimize costs—little or no overtime, no one working on vacation time, etc."

An alert managing agent is also quick to recognize potential cost changes and then prepare his or her client's budget correspondingly for the future. For example, Larry Kopp, board president of 345 East 69th Street, recalls how his co-op's managing agency, Douglas Elliman, countered the rising fuel costs spurred by the war in the Persian Gulf by focusing on even more efficient consumption and proper maintenance of its oil-burning equipment.

Expanding Role for Managers

It is this type of hands-on administration that characterizes the larger role that management firms are playing in the budgetary process. "In most cases, it's the agents who are writing the budgets," says CPA Stephen Beer of Czarnowski & Beer, a Manhattan accounting firm. "For most buildings, especially the larger ones, that's a more advantageous situation. The agent is usually more familiar with the building in its entirety: the tenants, the staff, the equipment and the building itself."

Whereas Beer was once asked to write more complete budgets, he now finds that the accountant's role is being minimized. "Now I'm there when the budget is completed to review it and make sure that nothing major was missed," he says. Apart from the continuous bookkeeping that he still attends to, he sees many of his previous responsibilities being divided up between the managing agent and the board treasurer.

Staying on Track

The one thing Beer feels still isn't being done properly is the monthly monitoring of the budget progress, which consists of comparing the actual expenditures to the projected ones. "This is something the board treasurer and agent should pick up on, especially if there isn't an accountant involved," he says.

As the party that handles all incoming revenue and authorizes and supervises all expenses, the agent takes the primary responsibility for monitoring finances. Management companies are certainly hearing the call. "We take a very aggressive role in monitoring our buildings' finances," says a Walter & Samuels executive. He feels that his job is made easier by the election of financially fluent people to board positions. "Most of the buildings we manage are smart enough to put the right people forward. They're being run like mini-corporations, mini-General Motors."

Arougheti points out that her firm does budget reviews every single month with its clients. In addition to that, she says, "There are two major reviews that we do: one at the six-month point, sometime in June, and then later in September." The firm monitors and notates everything from the rising costs of labor to tenants who are behind in their maintenance payments. Arougheti adds that she is disturbed by what she sees as the recession-driven reluctance of her clients to put aside funds for future, unforeseen expenses, although the new CIRA regulations are changing all that (see "The New CIRA Guidelines" on page 82).

Beer maintains that it is essential for boards to clearly delineate who monitors any deviations from the budget and who takes action to rectify such problems. "This constant regulation is especially important for condominiums that can't afford to borrow against their buildings the way co-ops can. All these expenditures have to be anticipated and planned for."

Planning for the Future

In addition to monitoring the budget from month to month, each year's budget process should include projections into the future. According to Andrew Cursio, a financial consultant with Shearson Lehman Brothers and board treasurer of his Upper West Side co-op, operating expenses have been rising at the rate of 5.7 percent per year, based on research done by the Council of New York Cooperatives. In addition, boards must plan for tax increases, tax abatement plans drawing to a close and capital expenditures, such as roof or boiler replacement.

Cursio points out that when interest rates are low, boards should look at alternative investments to help their reserves grow. "You have to do something to raise the money," he says. "My building bought a three-year annuity at 6.1 percent—that's twice what CDs were paying." Triple-A municipal bonds are another alternative, offering tax-free interest for five- to ten- year terms. Considering the tax savings, the yield comes to about 8 percent, says Cursio. Keeping a firm hand on the present and a watchful eye on the future is the goal of any prudent board's budget plan.

Co-op Income: Maintenance and Late Fees

By Stephen William Beer, CPA

The value crisis of the '90s has created the need for banks, prospective buyers and their attorneys to thoroughly scrutinize the details of a cooperative's financial statements. Furthermore, the issuance of the new CIRA guidelines by the American Institute of Certified Public Accountants on the disclosure of long-term capital budgets, and in effect the sufficiency of reserve funds, seems to have awakened shareholders to their liability for the replacement of the major components of common property. Since most cooperatives have instituted cost-cutting programs that would make the managers of corporate America proud, it is now time to concentrate on the top line—income.

Most co-op budgets are prepared on a break-even basis, which means that the income is calculated to be equal to the projected expenses. Since most sources of income, other than maintenance charges, are fixed, it will demonstrate the amount that maintenance must be raised in order to meet expenses. In reality, however, instead of approving the budget and imposing the necessary increase, the board will say, "We can't raise maintenance that much!"

Avoid Stop-Gap Measures

While in the past boards may have been able to limit increases, filling the gap by using reserve funds, mortgage refinancings and/or stretching out bill paying, the time to pay the piper has come. Nowadays, the first issue addressed by a bank in considering a co-op for refinancing is prior operating surpluses. Since generally accepted accounting principles require financial statements to be issued on the accrual basis, the use of these "stop-gap" strategies will be obvious. Furthermore, prospective buyers and their attorneys will quickly see trouble as well. In my accounting practice, I have had more calls from prospective buyers and their attorneys with questions about the financial statements of my cooperative clients in the last year than in the past five years. Prudent financial management has become a foremost responsibility of boards and they must avoid this "percentage increase phobia" if the shareholders wish to retain the value of their units.

As part of our audit procedures, we compare the annual results to the budget to reveal any errors. Many times, though, it is not that the annual results are out of line, but that the budget is off. This is usually due to the board adjusting the budget, in order to bring it in line with an acceptable percentage for a maintenance increase. Excuses such as "We had excessive repair bills last year" or "We spent so much money on the plumbing that nothing else can go wrong" will only lead to operating shortfalls. Whether we like it or not, expenses in New York City always seem to rise faster than the inflation rate. Boards must avoid the temptation to reduce the budgeted expense items solely for the purpose of limiting the amount of the maintenance increase to a perceived "acceptable" level.

Additional Income Sources

There are certain management policies and techniques that can increase cash flow and provide additional sources of income. Shareholders incorrectly assume that maintenance is due on the tenth of the month, rather than on the first of the month, with a ten-day grace period. Imposing a significant late fee for any payment received after the grace period is an effective cash management tool. In addition, it helps to provide added income without raising maintenance.

Instituting new procedures, such as applying shareholder payments received to outstanding late fees or repair charges before applying them to current maintenance charges, can quickly resolve a collection problem. Institute a policy of placing liens on tenant shareholder units for nonpayment of maintenance charges and instruct the managing agent to act quickly. The components of the monthly shareholder charges seem to have an effect on timely payment. Call it "tenant mentality," but shareholders seem averse to paying repair charges. They feel that in exchange for paying their maintenance charges, all repair expenses should be paid for by the cooperative, regardless of the terms of the proprietary lease. Perhaps this is why repair charges are commonly overlooked as a source of income. You may have a superintendent who cheerfully takes care of "inside apartment" repairs, but you should have a policy of charging a reasonable amount to the shareholder for his time and materials. In many older buildings, this can add up to a source of income comparable to that provided by late fees or laundry.

Other shareholder charges that raise income without increasing maintenance include sublet and transfer fees. If the board finds itself sympathetic to a resident's inability to sell his unit after the loss of a job, a marriage or simply the need to move to a larger apartment due to a growing family, the board can consider allowing him to rent his unit. But the co-op should be compensated for allowing this privilege with a sublet charge. I have seen charges as high as $100 per month, and with sublets on the increase due to a downturn in the present real estate market, several units paying these charges can go a long way toward limiting maintenance increases. Transfer fees can do the same thing, but with falling prices, they can become a burden to those who are not able to sell for as much as they paid.

Timely Collection Is Essential

These tight financial times also require that significant attention be paid to the timely collection of maintenance fees. A common red flag on the financial statement is a high amount of receivables due from shareholders. Buyers are steering clear of buildings with a history of arrears averaging over 1 percent of maintenance. Furthermore, now that market conditions have changed, it is not only sponsors who build up significant arrears. While foreclosing on an out-of-work neighbor is never appealing, the board must remember its fiduciary duty to the cooperative.

Compounding the collection problem is the separation between the board and the managing agent. Board members are usually able to review shareholder arrears only once a month. Many overburdened building managers have little time to enforce collection. It is not uncommon to notice that a vast majority of the arrears are due from only one or two shareholders. Therefore, it is imperative that the board monitor the collection process, as well as review the maintenance arrears report on a more frequent basis. I suggest requiring the agent to run the report either on the fifteenth day of the month or the day after the end of the grace period. Consider contacting delinquent shareholders at that point. Since agents usually distribute monthly reports to all of their clients at one time, it will probably be the fifteenth of the next month before the board sees these arrears. By adding this simple procedure, the collection process can be accelerated by one full month.

If the building continues to have problems collecting maintenance fees, the board should request that their attorney start notification or foreclosure proceedings after a specific period of time. This is especially important as the courts have been penalizing slow and haphazard collection procedures by awarding less than full arrears. Furthermore, banks holding mortgages on tenant units with excessive arrears are not stepping up and paying off the accumulations as they had in the past.

Being aware of the danger signals of shareholder default can go a long way in preventing the costly buildup of shareholder arrears. If collection procedures are not in place, new directors can quickly find themselves facing problems created by their predecessors. The simple implementation of the controls suggested above, along with prudent financial management, can help achieve adequate cash flow and desired operating results. This will not only protect the board and the shareholders from needless scrutiny, but support apartment values in the building as well.

Budget and Reserve Planning: Anticipate Spending

By Oskar Brecher

Co-op and condo managers and boards who have put off preparing their budgets until the eleventh hour may find the clock striking midnight on them. All too many boards and managers don't start thinking about the coming year's budget until the end of the year. But, in fact, budget planning should be a year-round process.

With the economy still tight, it is important to have a well-planned annual budget that will anticipate and prepare for maintenance and capital costs in an orderly, manageable fashion. That means planning not only for ongoing needs, but for large capital investments as well. Thus, budget planning and reserve fund strategies go hand in hand.

What to Look Out For

Capital improvements are one budget consideration that requires a multiyear plan. Co-op and condo board members must use forethought when budgeting money for such items as exterior renovations, plumbing and heating. When budgeting for the year, special attention should be paid to insurance costs. The current downward trend in insurance costs is expected to end, leaving co-ops and condos to face premium increases of at least 10 percent. In addition to monitoring insurance costs, it's advisable to watch the following items carefully throughout the year:

• **Payroll:** This may seem elementary. However, staffing levels must be reviewed regularly in order to cut or eliminate overtime and budget for vacation time. Proper scheduling can mitigate the problem of spending extra money on hiring part-time employees to cover for vacationers.

• **Property Tax Rates:** Real estate taxes should not increase significantly in the immediate future because they are already a political issue. However, the assessed value must be scrutinized carefully—and vigorously challenged if overstated.

• **Mortgage Rates:** They may rise as the economy recovers.

• **Utilities:** Energy-saving devices such as dual-fuel systems and fluorescent lights should be used and budgeted for.

• **Fuel Costs:** Fuel costs will probably remain unchanged next year.

• **Service Contracts:** The cost of such services as elevator maintenance and cleaning are not likely to increase in this competitive environment.

• **Delinquent Payments:** In this sluggish economy, set aside funds for possible delinquencies by shareholders and owners.

Reserve Fund Planning

Equally important to planning the budget is maintaining the reserve fund. After estimating the year's operating and capital expenses, a prudent board and/or managing agent will make sure some money goes into the reserve fund.

The position of a board on the reserve level is the main litmus test of fiscal responsibility. It is wise to maintain an appropriate level of funds to meet capital requirements as they arise. The replacement or renovation of major building components may be funded by special assessments, from reserves or by borrowing (especially in case of a cooperative). But reserve funds are an important part of the mix.

A purist in financial theory would define the adequate level of reserves as the minimum amount required to meet funding needs as they occur without having to resort to special assessments or borrowing. Your managing agent, with the help of an accountant and engineer, should be able to determine the useful life of your building's major components and come up with a theoretical reserve-fund level. If your managing agent cannot, such organizations as the Community Associations Institute can put you in touch with firms that specialize in the development of reserve-fund programs.

Those of you who care to follow such a business-school approach may want to ask your management firm to develop a "replacement reserve model" for your building, for the useful insights it provides. However, the theoretical levels must often be modified by practical considerations. Buildings in which shareholders and owners are able to fund capital improvement on demand, which is often the case on Fifth or Park Avenue, may not need any reserves. They invest their own money rather than having the building do it for them, and spend it when the building requires improvements. But properties whose owners have more modest resources should adhere more closely to the reserve levels determined by the financial model.

Cooperatives with unused borrowing capacity may need smaller reserves than identical condominiums. In times of economic uncertainty, reserves should be increased to compensate for the potential inability of individual shareholders to meet their obligations.

Three Different Strategies

Practical applications of the reserve-fund policy are illustrated by three of the buildings that we manage. One of the premier buildings on Central Park West, with approximately one hundred of the most desirable apartments in the city, has no reserve fund at all. The cooperative is lightly mortgaged and is confident that it can meet its obligations by special assessment or increasing its mortgage.

A middle course was elected by 58 West 58th Street, a condominium of 170 apartments in superb condition as a result of an ongoing preventive maintenance program. It maintains a reserve fund of between $200,000 and $600,000, depending on the status of the maintenance cycle.

An eighty-eight–unit cooperative at 150 Joralemon Street in Brooklyn is about to embark on a major capital improvement program, for which it has amassed almost $900,000 in reserve. This co-op has a prudent and conservative financial policy. Even upon completion of the proposed project, the reserve will be left with a substantial fund to meet future needs.

Each of these buildings has elected a specific and appropriate solution for its reserve requirements. Fully funded reserve levels, as determined by the financial model, are not always necessary, and are sometimes counterproductive. The question that has to be resolved responsibly by each board is: Where on the spectrum between zero and full funding is the right place to be? That depends on the circumstances of the building, its owners and the economy.

Preserve the Reserve: Investments That Work

By Andrew Cursio

Boards of directors of cooperative corporations, condominiums and home-owners' associations are being faced with new challenges in the management of their reserve funds. Preserving the reserve used to be easy. The traditional method of investing reserve funds was simply to invest the funds in low-risk savings accounts, money markets and certificates of deposit. Since 1990, returns on these types of investments have dropped from 8 percent to under 5 percent. The boards that continue to invest their reserves in these instruments are now losing money because their returns are lagging behind the rate of inflation.

Preserving the reserve means more than increasing the reserve fund account. According to a review of annual co-op and condo budgets conducted by the Council of New York Cooperatives, the cost of operations and capital expenditures has been rising an average of 6 percent per year. In order to preserve the reserve, the fund must provide a rate of return that exceeds that, while also providing an adequate return to help finance the future cost of capital improvements.

Managing the reserve fund can be a difficult task for board members, and every board will approach the problem in a different manner. For those boards who have not identified the expected future costs of building repairs and who have not properly planned for these costs, the only option to consider when investing the reserve fund is to stay liquid.

Long-Term Planning

Norman Prisand, a principal at Prisand-Newman, an accounting firm representing more than 150 co-ops and condos, has long stressed the importance of planning. "No big business would be without a five-year plan, and board members must realize that they are managing a big business. The long-range plan sets a framework within which the housing entity should operate and manage its activity. The object is to promote long-term stability."

The American Institute of Certified Public Accountants (AICPA) has recently implemented certain requirements to ensure proper planning. In order to help buildings more effectively manage and monitor the replacement of major building components such as elevators, boilers, plumbing, electrical systems, window replacements and sidewalks, the AICPA has recently issued an audit and accounting guide entitled Audits of Common Interest Realty Associations (CIRA). This guide requires co-ops and condos to make fuller disclosure about the condition of reserves in audited financial statements for periods ending on or after September 15, 1992. CIRA instructs boards to include footnotes about current estimates of future repairs and replacements of all major building components and funding policies to provide resources for these requirements. This schedule will help preserve the reserve because it will help the board of directors make more long-term investments and manage investment risk more efficiently by knowing when funds will be needed.

As many boards begin to address the CIRA requirements they are finding that their reserve funds may not be able to meet the future capital improvement and repair needs of their buildings, especially if they continue investing in low-interest-bearing money markets and certificates of deposit.

If co-op and condo boards do not take prudent steps to increase the returns on their reserve funds, shareholders could be faced with very large prices to pay when repairs and replacements must be made. Relying upon banks for large loans to finance these capital improvements can put unnecessary financial stress on shareholders that proper planning and investment of the reserve funds can avoid. The difference in potential income for the reserve fund between a $100,000 investment earning 4 percent and one earning 8 percent annually over a five-year period is more than $30,000.

Setting Investment Policy

A finance committee, which is solely responsible for the management of the reserve fund, should be formed and headed by the treasurer. The committee should seek out shareholders in the building who have a financial background to join and help out. It may also want to consider seeking the advice of investment advisors to enhance the committee's knowledge in accordance with its fiduciary responsibilities.

The finance committee should identify the adequacy of the reserve funds and execute a written investment policy to set the investment objectives for the reserve funds. This should define: (1) investment guidelines that address the target rate of return; (2) investment vehicles that will help achieve the desired rate of return; (3) guidelines on how the reserve fund should be managed and whether some funds should be placed under professional money management and (4) methods of monitoring and reporting returns to shareholders. This type of investment policy will create continuity for the board and is needed for any long-term investment program.

The selection of investments and the manner in which they will be invested (for instance, self-directed investments or professional portfolio management) will vary among buildings, based on the size of the reserve, investment objectives, target rates of return and liquidity needs, all of which should correspond with expected repairs and replacement costs identified in the engineering study of the building.

When selecting the appropriate investments for the reserve fund, the board must first understand the typical behavior of the various investment choices (see chart on following page).

1. Money market investments and short-term certificates of deposit will be virtually safe from loss and provide liquidity, but may not be good investments for the long-

Have Excess Cash Reserves Put You At A Disadvantage?

You may be sacrificing earning potential or opportunity cost if you are keeping more than necessary in lower-yielding, domestic short-term cash equivalents.*

Worldwide Yield Opportunities Guide

*Turn Opportunity Cost
To a Yield Advantage*

Use the table below to determine the potential advantage your excess cash reserves would earn from a longer-term investment seeking higher yields worldwide.*

Just by moving $100,000 invested at 7% to an investment yielding 8%— a yield differential of only 1%—you would enjoy the potential income advantage of $3,731 in just three short years.

Yield Differential**	Yield Advantage/Opportunity Cost			
	1 year	3 years	5 years	10 years
0.50%	$534	$1,852	$3,567	$10,240
0.75%	$802	$2,788	$5,383	$15,553
1 00%	$1,071	$3,731	$7,222	$20,998
1.25%	$1,340	$4,681	$9,083	$26,579
1.50%	$1,610	$5,638	$10,968	$32,299
1.75%	$1,881	$6,601	$12,875	$38,161
2.00%	$2,152	$7,572	$14,806	$44,170
2.25%	$2,423	$8,550	$16,760	$50,328
2.50%	$2,696	$9,535	$18,738	$56,639
2.75%	$2,969	$10,526	$20,741	$63,108
3.00%	$3,242	$11,526	$22,768	$69,738
3.25%	$3,517	$12,532	$24,820	$76,533
3.50%	$3,791	$13,546	$26,898	$83,497
3.75%	$4,067	$14,567	$29,001	$90,634
4.00%	$4,343	$15,595	$31,129	$97,949

*Of course, long-term investments are generally subject to greater fluctuation of investment return and principal value than short-term investments. Investments in foreign securities are subject to special risks such as those associated with currency fluctuations.

**Represents the difference in yield, assuming a base yield of 7%, between two hypothetical investments (having fixed rates of return) with interest compounded monthly. If base yield is other than 7%, yield advantage/opportunity cost will vary. The percentages used here are for illustration only and are not intended to represent current or future differences in yield between investments.

term capital needs of reserve funds because their growth rate seldom exceeds the inflation rate.

2. Fixed-income investments such as treasury bonds, mortgage-backed bonds, corporate bonds and municipal bonds will also sacrifice long-term potential and often lose ground to inflation, but under most conditions will provide consistent positive returns year after year largely in the form of interest payments, if the securities are held to maturity. Investments in municipal bonds, which are exempt from local, state and federal taxes, may provide added income benefits if your building is subject to Sections 216 and 277 of the Internal Revenue Code.

3. Stocks will hold far more long-term growth potential than any other financial asset class, but also the most short-term risk. Reserve funds that should be considered in this asset class are strictly those funds that will not be needed for major repairs or replacements over the next five years. Historically, common stocks have provided a higher rate of return than other investments and have outpaced inflation.

A Balanced Portfolio

The best route for most buildings in preserving the reserve is to develop a portfolio of investments that utilizes the potential to be gained from a combination of money markets, fixed income securities and common stocks. The more asset types in the reserve portfolio, the more favorable the risk/return reward profile of the reserve fund. The types of investments selected should coincide with the expected repairs and replacements schedule in order to manage investment risk.

In an effort to comply with CIRA, our fictional co-op board has identified the following capital expenditures over the next seven years:

Repair and Replacement Cost Schedule
December 1992

Component	Est. Remaining Life	Est. Replacement Cost
Furniture	3 years	$ 35,000
Elevators	4 years	80,000
Roof	5 years	100,000
Windows	7 years	175,000

The reserve fund that is available to meet these expenses is approximately $275,000. Only after properly identifying the estimated capital expenditure needs as illustrated in the above example can the board begin to create a portfolio of investments.

In order to meet the short-term expenses listed above, the board may want to invest in bonds by using an investment approach called "laddering" that minimizes any interest rate risk associated with selecting a particular maturity. Creating a bond ladder means buying bonds scheduled to mature at several dates in the future, rather than all in the same year. A ladder is especially effective when investors need money available on certain future dates and want to minimize interest rate risk. A

SELECTING THE RIGHT KINDS OF INVESTMENTS

This chart gives you a simple overview of various kinds of securities, grouped by investment category. As you review each investment option, consider whether it will (1) satisfy your investing objective(s), (2) generate the kind of returns you expect and (3) involve a level of risk you're comfortable with.

Note that actual risk and return potential may vary for specific investments in each category. This reference provides general direction only and there will be exceptions in each category.

	Investment Objective	Return/Growth Potential	Risk
Stock Investments			
Individual stocks	Maximum growth/ Growth	Very High/High	Very High/High
Stock mutual funds			
• Aggressive growth	Maximum growth	Very High	Very High
• Growth	Growth	High	Very High
• Index	Growth	High	High
Bond Investments			
Corporate bonds	Income	Moderate	Medium*
(investment grade)			
Municipal bonds	Tax-exempt income	Moderate	Medium*
U.S. government bonds	Income/Safety	Low/Moderate	Low/Moderate*
• Zero coupon bonds	Growth	Moderate	Low/Moderate*
Bond mutual funds			
• Corporate bond	Income	Moderate	Medium*
• Municipal bond	Tax-exempt income	Moderate	Medium*
• U.S. government bond	Income/Safety	Low/Moderate	Low/Medium*
Cash equivalent investments			
Certificates of deposit	Safety/Income	Low	Low
Treasury bills	Safety/Income	Low	Low
Money market funds	Safety/Income	Low	Low
U.S. gov't money mkt. funds	Safety/Income	Low	Low
Tax-exempt money mkt. funds	Safety/Tax-exempt income	Low	Low

Both maturity and credit quality of the issuer are important determinants of risk for bonds. Bear in mind that usually the shorter the maturity, the lower the risk and the longer the maturity, the greater the risk.

sample bond portfolio for our fictional co-op might look like this:

1. $35,000—Municipal or treasury bond maturing in three years to meet the expected expense for furniture.

2. $80,000—Municipal or treasury bond maturing in four years to meet the expected expense for elevators.

3. $100,000—Municipal or treasury bond maturing in five years to meet the expected expense for the roof.

While laddering bonds will not provide as much income as buying only long-term bonds, it is safer for the reserve funds because it entails diversification and eliminates the need for the board to gamble on the direction of interest rates. At maturity, the full principal value of each bond is repaid. If rates go up and the reserve fund is invested in long-term bonds, the bonds in the reserve fund might produce capital losses if there is a need to sell the bonds before they mature.

While an investment in a short-term bond mutual fund may be considered by the board, there are some disadvantages associated with bond mutual funds, especially when planning to meet short-term expenses. Since bond mutual funds are actively managed, they do not have a fixed maturity date. Without a fixed maturity date, the board will not be able to calculate the exact amount of money that will be available at some future date. For those boards who want to earmark a certain dollar amount to meet their short-term expenses and not have to worry about it again, investing in individual bonds in a laddered portfolio offers the best approach.

The remaining $60,000 of the reserve fund should be considered for investments in stocks. Stocks are volatile investments. Only those reserve funds that will not be needed in the next five years should be considered for an investment in common stocks. While common stock returns can vary from one year to the next, an investment in stocks over a five-year period will reduce the risk of loss and, more important, provide the board with an opportunity for returns much higher than bonds and the inflation rate.

This sample investment approach will help the board in a number of ways. First, by diversifying between stocks and bonds, investment risk can be managed. Second, the use of a laddered portfolio will help meet the short-term needs of the reserve funds and provide a higher return than an investment in money markets, shorter-term treasuries or certificates of deposit.

Finally, in this example, the board has designed a portfolio so that the proper funding is available to meet expected capital expenditures. Risk has been managed according to the type of investment selected, timing and amount of money required.

There is undoubtedly a balancing act between maximizing returns and preserving the reserve against the rising costs of capital replacements and improvements. Boards can no longer afford to let their reserve funds sit idle in the bank. Proper planning and management of building repairs and replacement costs can help to reduce costs to shareholders and help preserve the reserve for future expenditures.

Is Your Building Fiscally Fit? Detecting Early Warning Signs

By William Brangham

Just as doctors keep a watchful eye on the health of their patients through routine physical examinations, cooperative and condominium boards monitor their own fiscal fitness with regular financial checks. But while the warning signs pointing a doctor toward possible ailments are usually quite clear, the symptoms of fiscal maladies may be a little more difficult to detect.

"The number one sign that you're in financial trouble is when someone slips a foreclosure notice under your door," jokes Gary Kokalari, a former vice-president and regional manager of Washington Financial Management Group in Jersey City and currently a financial consultant for Merrill Lynch. "Unfortunately, as far as warning signs go, there are no scientific principles that apply. It's usually a combination of signals, each of which individually may be explainable, but when coupled with other signs probably means trouble."

Red Flags

Kokalari, who, in addition to his work in finance, used to preside over his own building's board, sees factors such as constant deficit spending, delinquent bill paying, a ballooning of shareholder arrears and erratic increases in monthly maintenance costs as red flags that should send an immediate message that the building isn't on stable ground.

According to an executive at Century Operating Corp., a Manhattan building management firm, the above factors certainly are primary warning signs, and they all fall under the budget category of a building's finances. "The budget is the key," he says. "Maintaining a realistic and diligent budget is the only way to keep your finger on the pulse of a building. It's still the best way to stem any future problems."

According to others, there are even subtler warnings to heed. For instance, consider the experience of Paulette Bonnano, vice-president of the National Cooperative Bank. As a lending officer, Bonnano is responsible for making quick assessments about a building's financial condition. One way in which she determines the soundness of a co-op, beyond the standard financial checks, is by visiting the building itself. "A co-op that's in disrepair, one that's being poorly maintained, is often a signal that something's wrong," she says. She describes the fine line that boards must draw as their budgets grow tighter: "If a board is in real financial trouble, how much money are they really willing to spend on physical upkeep at the cost of raising the maintenance fees? A building that's falling apart may be telling you something."

CIRA Requirements

Many investors see the new CIRA requirements, which assess the useful life left in a building's major components, as being a welcome budgetary tool that encourages long-term planning. Others note, however, that since the CIRA checklists aren't a mandatory requirement and are currently used only on a voluntary basis, they may be misleading. Kokalari says, "The CIRA requirements, while certainly well intentioned, can sometimes be used for the wrong reasons. A building that will look good on the CIRA checklist will certainly do it, while other buildings think they'd just be opening a huge can of worms." He says that the absence of the CIRA report from a yearly financial statement may be a warning. "If your building isn't following the guidelines, you may want to ask why. If there are problems looming ahead, then hiding your head in the sand is no solution."

Another possible indicator of a co-op's fiscal problems is an unusually large percentage of sublet apartments. "While I like to see flexibility on the board's part in relation to subletting, too many sublet units may be a sign of an investor building," says Bonnano. "Some people honestly have to sell, and the current market makes it harder to do so, but a majority in one building? That's a problem." She also points out that as far as a bank is concerned, "when you're lending to a co-op, you're supposed to be lending to owner property, but if half the units are sublets, then that's a different matter."

An accountant with the firm of Marin & Montanye, in Port Washington, Long Island, feels that there may also be discrepancies between various reports and financial statements. "Numbers can be deceiving," he says. While he says that blatant misrepresentation is not all that common and such behavior may result in prosecution, he notes, "It's clearly the duty of all parties to fully disclose their financial situations, especially in the case of sponsor buildings. But who willingly puts a noose around his own neck?"

Finding Help

That point highlights a concern echoed by others in the real estate community that valid information is often hard for tenants or shareholders to come by. While the basic indicators of trouble may seem obvious on the surface—failing to pay the bills, growing debts—there are those who feel that buyers, and owners in particular, need more education.

"What the co-op and condo community doesn't have is an entity that can assist the individual home owners. Current organizations just aren't geared to their needs," says Roberta Hendler, head of RLH Associates, a co-op consulting firm in Manhattan. She feels that one of the best ways for boards and individuals to lessen the chance of fiscal surprise is to broaden the network of information, advice and knowledge. "Talk to anyone and everyone you can about co-ops," she says. "Get referrals, call outside agencies, talk with other professionals and exercise your rightful access to information."

Along with all the sleuthing that must be done, Hendler sees a larger focus that helps fuel the fires of fiscal investigation. "You have to think of your role as that of a co-op home owner, not a shareholder. The term shareholder implies some sort of an arm's-length relationship with your property. Thinking of this as your home, in which you have vital and vested interests, gives you an added sense of empowerment to learn all you possibly can," she says.

Through a widening recognition of the warning signs of financial problems and an increasing understanding of exactly what is at stake, boards and individuals alike will be better prepared to avoid future financial disasters.

Consider a Credit Line: Ready Money at Lower Cost

By Gregg Winter

When the time to refinance arrives, there are several compelling reasons why boards should consider obtaining a line of credit along with their new underlying mortgage. It will never be less expensive to arrange this type of subordinate financing than when a building is refinancing its mortgage. Even if the board doesn't anticipate needing additional funds for three or four years, in many cases, credit lines can be put in place at the time of a mortgage refinance with no additional closing costs and no annual fee.

Once a credit line has been established, the board can draw upon it at will. Typically, a credit line's interest rate will be floating according to a spread over prime. Although the most common spread is 1 percent over prime, the best buildings may qualify for an even more advantageous spread of .25 percent to .5 percent over prime.

Get Access Now, Pay Later

There are several advantages to a floating-rate credit line over a larger fixed-rate mortgage. For one thing, your board does not needlessly have to pay interest on money it does not yet need. A credit line is simply an agreement to borrow money at a later time, quickly and easily, if and when it is needed.

In one case, a fifty-unit, 85-percent-owner-occupied cooperative in Brooklyn Heights was seeking to replace its mortgage. The rate on the old mortgage was nearly 10 percent. A new $1.1 million ten-year fixed-rate mortgage was obtained at 8.18 percent, along with an unsecured credit line of $200,000 floating at 1 percent over prime. By increasing the mortgage amount, the co-op would be able to cover closing costs, replace its water tower and take care of other maintenance such as pointing and waterproofing. The $200,000 credit line would be available for future capital improvements. Since it was possible to arrange the unsecured revolving credit line without any annual fee, the board did not have to borrow money it did not anticipate needing for three or four years, thus minimizing the interest costs.

In another situation, a seventeen-unit loft cooperative is refinancing its underlying mortgage to obtain a much better rate and a longer term. The board is also contemplating the purchase of the two ground-floor commercial co-op units, currently being used as retail stores. The new lender agrees that the proposed purchase makes good economic sense, and has approved a credit line that would allow the board to proceed. If, however, for any reason the purchase of the stores is never consummated, the board will not have needlessly borrowed the money. If the board does purchase the stores, the profits generated are expected to be able to repay the credit line within five years.

Tax Savings

From a co-op board's point of view, an unsecured line of credit has several distinct advantages over a secured credit line. However, it is also more difficult to qualify for. One advantage is that there is no mortgage recording tax due or payable on an unsecured credit line. In New York City, mortgage recording tax is a big-ticket item: All commercial mortgages of more than $500,000 are taxed at the rate of 2.75 percent. Thus, on a $600,000 unsecured line of credit, a co-op corporation would save $16,500 in mortgage recording tax. In addition, because the unsecured line is not a mortgage, the board can borrow then pay it back, borrow again and pay it back again at will. This is what is known as a revolving line of credit.

A secured credit line can usually be drawn to its maximum only once. If, after borrowing from a secured credit line, and over time, paying it all back, the board wants to draw upon the available funds again, technically they would be required to pay the mortgage recording tax again. When a secured credit line is first established, the mortgage recording tax is paid on the full amount of the credit line.

If your board qualifies, it is clearly a better choice to obtain an unsecured, revolving credit line than a secured credit line. Depending on the lender and your negotiating strength, it may well be possible to arrange such a credit line without any nonuse fee. Some lenders will charge a fee between .25 percent and 1 percent of the unused available amount of the credit line on an annual basis. For example, if a co-op board has a $250,000 line of credit with a nonuse fee of 1 percent per year and the board has drawn $150,000, the bank would charge 1 percent of the unused portion, or $1,000, to maintain the availability of the unused $100,000 balance of the credit line. This fee can often be eliminated during negotiations.

Short-Term Saves Money

If a co-op has a yield-maintenance prepayment penalty on its long-term fixed-rate first mortgage, it is virtually prevented from refinancing before the end of the mortgage term (most often ten years). Therefore, if additional funds are needed during the term of the mortgage for capital improvements or repairs, those funds will have to come from the building's reserve fund, an assessment of the shareholders or a credit line that the building has established for this purpose.

Not surprisingly, many co-op boards are choosing the latter for their short-term borrowing needs. One of the benefits of borrowing from a credit line for a specific project is that the co-op board can control the schedule of repayment, sometimes paying interest only and sometimes paying down the principal balance.

For example, if your board has a credit line and borrows $100,000 to replace an elevator, rather than adding that $100,000 to the building's permanent mortgage, the board might well decide to do the work and to fully repay the $100,000 over a period of three to four years. The disciplined use of a credit line can help to keep the lid on what could otherwise become a never-ending upward spiral of your underlying mortgage balance. This approach only works, however, if the board views the credit line as short-term borrowing and makes careful and realistic repayment plans before borrowing and spending the funds. Most credit lines must be used and repaid within five years.

It is important to note that not every lender active in the cooperative underlying mortgage market offers credit lines. The size of your mortgage and the quality of your co-op corporation, as measured by factors such as location, number of units, percentage of owner-occupied apartments and recent resale prices of apartments, will affect which lender and which approach make the most sense for your building. The starting point for a co-op board must always be a sound long-term financial plan. The correct approach to take with financing should always be dictated by that plan.

CIRA Guidelines: Long-Term Financial Audits

By Kate Shogi

In real estate as in life, the future is paved with uncertainty and nothing is a sure thing. However, in 1992 the American Institute of Certified Public Accountants (AICPA) issued a guide for its members that is designed to help the board of a co-op or condo predict and prepare for impending building improvements. The audits of Common Interest Realty Associations (CIRA), the first set of qualified accounting guidelines for co-ops and condos, was created to help shareholders and prospective buyers analyze a building's finances in a more sophisticated way. In addition, they provide an excellent tool to assist accountants and board members in addressing the issue of long-term capital budgets.

Complying With CIRA

The road to compliance consists of several elements. The CIRA guide requires a board to produce a review of the building's major components—the elevator, the roof, the boiler and the electrical and plumbing systems, for example—and determine the components' remaining life and estimated repair or replacement cost.

The board must then specify how these capital repairs or replacements will be funded, although there is no requirement stating how to finance them. These findings will then supplement the building's certified financial statement. If the board does not disclose the findings and funding policy, the accountant must make a note of that in the annual financial statement.

The first step that should be taken involves hiring a qualified outside investigator—a contractor, engineer or architect—to perform the review. You should be looking for "somebody competent and able to give a credible evaluation," says Marvin Schwartz, a partner in the accounting firm Jacobs and Schwartz. Keep in mind that although it may be recommended, you do not necessarily need to hire an engineer. You may have service contracts with a contractor who you feel confidence in. Charles Marino, whose firm, Braxton Engineering, has performed several such investigations, recommends performing a "total and thorough survey of all of the systems within a building [as opposed to] the 'mini,' which merely examines the major components." This comprehensive information will cost anywhere from $1,500 to $6,000, depending on the size, complexity and age of the building; the average for a one hundred–unit building is between $2,000 and $2,500. "If the building is relatively new or in good repair, the engineer's job is easy," Marino says. "But in a prewar building, we typically find that they need a lot of exterior work."

When the inspection is completed, the board is provided with a report, which typically has three columns, listing the item, the item's remaining useful life in years and its current estimated replacement cost. It is then up to the board to work in conjunction with the building's accountant to review these findings and determine future financing.

No Boon to Boards

Although the CIRA requirements are a boon to the buyer, shareholder and lender alike, many boards are not happy with the idea of disclosing figures that are so seemingly large, especially in an era of sharply rising operating costs and higher taxes. Suppose, for instance, that an engineer comes in to assess your building's systems, and announces that the elevator will need to be replaced in twenty years to the tune of $200,000. "Technically, if you were going to follow a grid line, you would set aside $10,000 a year for twenty years," says Marino.

Certainly, that would seem the sensible route. However, not all boards fund these items as a yearly amount. "It may not be financially feasible at this particular time," cautions Schwartz.

Stephen William Beer, a certified public accountant with Czarnowski & Beer in Manhattan, echoes that sentiment in an explanatory guide to the CIRA accounting practice. He writes: "…most boards tend to postpone funding for future major repairs and replacements until an emergency occurs…only then do they finance them or make capital and/or special assessments."

Schwartz targets the sluggish real estate market as a reason for the unpopularity of the new guidelines. "In this marketplace, to increase maintenance for reserve funds is not a popular plan, as many stockholders can't sell their apartments." In addition, he says, "They don't want to hear about the future when the marketability of their apartments is so low."

In the past, many buildings would take out equity loans or refinance in order to make capital improvements. But nowadays, the hesitancy on the part of many banks makes these funding options much harder to come by, and many boards are left wondering how best to proceed. Nevertheless, the regulations are already in effect, and are naturally causing some confusion. "Up until now, financial statements have given the history of the [co-op or condo]; they have not addressed the issue of capital improvement," says Martin M. Marin, a former partner in the firm Marin & Montayne on Long Island. "This is the first time that the future is being addressed in a financial statement." He adds, however, that New York is not alone. "New York is lagging nationally. Many states have voluntarily gone into this—they've addressed this problem for years."

In order to best fulfill your compliance with these new regulations, it's a good idea to educate yourself and talk with your accountant, who should be well versed in the matter of CIRA requirements. The sooner you prepare a financial plan for your building's boiler, the better you'll be able to prevent it from permanently shutting off in February. Remember, these requirements don't need to be regarded as a headache. Instead, think of them as a mechanism that can be used to help determine your building's future fiscal stability.

Responding to CIRA: Should Buildings File or Not?

By William Brangham

Everyone wants to be able to predict the future. Unfortunately, that talent is still out of our reach. Instead, we predict, we hypothesize and we plan ahead. With that sentiment in mind, the American Institute of Certified Public Accountants (AICPA) offered the co-op and condo community a set of guidelines in 1992 that they felt would help building owners and potential buyers predict and plan for the future.

Known as Audits of Common Interest Realty Associations, or CIRA, these guidelines encourage buildings to investigate and disclose the total costs of all current and future capital improvement projects. Buildings are also encouraged to specify where funds for these future projects will come from. The requirements are not mandated by law; a building chooses whether or not to file a CIRA report.

At first, the CIRA guidelines were viewed as a welcome budgetary tool. Everyone praised their intent and lamented the lack of long-term focus in many previous budgets. However, now that it's come time to actually start complying, not everyone is so enthusiastic.

"Initially, it sounded like a very good idea, but the more we looked into it, the more pitfalls we saw," says Oskar Brecher, managing director of American Landmark Management. Brecher, like several other managing agents, finds that complying with the CIRA guidelines is often more trouble than it's worth.

A completed CIRA report consist of three columns. Column one lists the item or piece of equipment, column two notes its estimated life expectancy and column three notes its replacement cost. Many point out that an accurate assessment of the second column, the life expectancy, hinges on too many variables to make the predictions reliable. "Take a boiler, for instance," says Matthew Newman of Walter & Samuels, a Manhattan management firm. "Let's say it's forty years old and its life expectancy is forty years. That boiler could still last another twenty-five years, so how do you punch that in?" Newman also points out that column three, the replacement cost estimate, is troublesome. "When calculating costs in the future, do you use current prices or future costs? What about inflation assumptions? What about interest-rate assumptions?" he asks. "So you end up doing it in today's dollars, and what's the point?"

The real issue here seems to be one of perception. Critics feel that the CIRA reports seem to offer imprecise information as factual data. "The problem with the reports is not so much that they ask you for reasonable judgments," says Brecher. "The problem is that they take what is a degree of probability and translate that into a certainty just by the sheer fact that the reports exist." The very fact that these reports are put alongside the financial statement gives them added importance, says Brecher, and, despite any disclaimers, they're weighed too heavily.

Accountant Stephen Beer of Czarnowski & Beer understands these concerns but disagrees. "First off, as an accountant, I would rather know where the building was than not to know. Second, the whole program is designed to be a set of estimates, not exact data," he points out.

A recent advisory issued by the Council of New York Cooperatives expresses outright skepticism. The open letter, which advises against producing CIRA reports, states, "Although AICPA does instruct the auditors to apply certain limited testing procedures to the information they receive, in the end, they disclaim responsibility for the validity of the information as a whole. The cooperative and condominium do not enjoy similar protection."

Brecher also voices concern, saying, "The producer of the information (the building) assumes some latitude in terms of how that information is being used, while the receiver (a potential buyer) expects it to be very precise."

The council's advisory also notes that the costs of producing the CIRA reports may vary widely, and they quote prices ranging anywhere from $3,000 to $20,000 for a "competent engineering study." Newman sees a corresponding problem. "It's such an ambivalent situation where you get engineers saying, 'I can't do [the report] for less than $10,000,' and others who'll do it for $2,000. You have to wonder what's the right price and what am I getting? Is one overkill or is another not doing the job? I can't answer that, and I don't want to be the one to pay to find out," he says.

The council advises that if a building does, in fact, file a CIRA report, it should include a potent disclaimer that emphasizes the hypothetical nature of the information. They advise boards to say that "the information was assembled on a best-effort basis, but no representation is made as to its accuracy or applicability."

Brecher notes that, despite any disclaimer, boards may shy away from CIRA reports because they feel that the report is almost a tacit guarantee to building residents against any unforeseen future costs. "What if somebody makes a purchasing decision based on these documents, and then it turns out that a couple of years down the line things are totally different from what was anticipated? The buyer then feels he may have been misled."

Despite their concerns, many managing agents and accountants seem to think that the CIRA debate will be resolved when banks routinely start asking for them. "As more and more buildings refinance, as more and more banks ask for the reports, more and more buildings will start doing the CIRAs," says Newman. "Then, people who are looking to buy an apartment will say, 'Well, why did this building do it and not this other?' and they're going to start asking questions."

Beer feels that this snowball effect is proof that in the long run, CIRA reports are valuable. He says, "The fact that banks will probably start asking for this information gives you evidence that this is important information that needs to be known."

Underlying Co-op Mortgages

- *Refinancing your building's mortgage*
- *Working with banks*
- *Terms and rates*

Building Refinancing: Restructure Mortgages With Care

By Steven M. Alevy

The financing of your co-op's underlying mortgage is one of the most significant factors in the fiscal integrity of your building, impacting the value of each individual unit. The recent growth in the co-op lending market, with many new players entering the field, and the advent of a more fluid secondary market for co-op mortgages, has given co-ops the opportunity to tailor their loans to fit the exact needs of the building.

When your current underlying mortgage needs to be refinanced— whether it is because a balloon payment is coming due, the building needs funds for capital improvements or interest rates have dropped significantly—the board should take the time to study all of its options. It is important for the board of directors to work with a professional mortgage broker who can educate, inform and advise the board on what refinancing arrangement would best satisfy the building's needs.

The primary mortgage market is comprised of savings banks and commercial banks, which raise funds through the deposits of their customers. The secondary mortgage market consists of insurance companies, pension funds and government funds such as the Federal National Mortgage Association (known as Fannie Mae) and the Federal Home Loan Mortgage Corporation (known as Freddie Mac). The secondary market's source of funds is through insurance premiums, Wall Street and the securitization of Mortgage Backed Securities. Because the secondary market has a lower cost of funds, it is able to offer lower interest rates to the borrower.

Lenders are in the business of lending money to make a profit; their primary concern is safety of principal. Because the safest loan for anyone to make is in U.S. Treasuries, their yield serves as a barometer for all other interest rates. For example, a five-year loan will be priced at a certain point spread over the five-year U.S. Treasury, which is currently trading at about 5.7 percent.

Another important factor in determining the interest rate of a loan is how long you are borrowing the money for. A lender will charge a higher interest rate for a thirty-year loan than for a fifteen-year loan. If the interest rate is significantly higher for the longer-term loan, it may not pay for the building to take that option.

A short-term loan, from five to seven years, offers the advantage of short-term savings, but you will be gambling on where interest rates will be when the mortgage matures. On the other hand, if you choose a long-term loan, say twenty or thirty years, and rates drop, you will not be able to take advantage of the lower rates, because these loans cannot be refinanced without a hefty prepayment penalty.

If your co-op must reduce its maintenance in order to maintain values or improve unit sales, a short-term mortgage should be given serious consideration. On the other hand, if your co-op can afford to pay a little more for the long-term security of a low rate, a long-term loan should be considered.

In addition to the payment of interest on the money you borrow, lenders usually require that throughout the life of the loan you make monthly payments towards reduction of principal. This reduction of principal is known as amortization. A "thirty-year amortization schedule," for example, means that the monthly contributions to reduction of principal are based on a thirty-year schedule, so that the loan amount will be reduced to zero at the end of thirty years. The longer the loan term, the more interest you pay with each monthly payment. And since the interest portion of your payments is tax deductible, a longer-term loan means a higher monthly tax deduction on your maintenance payments—another consideration to take into account when weighing the building's options.

On the other hand, reduction of principal increases the value of each individual unit and can lead to lower maintenance fees. A smaller mortgage in the future will be easier and cheaper to arrange, because a lower loan-to-value ratio will be more desirable to a lender, resulting in a lower interest rate. And lower mortgage payments mean lower maintenance fees.

Before considering any type of refinancing, begin with an assessment of the building's capital improvement needs for the long run, and its financial condition. Next, consult with your team of professionals: the building's accountant, lawyer and managing agent. Then hire a reputable mortgage broker to help the board navigate the rough and challenging waters of refinancing.

Underlying Mortgages: A Practical Guide to Refinancing

By Patrick Niland

Refinancing your underlying mortgage is like open-heart surgery on your cooperative's financial structure. It will affect not only the monthly maintenance but also the market value of every apartment. You don't want to rush into such an important decision. Get involved. Refinancing is the most important decision your board will make during its tenure. All board members should play a role. And it makes sense to consult all of your co-op's professional advisors.

Do a Background Check

Ask your attorney to verify that your existing loan will allow you to refinance when you want to. Check whether other liens or violations have been filed against your property. Getting an early start on the legal aspects of refinancing can prevent a lot of last-minute headaches. Don't be like the board member who recently told me that he didn't want to "start the lawyer's meter running just yet."

Direct your accountant to analyze your expense history and recommend a prudent level for your reserve fund. Two to four months of operating expenses is the generally accepted target but your accountant may feel that more or less is warranted in your situation.

Check with your managing agent for expected increases in real estate taxes, labor costs, fuel prices and other operating expenses. Get his input on needed major repairs and capital improvements. Now is the time to rely on his experience. Remember, that's why you hired him in the first place.

It has always been a good idea to hire an engineer to assess the repair and maintenance needs of your building over the five, ten or more years covered by your planned new loan. But now, in light of the new CIRA reporting guidelines, it is foolish not to.

Refinancing is a time-consuming and expensive process. But, if handled successfully, it can dramatically improve the long-term financial health of your co-op.

Have the Answers

The key to doing it right, says Sheldon Gartenstein, regional manager of the National Cooperative Bank, is to plan ahead. "Those who don't," he says, "are stuck!"

As managing partner of First Funding Group, a mortgage brokerage firm, it continues to surprise me that at least 25 percent of the board members who call my mortgage hotline can't answer even the most basic questions about their co-op. Yet they persist in asking, "What's your rate?" They fully expect to get a detailed loan proposal without revealing any of the essential information about their building.

For such people, I have a stock answer: "From 7 percent to 12 percent." Thankfully, some then realize that no one can possibly answer their question without more specific information. The rest continue to drive loan officers and mortgage brokers bananas.

If you are hoping that the lender won't ask certain questions or, worse, are actually withholding information, don't even consider it. Know everything about your building and be ready with simple, honest answers. Have all of the key facts (address, number of units, percent sold) at your fingertips and the rest in an organized file for easy access (see the Refinancing Checklist on the following page). Don't try to hide anything; you can't. Skeletons in the closet have a nasty habit of appearing just before the closing. No building is perfect, so be up-front with the loan officer.

It surprises many board members to find that all lenders are keenly interested in their co-op's sponsor. You should be prepared to give comprehensive information

Refinancing Checklist

Before searching for a new mortgage loan, the board should assemble, verify and review the following information:

✓ The offering plan (the prospectus or "black book")

✓ Any and all amendments

✓ Financial statements for the last three years

✓ Federal tax returns for the apartment corporation (IRS Form 1120) for the last three years

✓ The current balance in the cooperative's reserve fund

✓ A budget for the coming year

✓ An operating statement from the managing agent showing income and expenses to-date for the current year

✓ A recent maintenance roll showing each apartment, the number of shares assigned to that apartment, the number of rooms and baths and the monthly maintenance charge for each apartment

✓ A list of those shareholders whose maintenance charges are past due

✓ A list of all sublet apartments, indicating the reason for each sublet, how long each has been a sublet and the rent collected by the shareholder from the subtenant

✓ A list of all sponsor and/or investor apartments, indicating the unsold shares involved, the rent that the sponsor or investor collects from each tenant, the lease expiration date and which of these units are rent-controlled or rent-stabilized

✓ A summary of any commercial leases, indicating square footage, annual rent, lease expiration date and the type of business occupying the commercial space

✓ A list of resales within the previous three years, indicating apartment sold, sales price, number of shares involved and closing date

✓ A list of capital improvements made to the building within the previous three years

✓ A schedule of the intended uses of the proceeds from the planned refinancing

✓ The property's block and lot number

✓ The property's lot dimensions

✓ The property's assessed valuation and the status of any tax abatements

✓ A recent photograph of the building

about your sponsor (and any other holder of unsold shares), including a list of all units owned, the rents collected, lease terms and whether the sponsor has used the unsold shares as collateral for other loans. If the sponsor won't cooperate by providing this information, don't expect much from the lender.

If you don't care or try enough to get this information for the lender, don't expect the lender to care or try enough to give you a new loan.

How Much to Borrow

Borrow what you need—nothing more, nothing less. Remember, money without a stated purpose always finds one. Don't be tempted to borrow more just to round out the total or to "put a little something in the bank." That "little something" can earn only 3 percent to 5 percent at today's money market rates but will cost you additional interest at whatever (higher) rate you're paying on your new loan.

Be sure to borrow enough. Nothing can be more costly than being forced to refinance at the wrong time because the board failed to plan well enough ahead. Since closing costs can add up to 2 to 3 percent of your new loan amount (up to 10 percent for very small loans), you'll want to get as much mileage from each refinancing as possible.

Therefore, do your homework. Know how much it will take to keep your cooperative financially sound over the life of your new loan, including the effects of inflation, legislative changes and unforeseen events.

Don't borrow extra money to avoid raising maintenance fees. Balance your budget each and every year. Set maintenance levels to cover your expected operating expenses on an ongoing basis. Board members who believe that a refinancing can repair the damage of deficit spending need only look at the federal government to see what awaits them in a few years.

If you think you can duck the political heat of a maintenance increase by depleting your reserves instead, then you don't belong in the kitchen. Using your reserve fund to subsidize maintenance charges is like spending your IRA at the grocery. You can eat steak for a while but, sooner or later, you end up in the soup.

Weigh All the Options

Don't assume that the lender with the lowest interest rate will give you the best loan. Compare offers from various sources to get a feel for the overall market. But don't become obsessed with the rate alone. Interest rate is just one of the many factors that make up a good loan. Other terms, if overlooked, can cost you many times the few percentage points that you might save on the rate. I am now representing a co-op in Queens that needs money for a new roof and major elevator repairs. Unfortunately, their existing loan does not allow any secondary financing or prepayment. The "great rate" they have (which, in today's markets, is not all that great) is small consolation to the shareholders on the top floor. And the price tag on the solution to their problem is about twice what it would have been if they had included provisions for secondary financing and/or prepayment as part of their refinancing. Don't be penny-wise and dollar-foolish. Look at all of the terms being offered by each lender.

Consider the services of a mortgage broker to help your board navigate these stormy markets. A good mortgage broker can save you much more than his fee. But hiring more than one broker can ruin your chances of getting a good deal.

Get recommendations from other buildings, your managing agent or your attorney. You might want to interview several brokers. Be sure to check their references. But hire only one. Having more than one broker represent you will get you less than one loan. Hiring the right broker will get you a better loan than you could have arranged on your own. There is nothing more annoying to bankers than to receive three or four phone calls from different people requesting financing for the same building. This can give such a bad impression that in some cases the bank will stop taking calls from that building entirely.

Refinancing an underlying mortgage is serious business. As a board member, you have a fiduciary obligation to give it your serious attention. But don't be intimidated by the process. By enlisting the aid of professionals whom you trust, you will get a good loan and secure the financial future of your cooperative. And your shareholders will thank you.

Long-Term Financing: Lock in Rates, Budget in Costs

By Gary Q. Kokalari

Long-term mortgage financing offers significant advantages to co-op board members and their shareholders. In today's economy, prudent board officers must weigh the advantages when refinancing. The historically low prevailing interest rates available in the credit markets present a real economic window of opportunity. Most boards can greatly reduce operating expenses by refinancing at lower rates.

Long-term fixed-rate financing also provides important operational advantages. By locking in a low interest rate for the longest possible term, a board can conduct its financial planning without any future speculation on the building's debt service costs. A self-liquidating feature provides even more comfort.

Long-term mortgages can also reduce borrowing costs on the corporation's financial statement. Co-ops are required to amortize the transaction costs of refinancing. These costs range from 2 percent to 4 percent of the loan amount, depending on the lender, appraiser, engineering, title, legal and brokerage fees. Since closing costs are identical regardless of the loan maturity, the amortized costs can vary dramatically each year.

Let's look at an example. If we assume total fees of 3 percent, the transaction costs on a $2 million loan would be $60,000. Annualized over a ten-year loan term, the costs would be $6,000 per year. Over thirty years, the costs drop to $2,000 per year. The differential per year is a savings of twenty basis points in interest costs (see graph on facing page).

Long-term refinancing directly benefits shareholders as well. Every board must

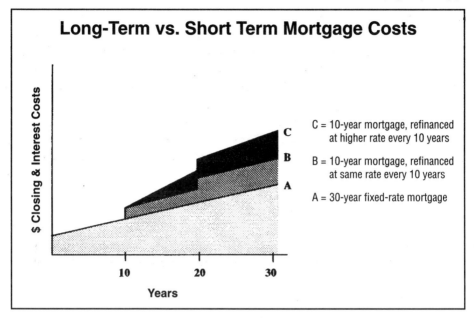

Long-Term vs. Short Term Mortgage Costs

C = 10-year mortgage, refinanced at higher rate every 10 years

B = 10-year mortgage, refinanced at same rate every 10 years

A = 30-year fixed-rate mortgage

take this into consideration when making the decision to refinance. A co-op is a corporation, and the board's mission is to protect and build shareholders' equity. Refinancing a mortgage for the longest possible term on a self-liquidating basis could be the single most important step taken by the board to meet this objective.

This benefits the shareholder looking to sell as well as those who intend to stay. For the shareholder wanting to sell in today's hostile environment, the market is much broader if the co-op's financial state is strengthened with a long-term fixed-rate underlying mortgage. For the shareholder wishing to remain or buy into the cooperative, the benefits are just as meaningful. More share loan lenders are focusing on the co-op's underlying mortgage with increased scrutiny to determine the value of the corporation's shares. When the co-op's capital structure is based on sound, long-term planning, shareholders can obtain better mortgage terms when they want to refinance their own shares.

Once boards want to go longer than ten years with their financing, lending sources are very limited. Finding lenders that offer long-term options and understand co-ops is even more difficult. Co-ops need to identify that financial resource which will take them into the twenty-first century with the ideal long-term loan.

A Risk Worth Taking: Floating Rates Can Mean Big Savings
By Gregg Winter

If your building could save thousands of dollars a year in interest payments, would you be willing to take a little risk? If your building's board of directors is not faint of heart, and is willing to keep a watchful eye on rates, there is a way to refinance with absolutely no prepayment penalty at rates as low as prime plus .25 percent.

This approach may not be for most boards, but it may be well worth considering for some. Depending on your board's current situation, the interest rate risks of a floating rate mortgage tied to the prime rate may be well worth the enormous rewards to be reaped by saving three to four full interest rate percentage points.

Many boards are facing the expiration of their J-51 tax abatement benefits. This factor alone can add as much as $250 per month to the average shareholder's maintenance. A board may be willing to take certain risks to avoid such an increase, cutting debt service to the bone via an innovative, floating-over-prime refinance.

One "white glove" Manhattan co-op was able to save $150,000 a year in interest payments by refinancing from a fixed-rate 10 percent to a floating rate, currently at 6.26 percent. This 100 percent owner-occupied, 150-unit building is in an excellent location, which qualifies it for the most competitive floating rate pricing: prime plus .25 percent. As of this writing, the prime rate is 6 percent. Therefore, as soon as the new loan closes, their debt service will plummet from 10 percent to 6.2 percent, an immediate monthly savings of $12,500, or $150,000 annually—a colossal drop given the loan amount of $4,000,000. The immediate benefits to the co-op are compelling, and the downside risks diminish with the passage of time.

Let's take a look at the long-term effects of this building's refinancing decision, given the fact that the floating rate can be fixed at any time during their ten-year term. Suppose the prime rate stays essentially stable for the next two years, and then begins to creep upward. As soon as prime goes from 6 percent to 6.25 percent, the board decides to convert from a floating to a fixed-rate mortgage for the remainder of the term. Since two years of their ten-year term have now gone by, the Treasury security that determines the rate at which they will lock will be of a shorter maturity; eight years instead of ten. The shorter the maturity, the lower the rate. As time goes by, the yield curve will increasingly work in the board's favor.

The longer the board floats, and the shorter the maturity of the corresponding Treasury security when the rate is locked, the better their odds of winding up ahead.

If, however, the board opts to float for only a short time—say one year—and then decides to lock when the prime begins to creep upward, and if the Treasury rates have also moved considerably higher, even though the board will be locking according to a shorter-maturity Treasury note, they could still end up with a higher average interest rate than they would have achieved by simply locking in the first place—a year earlier.

Ultimately, the decision comes down to a classic risk/reward analysis and the collective point of view shared by the board members.

However, with the nearly universal prevalence of a prepayment penalty for ten-year fixed-rate underlying mortgages, the above-described floating-rate converting to fixed-rate scenario is the only way to refinance now while totally avoiding the serious prepayment penalties that could prevent your board from taking advantage of the next significant dip in long-term fixed rates—should it occur.

If You're Refinancing, Be Sure the Building's in Top Shape

By Louise Brodnitz

- An Upper West Side cooperative had successfully refinanced its building, but was suddenly faced with $50,000 worth of roofing, repointing, structural and cosmetic work, all to be completed within a few months or the building would be found in default of the new mortgage.
- A converted loft in Soho searched for over a year for a bank willing to consider a loan for its building because it had no certificate of occupancy.
- A financially sound cooperative was well on its way to approval for a mortgage, only to have the loan fall through just months before the balloon came due, because the bank's condition report showed extensive work was needed on the building.

These cases illustrate the difficulties a building's physical plant can cause in the refinancing process. In today's economic climate, the percentage of sponsor-held units and the cash flow seem to be the only things bankers ask about when a co-op tries to refinance. Yet it is precisely because the question of a building's physical condition doesn't come up until the process is well along that this factor can become a costly snare in the refinancing game. By the time the physical plant becomes an issue, the application fees have been paid and valuable time has been lost.

In many cooperatives, repairs are typically done on an emergency basis as problems arise. Without a cyclical maintenance plan and a periodic condition report, cooperatives sail into refinancing only to find that nonemergency repairs must now be done under tight time constraints and with a portion of the loan amount (including a whopping contingency factor) held by the bank for that purpose. Worse, there may be problems the board was unaware of, which could prevent the loan from closing on time—or at all. Yet cooperatives hesitate to undertake regular inspections of their buildings until the refinancing lender arranges it for them.

Most banks will require three inspections as part of the refinancing process, resulting in the appraisal, the asbestos report and the physical condition report. Ordinarily, lenders will arrange for the appraisal and hire their own inspectors for the reports, charging the cost to the cooperative. However, a number of lending institutions contacted say that the inspections may be ordered by the co-op as long as the architect's or engineer's credentials are approved in advance by the bank. But why would a co-op take on the trouble of obtaining its own condition inspection?

The Importance of Ongoing Maintenance

According to Patrick Niland, managing partner of First Funding Group, a mortgage brokerage firm specializing in underlying cooperative mortgage loans, "the need for a physical condition inspection is at the discretion of the lender." If a co-op can demonstrate that the building is in good physical condition with a history of planned and budgeted maintenance, the lending institution may well waive the physical condition inspection. Further, when a co-op board has obtained an assessment of the building's health on a regular basis (at least every five years), followed an ongoing schedule for maintenance and capital improvements, and anticipated these items in the reserve fund, they can provide the lender with a high degree of comfort about the long-term value of the building and the commitment of its shareholders. There are other distinct advantages to this approach as well.

First, while banks can charge anywhere from $500 to $3,500 for a condition inspection, your co-op can control the cost of obtaining the report by getting competitive prices from several architects or engineers who do such inspections. Even more important, a board can get more mileage out of the inspection by including a cyclical maintenance plan, violation removal, Local Law 10 report or other inspection-related items in the scope of work.

Second, results of the report can give you information on exactly how large a loan you'll need to ask for. If your co-op needs $40,000 in repairs and cyclical maintenance of $10,000 annually, your loan should be large enough to include the lump sum repairs cost as well as a cushion for the anticipated annual expenses over and above the underlying mortgage amount coming due.

If this approach is simply not possible for your co-op, assign a board member to do a mini-inspection when the need for a refinance first arises, before approaching lenders. The following simple checks, which can be done by any board member, will help a great deal in avoiding surprises from the bank's physical condition report, and will allow you to get a jump on the restrictive correction periods banks allow.

1. Check building for department records: A fairly quick trip to 60 Hudson Street will net a copy of the current certificate of occupancy, a copy of the most recent Local Law 10 report and a list of violations (in secret code) for the building. A longer visit will be required to actually find out what those violations are and obtain copies. Lending institutions will rarely consider a loan for a co-op with a wildly inaccurate or nonexistent certificate of occupancy, and they will usually require that any violations be removed immediately, a highly time-consuming process.

2. Compile a maintenance history of the building: Prepare a fact sheet, noting the basics about your building—block and lot, size, age, the type of construction and heating system, fire protection system, elevators and so on. Find out the dates of all major repairs and capital improvements in the last ten years (such as windows and sidewalks). Indicate the age of the roofing, boiler, exterior paint or pointing, electrical and plumbing systems wherever possible. Attach the most recent Local Law 10 report, if any. From this data, project a budget for future maintenance and improvements.

3. Assess conditions: Take a tour through the entire building, even areas you think you've seen many times before. Look for things an inspector might see. In the cellar, make note of loose, hanging wires, debris blocking egress, badly cracked

or falling plaster, rusted or corroding metal, rotted, water-stained or deflecting wood members, damp walls. On the roof, check for evidence of standing water, cracks in the roof membrane, powdery masonry joints, cracked copings, tenant debris. In the corridors, check that lighting is adequate and that tenant debris is removed. Ask tenants to notify the board of any problems such as leaks so that they can be promptly corrected as well.

While the board may not be able to assess without professional help whether some of the problems encountered constitute emergencies or stabilized decay, many items can be set right immediately with little cost. For the larger problems the board can arrange for further investigation and thus have a plan ready when the lender brings up the issue.

Whether your co-op arranges for an inspection or leaves it up to the lender, the building itself is the corporation's only real asset. Knowing its condition and planning for its upkeep can make a great deal of difference in the loan you finally obtain.

Removing Obstacles to Financing: The Banking Industry Eases Up

By Anne Gaddis-Marcus

In the last several years it has been difficult, if not nearly impossible in many cases, to get mortgage loans on cooperatives. This is due to restrictive bank rules that were put in place largely because of excesses in the co-op market in the 1980s.

Those rules, according to Barbara Corcoran, president of The Corcoran Group, vary from stating that no more than 10 percent of the units of a co-op can be owned by the sponsor to presale requirements dictating that 45 percent of the units in a condo and 65 percent of those in a co-op must be sold before the bank will lend to individual buyers or the building itself. To further exacerbate the problem, banks often lump sublets with sponsor-owned apartments, which can spoil the profile of a building in the eyes of a loan originator, such as Freddie Mac or Fannie Mae.

Easing Restrictions

But in October 1993, the Federal National Mortgage Association, or Fannie Mae, issued guidelines that will make it easier for a large number of cooperatives to be qualified for share loans or to refinance underlying mortgages. The relaxed guidelines are expected to enable thousands of New Yorkers to qualify for bank loans in co-ops that previously would not have qualified. In November 1993, the Federal Home Loan Mortgage Corporation, known as Freddie Mac, followed suit, announcing its reentry into the multifamily market after a three-year hiatus.

Two weeks before Fannie Mae announced its new lending program, Corcoran and others spoke about the present lending situation at the New York Real Estate Congress, produced by *The New York Cooperator* and the New York Association of Realty Managers (NYARM).

"Banks are now beginning to talk about and understand that there is a difference between a sponsor or investor unit and a sublet. And an 80 percent presale can be an impossibility in a perfectly viable co-op that's been around for a very long time," said Mary Ann Rothman, executive director of the Council of New York Cooperatives. "Sixty percent comes closer to being a reasonable number, but, hey, what about 50 percent, 40 percent or even 22 percent?"

Other rules that some banks have been abiding by require that reserve funds be at least $1,000 per unit, that there be no AIRs (artists in residence) and that pro rata share rules limiting the building's leverage be in place.

"In the old days we used to wonder, 'Will they lend to the individual?'" said Corcoran. "The question today is 'Will they lend to the building?'"

At a financing seminar produced by the Community Associations Institute and the Mortgage Bankers Association in late 1994, Queens borough president Claire Shulman criticized what she described as "arbitrary criteria" set by the banks "that bear no relationship to the financial health of the building" in question.

And while she acknowledged the "laudable efforts" Fannie Mae has made "to get mortgage money flowing, and now Freddie Mac is following suit," she pointed out that serious restrictions still apply. "The 75 percent presale requirement that Freddie Mac has set virtually redlines my entire borough," she said.

Gary Connor, chief of the attorney general's Real Estate Financing Bureau, concurred, praising the lenders for going as far as they have, but calling on them to go further in closing the gap between bank requirements and the financial realities in many co-ops today.

At the Real Estate Congress, Rothman also criticized some of the banks' restrictive requirements, calling it "ridiculous" that in order to get a loan to buy an apartment, some lenders require an engineer's report, wherein it is stated whether or not asbestos was removed from the building. She said that a similar requirement could be instituted related to the current lead scare. "It's impractical," she said.

Things Are Looking Up

From a lender's point of view, there are three general types of cooperatives: "Those where substantially all of the units have been sold, those that have some sponsor ownership and those where 40 percent or more are owned by the sponsor," says Sheldon Gartenstein, vice-president of the National Cooperative Bank, which lends to co-op corporations. He says that with the first group, numerous lenders offer aggressive rates, terms get modified and the lender is even happy to throw in a free toaster.

With the second group, as long as there are no apparent serious underlying issues, there will be two or three lenders out there who will be willing to work out some sort of deal, says Gartenstein. He refers to the third group as "the one we've all read about." With these cooperatives, Gartenstein says, banks will rarely foreclose. "No institutional lender can afford to take over a property, destroy equity, become a manager of rental property and then face irate shareholders, local political pressure and banking examiners," he says.

But Gartenstein believes that things are looking up. "In the secondary market, Fannie Mae is a very exciting prospect because they have enormous resources," he says. "Borrowers will be able to benefit from very long-term fixed-rate, low-interest-rate financing."

Fannie Mae's new $500 million pilot program eases the guidelines for loans to co-ops in New York City by reducing the owner-occupied units needed to get financing from 80 percent to 51 percent. It also would allow loans in buildings with a small negative cash flow and in buildings with flip taxes.

"The dream of owning a home in New York City has been falling further and further from the grasp of hard-working citizens," says Congressman Charles E. Schumer, who worked with Claire Shulman and Fannie Mae president Larry Small to come up with a program that would help solve co-op financing problems. "The new relaxed rules recognize the economic realities of the times," he says. "Now it'll become easier for co-op owners to sell their apartments and for buyers seeking financing to make their dream a reality."

Fannie Mae, the nation's largest source of home mortgages, acts as a secondary market by purchasing loans from lenders. The new guidelines, which apply to loans that the agency takes over from issuing banks, will give lenders more capital for mortgage lending to consumers.

A Shot in the Arm for the Market

The Mortgage Bankers Association (MBA) also recently announced a proposal for solving the financial crisis that has engulfed New York's co-op and condo housing market. The program would restore liquidity to the market by providing financing to cooperative corporations and purchasers of individual co-op and condo units by issuing securities that would be backed by the subject share loans and underlying mortgages. These securities would be guaranteed by the credit of the state or of a state agency. State financial guarantees, however, would require legislative approval.

"Many solvent cooperative corporations are unable to secure underlying financing or end-loan financing based on the lending community's credit guidelines," says Mark Iannone, past MBA president and member of its board of governors. "This has placed many buildings in default on their underlying mortgage, resulting in the inability for units to be conveyed to purchasers. An entire segment of New York's affordable housing stock is presently dead in the water."

According to Patricia Niemas, MBA president, "The program would improve the economy of the state of New York by strengthening the ownership structure of owner-occupied affordable housing in the state, thereby preserving and increasing its supply."

Claire Shulman plans to press the state legislature to enact the MBA's program, "because it would pump additional mortgage money into co-ops, thereby giving the co-op market a shot in the arm."

And there's no doubt that the market could use a lift. Gary Connor blames conversion laws for helping to create the current financial difficulties facing many co-ops today.

"The attorney general's office has tried year after year since 1982 to get the law changed to make co-ops stronger by raising the percentage from 15 to 25 percent or more of sales required to convert, on the theory that if you sold out more units, you would have less investors in the deal and the risk would be lessened," says Connor. "But so far the law has stayed as is."

Shulman agrees, saying, "We have made some significant headway in reforming the conversion process." She adds, "We will be returning to Albany next year to press for additional reforms."

Finding Willing Lenders: Boards Can Help Shareholders Sell

By Barbara Dershowitz

For Adele Zasloff, it was the only logical thing to do. Zasloff has been board president of her enviably situated 188-unit midtown Manhattan cooperative for the past six years. When she realized that shareholders were having unusual difficulty selling their units despite lower asking prices and lower interest rates for buyers, she set out to discover why. And then she went into action—action every board can take to help shareholders sell faster.

The first thing Zasloff did was to look at the most common reasons for shareholders' inability to sell. She looked at the building's location and its physical and aesthetic features. No problem; hers is one of the best-maintained residences in a highly prestigious neighborhood.

Then she examined asking prices. But shareholders in Zasloff's building who were eager to sell, either because they had outgrown their studio or small one-bedroom or because they found themselves victim of the sagging economy, were willing to take far less than they had paid.

Zasloff then turned her scrutiny to the qualifications of prospective purchasers, and discovered, to her dismay, that even the most qualified deals were being delayed and often lost altogether.

"Why were people in the building having trouble selling?" muses Zasloff. "Because prospective buyers were having trouble getting co-op loans. It turned out to be because of the cooperative itself. Banks weren't disqualifying the purchasers; they were disqualifying the building."

Despite the fact that Zasloff's building is in strong financial health and 77 percent of shares are in the hands of shareholders, the building's debt service is high and there is a sponsor shortfall. "Banks have a lending decision formula based on debt," says Zasloff. "And because of the way our building's debt is structured, many refuse to even look at prospective buyers, no matter how qualified they are personally."

She decided to see what she could do to expedite the sales process for shareholders who wanted or needed to sell their units. "It seems to me to be very logical," says Zasloff, who sold real estate years ago. "When you want to help someone buy, you call up a bank and see what their criteria are for lending. So that's what I've done."

Zasloff has put in calls to most of the area's lenders to get their lending criteria and to find out whether or not they will work with qualified prospective purchasers in the building. She supplied the lenders with a package containing up-to-date information about the building, including the numbers of shares and units; the number and percentages of sold and unsold shares; the amount of sponsor shortfall; the latest structural and mechanical aspects of the building; a full financial disclosure and whatever other documentation each lender required.

Leslie Kaminoff, president of AKAM Associates, feels that boards shouldn't have to do this research themselves, that identifying viable lenders is management's responsibility.

"Every manager should put together an information package," says Kaminoff, "so that every time a shareholder goes to sell, they can say to their purchaser, 'We have these three lenders that have already approved our building.' It speeds up the process tremendously. It makes it easier to sell and the lender's time is cut because they don't have to look at the building again. All they have to do now is consider the purchaser's qualifications.

"What we've done that's innovative is to include a narrative that talks about everything that's been done in the property over the last three to five years," continues Kaminoff. "The narrative talks about what the board is planning to do, where they're getting the funds to do it and what sets this property apart from the one next door, like amenities and so forth. We've found that many properties have things banks don't know about, like storage and community rooms, which aren't things that the bank asks for in a standard application but certainly do make a difference to the lender.

"The other thing you've got to try to get across to the lender," says Kaminoff, "is the type of unit owner and the type of board in the building. Lenders need to see that the board is active and guiding the building financially. It gives the lender a sense of security in the value of the property. If they like what they see overall, they'll approve and lend in the building if the purchaser is qualified. More and more banks are doing this, and it's something we'll do for our boards."

As for the banks themselves, they're eager to share their lending requirements. Take Independence Savings Bank, for example. According to Joseph Morgano, executive vice-president of mortgage lending for Independence, the bank has always considered itself an old-fashioned neighborhood bank. "Our money comes in locally and stays local," says Morgano. "We're looking for business, and from the standpoint of rates, ours are aggressive because we want good loans." Morgano emphasizes that Independence has a responsibility to its depositors and to the purchaser of an apartment to ensure that the loans the bank writes are well documented and good risks.

"Our bank has always been in co-op loans, right from the beginning," says Morgano. "Our policy has always been on this basis: We will lend if the building is 65 percent owner occupied, if there is no sponsor shortfall, if the sponsor will agree not to leverage his shares and if the structural and major mechanical components of the building are in good shape. We're also concerned about the reserve fund. We look at lending as a partnership."

One phone call was all it took to get this information. And the message from Independence is clear: If a co-op doesn't qualify according to these criteria, then Independence isn't the appropriate lender. And no matter how qualified the purchaser, Independence won't write the loan.

"Once we determine which banks are willing to work with our building and which ones aren't," says Adele Zasloff, "then we'll inform shareholders. Of course, we'll include the caveat that lenders' guidelines change often, and that just because a bank may be willing to work with the building doesn't mean the purchaser is automatically approved.

"I have to say," Zasloff continues, "this process is a long one. But I think it's our responsibility as a board to provide the most helpful information we can to our shareholders. This is one valuable way to do it."

Keeping Your Building in Top Shape

- *Year-round planning*
- *Heating and cooling systems*
- *Energy and water conservation*

Annual Maintenance: Assume the Worst and Be Prepared

By Dick Koral

Professional engineer Arthur Spaet used to begin his lectures on housing maintenance by pointing out that every part of a building begins to deteriorate from the moment it goes into operation. In order to lengthen the life and improve the efficiency of your building's equipment, it is necessary to keep it properly maintained. The shareholder who does not flinch in the sure knowledge that "if anything can go wrong, it will" is set on the road toward formulation of a good policy for ongoing building maintenance.

The person in charge of organizing maintenance efforts should be a member of the board of directors and chairperson of the Building and Grounds Committee. We may liken the chairperson's role to that of chief executive officer for maintenance. The building superintendent acts as chief operating officer. That means the super is responsible for everything and reports to the chairperson only. (Ideally, there are members of the Building and Grounds Committee who share the work of the chair.) If the super reports to more than one person, then the responsibility is divided and there will certainly be items that fall through the cracks.

If the co-op or condo has a real manager—that is, one who tours the building and talks to tenants and staff daily—then the super should report to the manager and the manager should report to the head of Building and Grounds.

The beginning of the year is budget-planning time for most co-op and condo boards. One of the most difficult areas to plan is maintenance and operation because so much depends on the ups and downs of the weather and fuel prices. In planning, as much information on the previous year's operations should be on the table as possible. There may have to be a number of working sessions, because, inevitably, a lot of information will be missing.

A maintenance timetable should be established, itemizing daily, weekly, monthly, semiannual and annual equipment checks. As many building parts as possible should be considered and a budget established for the maintenance of each, from zero on up. (Don't neglect to set down the "zero" items. They belong on the list for reference in next year's budgeting.) Following is a list of only some of the "parts" and how you might consider them:

Roof: The roof is supposed to be inspected at least every spring and fall for cracks, deteriorated flashing and condition of the parapet wall. Was that done? If not, do it and report back to the next session of the committee so a budget can be determined for what needs to be fixed. Is there a water tank up there? What did it cost for its annual inspection and cleaning last year? What does the contractor say it will cost this year? Are there roof fans or air-conditioning equipment on the roof? Are they working, starting to make noise? If the building does not now have a written maintenance schedule, make one and under Spring and Fall, put Roof.

Walls: The exterior walls incur most deterioration in the winter freeze and thaw cycles. Were they inspected last spring? Did the inspection indicate a need for pointing of the bricks, or are any suspicious cracks developing? If the super is doing the inspection, be sure he has a pair of binoculars. If pointing is needed, get estimates from weatherproofing contractors now. Add Walls to the Spring maintenance checklist.

Windows and Doors: When were the windows and doors last inspected for damage, air leaks, locks, tight closure? Be sure to include all, including doors to the basement and roof. How long ago were the windows and doors caulked? After three years, even a good caulking may have to be redone. Failure to do so may increase the heating bill significantly. Caulking and weatherstripping of existing windows costs a small fraction of what new windows cost and, unless the windows are rotten, the results are almost as good.

Elevators: Are the shareholders satisfied with the performance of the elevators? Is the annual cost for maintenance over the last few years increasing faster than the inflation rate? Perhaps it's time to ask your current elevator maintenance contractor as well as two additional contractors to bid on overhaul and annual full maintenance for five years. You may want to have the help of an elevator consultant to evaluate the bids. After about twenty-five years, almost all elevators need virtual replacement. Since this may be one of the most expensive things the co-op has to do, it pays to do the research.

Compactor: What do the porters think about the machine? They would know if it needs basic repairs. Are roaches a problem?

Heating System: Before going into details, what has been the annual fuel consumption (gallons of oil or cubic feet of gas used) for the last few years? If usage is creeping up, is there a failure of maintenance? Find out why. Has the super asked for improvements and been denied? How much has that cost the building? Figure cost of improvements versus cost of fuel increase.

Have there been a significant number of heating complaints? Noise? Overheating?

Underheating? Are there patterns? What has to be done to satisfy the complainants? Set a timetable. What will the super do? What will outside contractors do? What will it cost? Does overtime need to be budgeted?

Water, Cold and Hot: By now, almost everyone has an inkling of the precipitous rise in the cost of city water, which used to be almost fixed and of not much consequence as compared to fuel, for instance. Because it was not metered, we all developed very wasteful habits of use: washing dishes in running water, allowing faucets to drip and toilet tanks to run, unrepaired, for long periods of time. Now strict maintenance to prevent these practices is imperative.

Even if your building is not yet metered, it will be shortly, so now is the time to look into water conservation. This is two faceted. One aspect is occupant education. After shareholders are told one hundred times (ten times will do no good), they will start to be more careful. They must also report leaks and running toilets immediately, and the building must repair such water-wasting problems at no cost, regardless of what the lease says about who is responsible for in-apartment items of maintenance! An accelerated maintenance plan has to be accounted for in the maintenance budget.

The law now requires low-flow/low-flush plumbing fixtures whenever one of these needs to be replaced. Economics may dictate that the building not wait, but replace all the showerheads, for instance, now. This is something for the Building and Grounds Committee to work on. When it comes to hot water, the cost is very high because the building is paying for the water as well as the fuel to heat it.

Other water problems to watch for include insufficiently hot water, water that is scalding or erratic functioning. Prompt reporting of such problems should be encouraged and the data logged in and analyzed, just as in the case of the heating system. Sooner or later, expensive piping replacements will be required. In the meantime, an examination of every apartment should be conducted and, while there, a check made for illegally connected washing machines or dishwashers, which contribute to erratic hot/cold supply.

Checklists: A Preventive Maintenance System That Really Works

By Chris Luongo

Fourteen years ago, as superintendent of a Hempstead, Long Island, apartment building, Vincent Occhipinti would routinely hop out of bed around 6 A.M. and immediately set off to walk the premises. He'd begin in the boiler room, where he'd crouch down near the pavement to see if there was a leak. He'd peek into the firebox chamber. Then he'd step into the elevator for a test ride to the penthouse, before finally taking the long walk down the back stairwell, stopping to inspect each floor for the odd blown-out light bulb, piece of stray garbage or crack in a ceiling. All the while he would scribble down notes and make check marks on a maintenance log sheet for future reference.

"This way I knew what I was confronted with for the day," he says. "And then I'd have my breakfast."

Today, as vice-president of management at Elm Management, Occhipinti has various managing agents and superintendents under his wing who, he ensures, never break his old habit of thoroughly inspecting their buildings through the use of daily, weekly and monthly maintenance checklists. By doing this, he says, they are able to anticipate and solve problems before they become catastrophes.

Other management companies rely heavily on checklists as part of their preventive maintenance programs, using property inspections that involve detailed reports, customized for each building. During their inspections, they check for such things as code violations, tripping hazards and lighting fixtures that could be replaced by more energy-efficient ones. The reports are then turned over to the board of directors.

At the Argo Corporation, agents carry around general maintenance checklists when they do their weekly property inspections, while individual building superintendents fill out separate service logs that track all service and repair jobs. The firm's director of management, Jeff Levy, explains that these service logs are extremely helpful in proving that an equipment failure was not due to negligence on the part of the building personnel. Levy points out how easy it would be for even the most conscientious of superintendents or managing agents to lose track of an item in the long list of building maintenance chores without the aid of some sort of log sheet.

"It's like when you go to buy groceries, how many times do you forget to pick up a loaf of bread?" Levy says. "Everyone's human."

The Danger in Not Using Them

Agreeing with Levy that even the simplest maintenance job can be overlooked, Argo vice-president Marina Higgins says she has been continually surprised to discover that many of the buildings her firm takes over had been previously operating without a preventive maintenance program in place. She says that these same buildings often have histories of problems that could have been prevented had the former management company taken a more pro-active approach toward maintenance.

"This is a chronic problem in the industry," says Higgins. "A lot of management companies think they don't need to employ the use of written tools."

According to Occhipinti, even the most seasoned superintendents aren't putting enough emphasis on preventive maintenance and often don't bother to use written checklists to keep their buildings operating smoothly on a daily basis. "You don't know how lazy some people can be," he says. "You can't manage a building from behind a desk."

Occhipinti says that the buildings that don't keep written maintenance logs end up paying for it in the form of machine breakdowns, sections of building facades that crumble into pieces, motors that sputter to a stop and brand-new boiler systems that shut down for good. He adds that these disasters often wind up causing tenants to fume when they find themselves without heat and hot water, and board members to swear under their breath as they shell out thousands of dollars to buy a new piece of equipment.

"Ninety percent of the buildings here just overlook a thing like a checklist," says Occhipinti, who requires that all buildings he manages keep detailed logs, which must be posted on the wall in the superintendent's office. "Every one of my supers must live by this, or else there's a written warning."

Dick Koral, director of the Apartment House Institute at New York City Technical College, says he can never stress enough to his students the importance of keeping careful records and maintenance checklists to stay on top of things. And, like the others who have already experienced the benefits of using them, Koral says he is "baffled" by the fact that so many managers are reluctant to give the checklist system a shot.

"It's hard to believe how many buildings don't pay attention to this, and will do things like wait until the first hot day to check the cooling tower for their central air conditioning," Koral says. "So often people are stubborn about this stuff. They'll spend hours deciding on what color to paint the lobby and only five minutes on the steps needed to maintain the boiler. I find this amazing."

The Checklist System at Work

Koral says that through the use of checklists, buildings will stand a better chance of minimizing fuel and electricity expenses, getting the most for their money out of the machinery and keeping everything from the elevators to the roof, the ceiling and the walls in good shape. "A managing agent or superintendent should be able to look at a log and see that all the things are attended to," he says.

A sample checklist that Koral hands out in his classes includes a master plan, which consists of a breakdown of all the seasonal maintenance jobs as they pertain to different sections of the building, along with individual checklists that separate the items into daily, weekly, monthly, semiannual and annual logs. Koral suggests that a checklist also include records on how each piece of equipment operates and the dates when it was repaired or serviced.

The items on the list that he recommends building personnel pay close attention to include the garbage compactors ("You've got to check them daily because if they plug up you've got a disaster"), the boiler tubes ("If they're all sooted up, steam will end up going out the chimney instead of into making heat") and all the controls that affect the boiler, the burner system and the elevators, pieces of equipment Koral says many buildings throw all their money into and then don't bother to maintain.

Managing agents and superintendents who do incorporate checklists into their day-to-day operations say that the fact that they have so few building-disaster stories to tell speaks for itself. Lori Fields, director of co-op management at Merlon Management, says that not only do checklists clearly define all the various sections of a building that need to be maintained, they also help her keep close tabs on fuel consumption "as a means of not only saving money, but as an early telltale sign of a boiler problem."

She recalls how a routine inspection in a West 23rd Street co-op boiler room revealed the cause of a rise in oil consumption to be a leak in an underground water pipe. "We then had a crew come in with sledgehammers," recalls Fields, "and we quickly fixed the leak."

Mark Prout, director of maintenance at 1199 Housing Corp., a colossal 1,594-unit Upper East Side co-op, says that ever since Elm Management took over the building and Occhipinti got him started on an extensive checklist system, flaws have been routinely detected before they've turned into problems.

"Each shift has its own preventive maintenance routine that involves doing things like checking the levels of water in the boiler, making sure the feed pumps are operating and that the oil level is up to par—all the important things," Prout says. "As I go along I check them off, and once in a while I even catch something that another guy overlooked. The system really works."

Servicing Equipment: What Should Contracts Cover?

By William Brangham

"It was a nightmare," recalls Lisa Gilbert, who awoke one morning to find that the heating in her Upper West Side apartment building had completely shut down during the night. "It was the middle of January. My father was visiting New York for the first time, and there we were, wrapped up in sweaters and blankets, huddling together first thing in the morning." She quickly called the superintendent, who had already fielded several calls from other frozen, irate residents. "All he would tell us was, 'Yes, the boiler's down and I'm trying to get it working again.' It was the weekend and so he left message after message on the repair company's answering machine."

Gilbert's story highlights a question that haunts many co-op and condo board members and residents: How can we prevent such a crisis from striking our building? The answer depends on whom you ask. Some will tell you that the equipment in your building is too complex and valuable to let anyone but a factory-trained representative take care of it. Others will say that a well-trained super can handle all but the most extreme repair work and that service contracts are nothing more than expensive insurance policies that you'll never use. On the other hand, without a contract, few firms will accept any emergency repair work because of the liability.

Assess the Equipment and Staff

Both answers may hold some truth, but your board and managing agent must determine which side to bet on, and for which pieces of equipment. Start by making a general assessment of all the equipment currently in operation in your building. "Evaluate how old the existing equipment is, what condition it's in, what may need to be done in the future and then check to see how knowledgeable the super is about the equipment. Then you go from there," says Burton Wallack, president of Wallack Management.

"In these tight economic times, we're finding that many co-ops like to have a contract on file that states their systems will be taken care of," says Richard Blaser, president of Atlas Welding and Boiler Repair. "Some companies will put you on the bottom of the list if you don't have a contract. Our company's philosophy is that everyone is treated the same. After the first year's warranty expires, we usually let the contract revert back to a time-and-materials basis. That is, you call me when you need me and I'll be there."

"I'm anti-service contracts," says Elizabeth Whitcomb Brown, board president of the Dorchester, an elegant East Side co-op. "I say to the board, let's try it for three years without one and see how much this piece costs us for basic maintenance. Then we'll really be able to gauge a contract's cost-effectiveness. The only contract our building has is for the elevator; I certainly don't want anyone to get stuck in there."

In fact, elevators are a special consideration in all buildings and are subject to monthly inspections by a New York City Department of Buildings certified inspector. These licensed inspectors are usually from an elevator repair company.

All Equipment Is Not Alike

Some contractors argue that the equipment they install will be more cost-effective to operate if it is taken care of by trained experts. According to Roy Antonoff, vice-president of Empire Mechanical, an air-conditioning sales, service and installation firm, "It's not common for the super to do the work on central air units. They're intricate machines. A service contract will guarantee that the work gets done on schedule and that it gets done right, which benefits the building in the long run." Recent tests show that the efficiency of a poorly maintained boiler or central air-conditioning unit can drop by 10 to 25 percent (see chart below).

Savings for Every $100 in Fuel Costs by Increasing Combustion Efficiency

To an increased combustion efficiecny of:

From an original efficieny of:	55%	60%	65%	70%	75%	80%	85%	90%	95%
50%	$9.10	16.70	23.10	28.60	33.20	37.50	41.20	44.40	47.40
55%		8.30	15.40	21.50	26.70	31.20	35.30	38.30	42.10
60%			7.70	14.30	20.00	25.00	29.40	33.30	37.80
65%				7.10	13.30	18.80	23.50	27.80	31.60
70%					6.70	12.50	17.60	22.20	26.30
75%						6.30	11.80	16.70	21.10
80%							5.90	11.10	15.80
85%								5.50	10.50
90%									5.30

From HRD's Energy Systems Operations Manual

Yet a boiler is not an elevator is not a security system. "We had an intercom unit put into our building a few years ago, and the installation company really encouraged us to purchase their all-inclusive service contract," recalls Brown. "It turned out that the contract would have cost us about $4,000 dollars a year. At that price, we'd be able to buy a brand new unit in ten years." Her building decided against it and then after three years, they assessed their own maintenance costs for the unit. Says Brown, "In the three-year period, we didn't spend the equivalent of one year's contract."

Some say that may be a fine approach for something as relatively simple as an intercom, but what about the boiler or the water tank? "If your trash compactor goes down one day, no one will panic. But what if you lose heat and hot water in the middle of February? You're going to be a little more concerned," says Blaser.

Preventive Maintenance

Edward Henry, board president of a 315-unit co-op on the Upper East Side, takes a middle-of-the-road approach. "Our building has three major service contracts: for the elevators, the mechanical system (that is, heat and central air conditioning) and the boilers. The contracts include routine maintenance, inspections and preventive maintenance. We 'preventive maintenance' stuff to death."

Henry points out that many major problems are already covered under the building's insurance policy. For example, if water leaks into the boiler and it is ruined, that would probably be covered. "We don't use the contractor as an insurance company. That gets expensive. For major repairs, we pay as they are needed," says Henry.

Contracts and Contractors

If, after assessing the existing equipment and the capabilities of the superintendent, a building decides that a service contract is needed, a broad range of estimates is recommended. Tim Waldon, formerly a service representative for Kelly Trane Co., specialists in heating, ventilating and air-conditioning (HVAC), says, "Call a firm's current clients and ask, 'What kind of a job have they done for you?' 'Are you satisfied with their work?' Good references are still the best way to tell."

When it comes down to choosing among companies, compare and cross-reference all the different estimates. "You can take two service contracts, put them side by side and they'll look almost identical," according to Lou Ballato, director of operations at Knudson Elevator, a firm that repairs, modernizes and services elevators. Ballato, who has lectured about the merits and pitfalls of service agreements at Hunter College, says, "It will seem that you're getting the same exact thing from two different companies until you read the fine print. I've seen contracts that leave out a guarantee to repair the single most important drive mechanism of the elevator," he continues. "Unless you knew what that gear is called, you'd never notice it was missing."

Ballato recommends getting advice from a specialized consulting firm to help you assess and compare contracts. "Whatever equipment you're talking about, a consulting firm's checklist is usually the most thorough," Ballato says. "Get them to evaluate what your specific equipment needs are and what a complete service agreement should look like."

In general, consultants tend to specialize in one type of equipment. For a list of firms, try contacting trade organizations or ask industry experts. Armed with professional input, you'll be much better off in negotiating a deal to keep your building's equipment running smoothly.

Maintaining Your Boiler: Water Treatment Stops Corrosion

By James J. O'Brien

Water conditions play a most important part in the failure of boilers and their tubes. Tube leaks caused by corrosion are the most common cause of emergency boiler shutdowns. Such problems can be nearly eliminated through proper maintenance and the use of regular boiler water treatment.

There are two methods of treating boiler water: through the use of chemicals and through cathodic protection. The primary cause of corrosion is the presence of oxygen and acidity in the boiler water. Chemical treatment, usually the injection of a nitrite corrosion inhibitor, works by neutralizing the pH level of the water and removing the oxygen, according to Dick Blake, technical director of The Metro Group, a boiler water treatment company located in Long Island City. Chemical treatment also breaks up an oil buildup on the water's surface, which can cause surges within the boiler, as well as removing salt from the water, which can add to the corrosive effects, says Dick Koral, director of the Apartment House Institute at New York City Technical College.

Because low-pressure boilers are designed to recirculate the heating water, the chemical corrosion inhibitor needs to be injected into the system only once each year. Companies like The Metro Group contract to do annual chemical injections as well as monthly checkups to be sure the water chemical levels are properly maintained. The Metro Group provides such service for ten thousand boilers in the New York City area, at a fee of about $200 per year.

An increasingly popular method of water treatment for the prevention of corrosion is cathodic protection, which is based on an electrochemical reaction in the water between two metals. By introducing a "sacrificial anode" or piece of metal—usually zinc or magnesium—into the water, the corroding reaction is absorbed by the anode instead of the steel boiler.

Cathodic protection has been used extensively throughout the country to prohibit corrosion on bridges, boat motors, pipelines, hot-water heaters and tunnels. For over twenty years the same technology has been applied successfully to the boiler industry. Cathodic protection is designed to provide complete, continuous protection against scale and corrosion in your boiler.

111

Blake, whose company uses both chemical and cathodic methods of water treatment, favors chemicals. He points out that with cathodic protection, as the sacrificial anode disintegrates, it leaves a by-product in the water, creating a buildup of metallic deposits that can cause pitting of the boiler's inside surface.

Our firm, Rockmills Steel Products, however, prefers the cathodic method to chemicals, and recommends it for the more than twenty thousand boilers we have built and installed in New York City. Pitting may result when using a zinc-based anode, but our firm recommends the Neutro-Chem Company's magnesium-based anode, which has been manufactured and sold for twenty years and has never resulted in metallic by-products during testing.

This system also has the advantage of no chemical carry-over in the boiler water and steam, and, therefore, no pollution problems. In addition, there is no human element involved to cause over- or undertreatment, and because the anode is a solid casting, there is no loss of chemicals due to leaks in return lines or during blowdowns.

Of course, no treatment can protect a boiler that has been poorly maintained and is in need of repair. The following are some general guidelines recommended by Rockmills to help keep your steel boiler healthy all year. In most buildings, this work is done by the super or other staff member. It is important to keep a written maintenance record of the type of work done throughout the year.

Water-Side Maintenance

1. Your new boiler should be washed out until it is free of oil, pipe-joint compound and all foreign material. This is usually done by the heating contractor. However, if the old boiler was treated with a boiler-sealing compound, some of the compound usually circulates through the system and after a few days of firing this may start to drain back into the new boiler. If so, additional cleaning will be required.

2. Do not allow fresh water to remain in the boiler without being heated. Do not add large quantities of cold water to a hot boiler. Whenever the boiler has been filled with fresh water, it should be fired and brought to steaming temperature in order to prevent the formation of air bubbles, which cause corrosion.

3. Check water level daily and maintain the proper water level in the boiler at all times. If it becomes necessary to add excessive amounts of make-up water manually or if the automatic water feeder is operating excessively, find the cause of the loss of water such as leaking connections, missing or defective valves, buried and leaking return lines and so on. In order to protect your heating plant, you must repair the problem immediately.

4. Blow down the low water cut-off and/or automatic water feeder weekly. This prevents dirt and sediment from clogging up the internal parts of the control.

5. Flush out the water column weekly. This prevents sediment from accumulating in gauge glass and connecting lines and giving a false reading. This is done with no pressure in the boiler.

6. Do not drain any more water than necessary out of the boiler. This adds to the necessity of the constant addition of make-up water, which introduces oxygen into

the boiler. The blow-down valve at the bottom of the boiler should be used every three to four weeks only to check the amount of sediment that may accumulate in the boiler. As a rule, draining a gallon or so will be sufficient.

7. Boil out or wash out the boiler thoroughly once a year. This can be done during the summer months. Also, boil out the boiler with an alkaline cleaner after installing new tubes to remove oil or other coatings from the tube surfaces. These protective coatings are commonly applied to new tubes to prevent rusting during storage and transit, and will cause corrosion if left on the tubes during operation of the boiler.

8. Make sure all piping, valves, nipples, plugs and so on are free from leaks no matter how small.

9. Maintain boiler water with cathodic or chemical protection to prevent water-side corrosion and scale.

Fire-Side Maintenance

1. Clean tubes whenever soot, scale or any residue accumulates.

2. Never allow soot or scale to remain in the boiler when it is out of service—especially if the boiler room is damp. (The sulphur content in the oil can become sulfuric acid and will pit and corrode all heating surfaces.)

3. Maintain a smoke-free fire—smoke creates soot and air pollution.

This guide is to be used for normal operating conditions only. If unusual or unsafe conditions exist, call your heating contractor or service company.

Off-Season Overhaul: Get the Heating System in Order

By Mark Klein

The months immediately following the end of the heating season are prime time to reassess your building's heating equipment. At this time, problems are still fresh in the minds of the staff. If you wait too long, the necessary parts and vendors may be unavailable in time for the start of the next season, or only available at premium prices.

There have been many recent advances in heating plant equipment and an array of new products are on the market. While some are excellent, many are not worthwhile when payback periods are considered. By properly maintaining existing equipment your super can collect the base-line data required to determine whether or not changes and modernization are warranted. Often, after addressing the following items, it will be discovered that major equipment replacement is not necessary.

The Boilers

A successful summer heating plant overhaul usually starts with the boilers. The boiler firebox refractory, boiler tubes, hand-holes, sheets and mudlegs should be inspected. Throughout the year, the fire tubes should be brushed every sixth week or 750 hours of operation, whichever occurs first. On occasion, your staff will notice that they cannot pass a rotating brush through the tubes because of blockage by solidified soot. A boiler with blocked tubes will not allow the efficient transfer of heat from the burning fuel to the water in the boiler, with a subsequent loss of thermal output and a considerable increase in fuel consumption. In addition, on the coldest days you will need additional boilers on line in order to maintain adequate apartment heating levels if you operate with blocked tubes.

Contact your boiler repair company to turbine brush the boiler tubes that your staff cannot clean. In preparation for brushing the tubes, the back connections and boiler breechings should be cleaned and vacuumed. The main breeching should be cleaned at least twice each year to remove the soot that accumulates so that proper draft and safe, efficient operation can be maintained.

The boiler refractory and/or fire brick should also be closely inspected at this time. It is reasonable to expect that the refractory will sustain some damage in the course of the heating season. But the continued operation of a boiler with damaged refractory material will result in serious damage to the surrounding areas of the boiler as well as additional fuel usage.

Once these steps are taken, the boilers should undergo a complete inspection by someone qualified. All hand-hole covers should be removed and both the water sides and fire side of the boiler should be checked for problems, which, if allowed to go unresolved, can result in catastrophic failure. The mudlegs should be cleaned out and all hand-hole gaskets should be replaced. A hydrostatic test should be performed on the completion of this work to test the soundness of all boiler tubes, sheets, manholes and hand-holes. If the boiler fails the hydrostatic test, the necessary welding can be done at this time and the boiler retested.

The Heating Control System

The heating control system should also be given attention before being laid up for the summer. Many moderate-to-large-sized residential buildings are equipped with Vari Vac subatmospheric heating systems. These offer extremely efficient service, but only when in perfect operating condition. A Vari Vac system that is not properly calibrated, or which has one or more of its components out of order, will consume significantly more fuel than a less sophisticated system.

The control panel, the "brain" of the system, receives information from a variety of sensors. It is usually located in the boiler room, each building having an individual panel that not only provides control of the heating operation, but also a means of monitoring the status of the other components and the actual amount of heat both required and supplied. In the event of a failure of the other components in the system, the control panel provides the means to manually control the heat supply to the residents until repairs are made.

The Vari Vac control panel should be professionally cleaned and calibrated at the end of each heating season. Frequently the control panel takes the blame when the Vari Vac system fails to perform and is all too often replaced by a "more modern" model. Unfortunately, the replacement of the control panel will never restore proper operation to a system plagued with the other malfunctions. Only consider installing a "more modern" Vari Vac control panel after the entire system is proven to be in operating order.

The heat balancer, motorized zone valve, outdoor selector, differential controller, auto timer and vacuum pump controls should also be professionally checked and calibrated. No Vari Vac system can operate with defective vacuum pumps. The pumps should be dead-end tested by the staff to determine if they can produce the vacuum necessary to distribute heat efficiently throughout the building under all operating conditions.

To dead-end test, close the condensate return valve nearest to the vacuum tank; test the pumps individually on hand (continuous) operation and watch the main vacuum gauge. The vacuum in the tank should rise rapidly to approximately twenty-seven inches of mercury. If this does not occur, try the test with both gate valves on the discharge piping closed. If vacuum is achieved, the problem is only in the vacuum check valves on the discharge piping. This can easily be corrected by your in-house staff. If adequate vacuum is achieved, turn both pumps off for several minutes to check the vacuum tank and associated piping for leaks. Any problems occurring with the vacuum pumps should prompt an immediate call for professional service.

In the event that the pumps have tested well and the piping system throughout the building has tested poorly, you will have to make the decision as to whether or not to abandon the Vari Vac system and select another type of heating control system. This may be the best course of action if modifications to the apartment convectors have been made or thermostatic valves have been installed on the apartment convectors in an attempt to resurrect a nonfunctioning Vari Vac system. Replacing apartment convector valves, re-orificing each convector and repairing vacuum leaks throughout a large development can easily result in an expenditure of several hundred thousand dollars.

Steam Traps

Few managers realize the importance of the steam traps located throughout the system, without which it is impossible to supply adequate heating. There are two basic types of steam traps you will encounter in your steam distribution system.

The thermal element steam traps, located in each apartment convector, all need to be working in order for heat to be distributed evenly throughout the building. A large supply should be kept on hand for use by your staff when checking apartment heat complaints. A nonworking convector can usually be returned to service by replacing a nonopening thermal disk in the steam trap of that convector. Inordinately high condensate temperatures are a sign that many apartment thermal elements are defective and passing steam.

In addition, heating problems in particular apartment risers are often traced to "blown" steam traps that will not close in the convectors on the floors below the problem apartment. Thermal element steam trap replacement is one procedure best done during the heating season.

Each major steam riser is equipped with a float and thermal trap that prevents the buildup of condensate in the steam risers, blocking the flow of steam to the apartments. It is essential that these traps be serviced annually. The thermal cage should be replaced whenever these traps are opened for replacement of the float and seat mechanism. These traps should be infrared scanned during the heating season to determine if there is an adequate temperature drop across the trap.

Steam main drips are serviced by float and thermal traps so large that the malfunction of only one can prevent the proper operation of the entire heating system. In buildings where the condensate return from the domestic hot-water generator is piped directly into the building return line, a malfunctioning trap will also disrupt heating system operation by destroying circulation, due to loss of vacuum throughout the system. If you receive heat complaints during periods of peak domestic hot-water usage, and your boiler plant or the utility is providing adequate pressure, the culprit is usually the domestic hot-water generator steam trap.

Proper attention to the maintenance items touched upon above will ensure that next winter you will be in a position to provide adequate heat to the residents of your building at the lowest possible cost. If the work is done professionally, the costs incurred in your summer overhaul program will be returned many times over through fuel cost reductions in the coming year, and will be far more beneficial than the needless replacement of serviceable equipment.

Heat System Upgrade: Proper Maintenance Reduces Fuel Costs

By Dick Koral

In June, most people's thoughts turn to sunny days at the beach. But those who have experience running a building know that the time between heating seasons, when the boiler can be shut down, is ideal for performing the necessary maintenance procedures. Since summer is a busy season for boiler repair crews, management should schedule maintenance and repairs by late spring.

Consider Separate Hot Water

Most multifamily buildings in New York generate their domestic hot water (DHW) in their heating boilers. Not only is this a wasteful practice, but boiler maintenance requires shutting down the hot-water supply, which is an inconvenience. So June is a good time for thinking about installing a domestic hot-water system that is independent of the heating boiler. If the boiler is fired by natural gas, it goes without saying that the separate DHW heater will also be gas fired. If the boiler is oil fired, many building companies choose gas-fired water heaters, because they are easier to maintain.

An effective building heating system consists of many basic components: the fuel delivery (by gas main or oil truck and storage tank); the boiler and burner and their controls; the central heating control; the flue and chimney; the steam or (heating) hot-water distribution system, which includes piping and radiators or convectors in apartments and, by extension, the walls, windows and roof, which help to keep heat in. Neglect any one of these and you'll regret it.

Before proceeding with scheduled maintenance, an analysis should be made of past performance and current conditions. How did the fuel consumption in the past twelve months compare to previous years' consumption and the city's average of 850 gallons of No. 2 oil per two-bedroom apartment? Generally, consumption of more than 650 gallons can economically justify the cost of a lot more than routine cleaning and adjustments.

Annual Maintenance

A chimney needs to be inspected by a professional every few years, then repaired and cleaned as indicated. Broken bricks in the boiler's firing chamber must be replaced before the boiler itself can be cleaned. Any boiler tubes that have been temporarily plugged due to leaking during the winter need to be replaced. Parts of the boiler that come in contact with water must be chemically cleaned after all the water in the boiler has been drained, and the innards flushed thoroughly. All burner and boiler controls should be checked and reset, as required. If the fuel is heavy oil (grade four or six), the fuel tank should be cleaned out every few years.

As a result of all these measures, it is not unlikely that boiler plant efficiency could reach 10 percent higher next fall. (A 10 percent fuel cost savings would pay for all of this work, with money left over.)

Usually neglected because it is so labor intensive is a check on the steam-heating distribution system, especially the radiators, with their inlet valves and either air-vent valves or convectors, or, in the case of two-pipe systems, steam traps. Because these are not usually well maintained, New York is a winter symphony of banging pipes when the steam comes up and wailing tenants who are either too hot or too cold, depending on which apartments they occupy.

The Building Envelope

Finally, there are the walls, windows and sometimes the roof that must be maintained, which is a lengthy subject in itself. It can be summarized by noting that even the best heating system is inadequate if it is located in a leaky barn.

Murphy's Law states that if anything can go wrong, it will. We think Murphy must have lived in a New York City apartment building. The principles are simple, the details complex. Managers and boards need expert guidance to institute proper maintenance programs for their buildings. Some contractors are very good at heating systems. They are even better when the building has retained an independent engineer to inspect the systems, prescribe ("specify") the measures, prequalify the contractors who will bid on the work, help select the winning bid and check that the work conforms to his specs.

Spring Cleaning Time: Do Heating System Maintenance Now

By Dick Koral

Now that spring is almost here, it's time to arrange for your building's annual maintenance of the heating system. Many of the good heating service firms will soon be booked up for all the heating system service work that needs to be done during the nonheating season, so don't put this off.

It's also early enough to be taking note of all the faults your heating system demonstrated this winter: overheated and underheated rooms, breakdowns of either heat or hot-water delivery, banging radiators and so on. The board should ask the manager for a report on these now. What were the individual complaints that the super responded to? Boards should be able to view a log (written record) of these. They are usually symptomatic of general problems.

Among the items that should be addressed at this time are:

1. Chimney inspection and repair: Have this done first, because the debris from repairs will settle at the base of the chimney.

2. Chimney cleaning: It is important to have a clear path for the boiler to vent itself, so this is best done before the boiler is cleaned.

3. Boiler cleaning: This should be done before repairs if the cleaner has to crawl though the combustion chamber, which may do damage to the brickwork.

4. Boiler repair: Hint—specify American-made boiler tubes. Only slightly more expensive, they last a lot longer.

5. Faulty controls replacement: Some of these may have been rewired temporarily during the heating season in response to some problem.

6. Hot-water heating coil: Check the hot-water heating coil in the boiler by turning off the automatic make-up water supply for a day and observe the boiler gauge glass. If the water level has risen over a day or two, the coil may be leaking. (If the water level drops more than about a quarter of an inch, the coil is okay but there are steam or steam condensate leaks in the system that must be discovered and corrected as soon as possible.)

7. Oil tank cleaning: Have this done if sludge or water has accumulated. Often, water drains into the tank during rain storms from a deteriorating fill box in the sidewalk, which should be replaced. To avoid the problem and conform to the requirement that the box be flush with the surface, make sure that the new box is about one-half inch above the level of the sidewalk and that there is gently mounded fresh cement around it.

To be assured of a thorough tank-cleaning job, specify "cut, clean and squeegee out." This means that the cleaning contractor will cut an access hole at the top of the tank, if none exists, to permit an employee to climb inside. Specify that clean oil be returned to the tank. Request that the employee who enters the tank note the condition of the oil gauge dip tube inside the tank (the tube extends from the top of the tank to within four to six inches of the bottom).

One indication that there is an excessive accumulation of sludge is a sluggish oil gauge, which might take an hour or more to indicate the true level of oil in the tank after a delivery. Get the super to check this at the next delivery of oil.

8. Tank gauge (petrometer) check: Consider using a "stick" for a more accurate reading of oil content and a check before and after, on delivery. (A chart for calibrating the stick is available at no cost from the Apartment House Institute at New York City Technical College. For installations where there is not sufficient headroom above the tank, a folding oil stick can be purchased.)

9. Burner check: Consider overhauling or rebuilding. An overhaul is replacement of worn parts and adjustments. Rebuilding (usually in the contractor's shop) includes replacement of all working parts to make the burner "like new." This costs about half what a new burner would cost. Ten to twelve-year-old oil burners are likely candidates for rebuilding.

10. Basement-floor moisture check: Check for this in the vicinity of buried condensate return lines, indicating the possibility of a leaking condensate return pipe. (See item 6.) If buried pipe is not brass, expect the worst. (Condensate and steam leaks result in excessive need for make-up boiler water, which, rich in oxygen, eats up steel boiler tubes. Its carbon dioxide content will corrode cast-iron boilers, too.)

11. Checking of air-vent valves on basement steam mains (the service company's job) and on all radiators (the super's job): If they are not functioning, they are likely the culprits that cause overheating and underheating. Replace all defective ones.

12. Checking of thermostatic mixing valve for domestic hot water: It controls the temperature of the water sent to the apartments. Reset or repair, as required. (On some boilers, the water level may have to be set higher in the summer to compensate for lower boiler water temperature.)

Reduce Your Fuel Usage: Heat Computers Offer Sure Savings
By Robin Shamburg

Today's complex computers do everything from cleaning the pool to paying one's taxes. So naturally, it was only a matter of time before the high-tech computerized world came to the rescue of inefficient apartment heating. Many co-ops and condos are finding a way to reduce their operating costs by installing computerized equipment to monitor existing heating systems.

The heat computer began as the brainchild of Gerald Pindus, president of U.S. Energy Controls, a Brooklyn-based company that installs and maintains energy systems. In 1973, when he was owner and manager of a Bronx apartment complex, Pindus was faced with the challenge of keeping his buildings cost-effective during the oil crisis. "We began to investigate the causes of oil waste in multifamily residential buildings," recalls Pindus. "We discovered that, in the majority of cases, the most obvious cause of waste was building overheating."

According to Pindus, the culprit was the basic time controllers that operated a building's boiler system based on outside temperature. Still widely used in most co-ops and condos today, these controllers provide very limited regulation of the heat supplied by a boiler. They simply turn on a boiler whenever the outside temperature falls below a specific level—fifty-five degrees Fahrenheit during the day as required by New York City law. Even when the building is warm enough, the boiler will continue to cycle as long as the outside temperature remains below this level. In an attempt to maintain a comfortable indoor temperature, residents throw open their windows, causing valuable heat to escape.

A High-Tech Alternative

In an effort to improve on this low-tech system, Pindus consulted with an oil burner expert and a computer expert to design a microprocessor-based system that would regulate boiler activity based upon indoor temperatures. The system is triggered by a network of temperature sensors placed throughout the building—in corners, hallways and particularly cold areas known to generate complaints. These sensors are linked to a computer receiver in the boiler room that analyzes the readings to provide an accurate temperature picture of the building.

In this way, the heat computer performs two distinct functions: First, it monitors apartment temperatures and restricts boiler cycling to periods when heat is needed. Second, the computer provides what Pindus terms "hard printed facts" concerning fuel consumption, steam and vacuum pressure and an entire wish list of system specifics—including how much heat is going up the chimney.

Some models are equipped with an alarm that will automatically dial a specified telephone number to alert the manager, super or plumber in the case of system trouble. Building managers may opt for a printer on the premises to print out information, or may access the same information by modem from a remote terminal. With a modem, the computer can be dialed from any telephone to set the desired daytime and nighttime temperatures.

A Worthwhile Investment

Today, there are several manufacturers of heat computers serving the tristate area. Prices for installing a twelve-sensor system to service a one hundred—unit building average between $5,500 and $12,000, with a five-year parts and one-year service warranty. According to David Suthergreen, a former vice-president of Optimum Applied Systems, a firm that manufactures, installs and services its own heat computer, a building's fuel consumption can be reduced by as much as 25 or 30 percent through computerized monitoring. With this kind of efficiency, says Suthergreen, the system will pay for itself in one to three years, depending on the price of fuel.

Larry Zucker, president of Compusave Fuel Systems, manufacturers and installers of wireless heat computers, estimates that the building's board may see a payback "in as short a period as a single fuel season—depending on how the building's superintendent has been running the building." Alan Tabachnikov, vice-president of construction management at Energy Investment Systems, a company that provides energy management audits for multifamily buildings, estimates a payback period of two to five years. But, he admits, the savings are often relative and sometimes hidden.

William Haugh of Haugh and Walsh, a Queens-based firm that uses heat computers in the thirteen apartment buildings it owns and manages, says that he has found "phenomenal savings" through effective energy monitoring. "Because the apartments are no longer overheated, we've seen a substantial decrease in oil use," Haugh says. "As a building owner, there's nothing more aggravating than seeing windows wide open in the middle of winter."

A Helpful Budgeting Tool

In addition to reducing fuel consumption, the heat computer can play a significant role in a building's long-term planning. Joseph Barocas, sponsor and manager of a sixty-five–unit Queens co-op, says that the information generated by his co-op's fuel computer was very helpful in planning the building's annual budget. "Our system enabled us to project fuel bills and maintenance expenses that we otherwise might have only been able to guess at." In addition, because the computer maintains a record of heating functions over an extended period of time, managers and board members can review costs and flag any potential system problems before they result in costly repairs and inconvenient shutdowns.

With all these capabilities coupled with the ever-present need to conserve our natural resources, it may seem surprising that more co-op and condo boards aren't equipping their buildings with these computers. Tabachnikov says that of the twenty thousand apartment buildings with over thirty units in New York City, just one thousand are equipped with heat computers. One reason, he says, is that most management firms are reluctant to invest in the installation costs because they haven't yet seen the savings such a system would bring. But, says Tabachnikov, "Overheated apartments are a luxury that buildings simply cannot afford."

In a study conducted by Peter H. Judd, former assistant commissioner of New York City's Energy Conservation Division, it was found that "The average fuel use per apartment was 865 gallons of oil per year. A reasonable average use should be 650 gallons per apartment per year, attainable with standard equipment and attentive maintenance." The only way to remedy this type of waste, which stems primarily from inadequate controls, is through effective monitoring.

"If you speak to private owners, co-op management firms or even the New York City Department of Housing—which so far has installed heat computers in thirty-five of their buildings—you will see that these computers are beginning to proliferate," says Pindus. "Management is beginning to see that you can't run a building these days without information."

Ultimately, however, the decision for a building to install a fuel computer should be based upon necessity. Suggests William Dichter, president of a Mamaroneck co-op that purchased a computer one year ago, "The first thing a board should do is take the building's fuel bill and divide it by the number of units in the building.

See how it hits against the local average fuel consumption. If it's fairly similar, leave it alone. But if it's significantly higher, then it's time to install a fuel-monitoring system."

Keep Cool: Maintain and Update Your Air-Conditioning System
By Dick Koral

Over the next five to ten years, profound changes are likely to take place regarding your building's air-conditioning system. As environmental impact is considered, many refrigeration coolants will be banned. That, and the rising cost of fuel, will cause most Americans to reevaluate their current cooling systems. Whether your building has window-mounted or through-the-wall units in individual apartments or a central air-conditioning system that operates with refrigerants, climate control has become a special problem.

We recommend that each housing company retain a qualified engineer to guide its air-conditioning policy during this crucial period, when many buildings will be forced to change refrigerants and, probably, equipment. Even if there is no central air-conditioning in your building, the problem is too technical to be left to each shareholder to solve. The engineer should survey the equipment in each apartment. The oldest units might be very costly to run now, and ready for the scrap heap (with environmental safety in mind, of course!). A master contract to overhaul equipment in the apartments would save every shareholder from bad luck with poor contractors.

Alternative Coolants

Nonabsorption air-conditioning systems, which use refrigerant compressors, use "halogenated hydrocarbons" to create cool air. When released into the atmosphere, they contribute to the destruction of the ozone layer high above the earth, which protects us from the harmful effects of the sun's ultraviolet rays on our skin. Some refrigeration compounds have been banned and some companies, like Du Pont, which invented Freon, one of the compounds containing chlorine and fluoride (chlorofluorocarbons) used in refrigeration, have stopped manufacturing them. Mechanics who must repair air conditioners can no longer release the gas but must use very expensive, bulky equipment to capture the gas for safe disposal.

Many apartment houses with central air-conditioning systems do not use these refrigerants, but instead have "absorption" systems that use steam from the heating boiler in summer to make chilled water. The refrigerant in these systems is harmless water!

Substitute refrigerants have been and continue to be developed. They are not cheap. Since these substitutes are not quite as effective as the old refrigerants, changes often have to be made to the air-conditioning systems if the required capacity is to be maintained.

Maintenance Is Crucial

If your building has a central air-conditioning system, it has probably received an annual overhaul every spring. To operate efficiently, the cooling tower on the roof must be cleaned, refilled with clean water and dosed with chemicals that prevent the growth of algae and bacteria. The coil where the water from the cooling tower picks up the heat from the hot refrigerant has to be cleaned. Motors, pulleys and other moving parts have to be lubricated, and the compressor must be checked. If the system needs a topoff charge of refrigerant because some has leaked out, then the leak has to be found and repaired.

We recommend that, this spring, the above work, especially concerning the compressor and the refrigerant piping, receive the most profound attention because, after this summer, it may not be possible to buy more refrigerant of the same type. With the air-conditioning system in tip-top shape, the consumption of electricity (or fuel, if an absorption system) will be minimized. Energy costs for any air-conditioning system are very high, and will be higher with the implementation of the proposed new energy tax.

The overhaul should not be restricted to the roof. Each window or through-the-wall air conditioner and each fan-coil unit under the window, in the case of centrally supplied cooling, needs to be clean in order to function efficiently. In the case of window and through-the-wall units, the inside cover must come off, exposing the filter. The filter is then removed, exposing the cooling coil. If dust clogs the spaces between the aluminum fins, the coil must also be cleaned. A vacuum cleaner may do the trick. Then the filter must be cleaned or a new one procured, and carefully replaced. Likewise, the coils and filter of the fan-coil unit have to be examined and cleaned, as required.

Especially important: If replacing a room air conditioner, do not accept the recommendation of a contractor or retail store as to what capacity unit to purchase. They usually exaggerate the size—a waste of purchase money and operating expense. Use the calculation form published by the Association of Home Appliance Manufacturers of Chicago and also available from Con Edison. And buy the unit with the highest "EER" rating available. It will repay its slightly higher cost quickly in energy savings.

Elevator Maintenance: The Importance of Ironclad Contracts

By C. Jaye Berger, Esq.

Elevators are one of life's necessities when you live in a high-rise building. Yet unreliable elevator service is a common complaint among apartment residents. As we all know, nothing is more annoying than having to wait indefinitely for—or worse yet, in—an elevator. The key to smooth elevator operation is a solid maintenance and repair contract with a reputable elevator company. This is not always an easy item to negotiate. But with the help of the right professionals—an attorney and an elevator consultant—your building should be able to rise to the occasion.

To begin with, repair and maintenance contracts should be separate documents. You do not want a situation in which the maintenance contract is terminated, causing any unpaid balances for repairs to become accelerated and due in one lump sum. In addition, because maintenance contracts tend to involve large sums of money, they should be carefully reviewed by an attorney familiar with this area before they are signed.

It is also recommended that co-ops and condos work with elevator consultants, since elevators are complex pieces of equipment. The board will need someone to explain which parts of the elevator are or should be covered by the agreement and which are not. If the expert prepares any general conditions, they should be reviewed by an attorney, since they will be used for bids and will become part of the general contract. If the co-op's attorney disagrees with any of the document's language, it must be changed before handing it out for bids. In any repair contract, payments should be made in accordance with a predetermined schedule that relates to the amount of work done. A representative of the co-op should review each phase of the work before each payment is approved.

The extent to which emergency repairs are covered by your contract is important. Other things to consider include: What kind of response time can be expected? What guarantees are there as to when the equipment will be working again? At what point, if any, will the co-op be charged for additional services?

Responsibility for elevator tests and corrections of violations will need to be discussed. Certain tests can potentially harm the elevator and repairs may have to be made. Who will be responsible for this? When notices of violations are issued, there is usually a time period within which they must be corrected. If additional time is required, who will be responsible for securing this? Will all violations be the responsibility of the contractor to correct?

If any notices must be given by either party under the contract, the form of notice should be specified as well as the amount of time allowed for such notice. For example, is telephone notice of an accident sufficient or must written notice be given as well? Is immediate notice required or is notice within a certain number of days sufficient?

Some maintenance contracts stipulate a fixed price, but can be subject to increases due to various factors. The co-op should have a clear understanding as to the circumstances under which prices can be increased and should try to negotiate a cap, if possible.

These and other issues must be negotiated as part of any contract concerning elevators. A little time spent consulting with knowledgeable legal counsel before signing a contract can mean less time will be spent with problems later on. It can be very useful to have a meeting with all parties present to review any problematic terms before signing the document. Once you have resolved these issues, an experienced attorney can draft any necessary amendments into the agreement.

Raise the Comfort Level: Make Sure Windows Are Up to Par

By Angelina Esposito

The current temperature is nineteen degrees and with winds gusting up to thirty miles per hour it feels more like twenty degrees below zero. While weather advisories are flashing on your television screen, warning people to stay indoors, the winds are whipping at your window causing a rattling noise, while freezing air seeps through.

If you have ever experienced a winter like this, you understand the importance of preparing early, even while the summer heat still bakes the city sidewalks. The first step in the preparation process is to make sure your windows will not allow heat to escape or cold air to enter. Besides having cold rooms, noisy windows and increased fuel bills, there are many less obvious signs of a faulty window. Some indications include a window that slams shut or does not open, close or lock easily, one that has a rotted sill, or cold glass. If any of these problems sound familiar, you have two options: replace or repair.

Replacement Windows

When deciding to replace your windows, there are three benefits to consider: comfort, ease of operation and reduction of fuel costs. According to Robert Ecker, vice-president of Ecker Manufacturing, New York's largest window manufacturer, the biggest benefit of new windows is the improved quality of life. "Replacing enhances a person's life and apartment," he says. "The apartment immediately gets quieter and warmer."

So when is it time to replace? And what are the financial benefits? Bob Peterson, energy conservation specialist at Con Edison, advises, "Windows can fall out if they deteriorate." Dick Koral of the Apartment House Institute agrees, suggesting that you know it is time to replace your windows "when they are so rotten they threaten to fall out."

The installation of new windows is an investment—about $250 each for the popular double-hung luxury aluminum window manufactured by Ecker, for example—but the rewards are tangible. According to Sally Karpen, sales associate at Ecker, deciding whether to replace is a question of when the building owners decide to upgrade the look of the building and improve the electric bills. If your windows are beyond repair, if the wood begins to rot and the metal begins to rust, if the sashes become loose and fall out, if you experience drafts and high electric bills, then it is time to invest in new windows. Replacement can result in savings of 10 to 30 percent on a small building's heating bills, and up to 20 percent in bigger buildings, according to Ecker.

Due to advances in technology, windows installed prior to 1980 will eventually have to be replaced. Prior to that time, windows were not made with insulated glass. They were not technologically designed to keep freezing air out, but rather acted as a conductor of the cold. Today's windows are made with double-pane glass, designed to resist the winter cold. "Air infiltration and the conduction of heat through the single glazing (88 percent and 15 percent respectively) are the largest source of heat loss in most old windows," says Richard C. Apfel, vice-president of large-volume sales at Skyline Windows. The newer windows made with insulated materials and weatherstripping "can result in a reduction of overall heat loss of up to 85 percent," leading to a substantial fuel savings, he adds.

At Two Fifth Avenue, the board decided to replace all of the co-op's 3,200 windows last year, primarily to reduce noise and drafts. Skyline Windows began the project in September 1992 and completed it the following April. The job cost approximately $300 per window, which included installation, screens, removal and reinstallation of air conditioners. According to board president Tom Marcosson, the board expects to save approximately $40,000 per year on fuel costs as a result of their investment.

When replacing windows in the entire building, Koral suggests contacting a window consultant to guide you through the replacement process or locating three co-ops that had good experience with their contractors and soliciting bids from those companies.

Although individual apartment owners may decide to replace, Karpen explains that it is wise for the entire building to undertake the project together. Replacing all the windows at once is substantially cheaper than doing it one at a time, she says. It also keeps the look of the building consistent and creates building-wide energy savings. When individual apartment windows need to be replaced, owners must get permission from the board before installation, and often must match the new windows to the others in the building.

Repairs and Upgrades

When replacement is not necessary, repairing your existing windows or making additions can be equally beneficial. While some repairs have to be done professionally, others can be accomplished with do-it-yourself kits.

A common problem with windows that can be easily repaired is dried-out weatherstripping—the soft material installed between the window frame and the building wall. Over the years the weatherstripping becomes dirty and eventually wears out, allowing the window to leak air. According to John Bentley, lead mechanic at Window Restorations, "By replacing the weatherstripping you can prevent 80 percent of your heat from escaping and cold air from entering."

If the window tracks are kept clean, new weatherstripping should last ten to fifteen years. If not maintained, it may have to be replaced in as little as two years. Check the weatherstripping; if it appears to be smooth and pliable, it is in good condition. If it is hard, it needs to be replaced, says Vincent Rua, president of Skyline Windows. As long as the window frame is not damaged, the weatherstripping can be replaced.

Other problems that can be repaired include changing the lock if it does not close properly, to eliminate heat escape, balancing (needed if the window slams shut) and corking to tighten the gap around the window frame and building wall.

Add-Ons

Other alternatives to window replacement include the installation of storm windows or window film. If a window is not rotted to the point where replacing is warranted but is losing heat, storm windows may be the answer. According to Richard Peritz, president of MetroSolar, an authorized 3M dealer, by installing storm windows, a single-pane window becomes a double-pane and a double-pane window becomes a triple-pane. Storm windows reduce heat loss on a single-pane window by 55 percent, according to Peritz. There is no major construction involved or appearance changes to the building's exterior. They also aid in the reduction of cold-air admittance and noise, infiltration of air, dust and most damaging ultraviolet rays, and they increase safety, he adds.

The average cost of a small job with a complex window structure is $12 per square foot, according to Peritz. "By installing a storm window, you can have an annual savings of $20 per window on your electric bill," says Peterson. Equipped with a magnetic lining, the storm window can be easily installed and removed by the individual, then stored away under a bed, in the attic or anywhere out of the way.

If your existing window is in good condition but is losing heat, another alternative is Vista Window Film, introduced by Courtaulds Performance Films. This film is used on windows where appearance, as well as energy savings, protection and comfort, is your main concern. After application, it is virtually invisible.

Besides eliminating harmful effects of ultraviolet rays and heat buildup and protecting furnishings from fading, the film reduces energy costs and prevents interior heat loss by reflecting the heat back into the room and limiting the amount that escapes. The film costs approximately $4 and up per square foot, depending on the size and complexity of the job, according to a representative of Vista. A study done by the Industry Association shows an average savings of forty to fifty cents per square foot of filmed window per year. The savings vary according to the number of windows filmed, the location of the windows and the climate.

Whether you decide to replace, repair, add-on or do-it-yourself, now is the time to get started. Winter is right around the corner and Jack Frost will be nipping at your windows soon.

Water Costs on the Rise: Meters Lead to Conservation Efforts

By Kate Shogi

There are many compelling reasons New Yorkers should be conserving water. Our reservoirs are slowly becoming overtaxed, droughts seem to arrive with alarming regularity and New York City's total water consumption is spiraling upward.

In case you're not convinced, New York City's Universal Metering Program is likely to change your habits. In an effort to charge property owners for the exact amount of water that a building uses, the Koch administration announced in 1988 a ten-year, $290 million program aimed at installing water meters in all private homes and multiple dwellings. The plan encourages conservation because it will replace the current flat-rate billing system with a metered system requiring that consumers pay for what they use.

"When you meter, people conserve," says Jay Haas, a spokesman with New York City's Department of Environmental Protection, Bureau of Water and Energy Conservation. Even if your building doesn't have a meter yet—and chances are it doesn't, because, according to Haas, only 213,000 of the estimated 630,000 meters have been installed—it's never too early to get into good conservation habits. In addition, for fixtures, it's the law.

Effective this year, New York State has set conservation standards and criteria for plumbing fixtures that have been incorporated into the building code. For example, if you purchase and install a new toilet, it must use no more than 1.6 gallons per flush—a drastic change from the five to seven gallons routinely used in toilets of the past. While the law is not retroactive—you don't have to replace older fixtures for newer, more efficient ones—it's probably a good investment.

Fortunately, there are many steps that you can take to whip your older fixtures into shape and make your home less wasteful. According to Fred Weintraub, a licensed plumber with M. Farbman & Sons, there is no shortage of water-saving gadgets. "The market has absolutely complied [with water-conservation efforts] and responded," he says. "There are about 130 to 150 manufacturers that produce low-flow fixtures."

There are five key areas of water consumption in a home—leaks, toilets, showers, faucets and appliances. Hundreds of gallons can be saved by doing something as simple as not running water while shaving. What follows is a list of some suggestions and ideas.

Fix That Leak

The first step that needs to be taken is to pinpoint and repair all leaks. According to the DEP, most leaks, aside from those in toilets, are in faucets and can usually be repaired by replacing worn washers. Consider that a slow drip can easily leak up to fifteen to twenty gallons a day. According to John Rakos, a consultant with the water management firm Consumer's Advantage, a faucet that is one-quarter open and leaking around the clock wastes roughly 150 gallons per day—which could cost a building hundreds of dollars per year.

Less easy to spot but just as wasteful are toilet leaks, which occur when the flushing mechanism is not adjusted properly or parts become too worn. These leaks often occur at the overflow pipe or at the plunger ball; look for leaks by checking the height of the water level or by dropping a little food coloring into the tank and waiting to see if it shows up in the bowl.

Increase Toilet Efficiency

Toilets are notoriously water hungry, claiming up to 40 percent of the total household water usage. There are two ways to reduce this: Don't use the toilet for things it wasn't meant to flush—a DEP handout mentions spiders and cigarette butts—and cut down on the amount of water per flush. There are many new methods for controlling the amount of water your toilet outputs; according to Rakos, it's a matter of choosing what works best in a specific scenario. There is a dam-type method, which works by blocking an amount of water held from going down; a forced-closure device, which closes the flapper valve at a premature level, and a float-type device, which attaches to the flapper and holds it open to a certain water level. Rakos recommends three devices: Frugal Flush, Mini Flush and Float-A-Flapper; these range in price from roughly $10 to $16 in cost.

Less precise but DEP-sanctioned is the method of filling a plastic bottle with water and popping it into the tank, staying clear of the flushing mechanism. Be sure not to displace too much water, as you'll end up having to double-flush, which wastes more water than you'd save.

Shower Frugally

"Conservation, especially in showers, has gotten a bad rap," sighs Rakos. Most New Yorkers are familiar with the dime-sized plastic discs that the city sent around years ago to be installed in showerheads. These discs cut into water pressure drastically, leaving many people frantically taking apart the shower head while covered with soap. However, an unaltered shower head can pour out between five and ten gallons per minute; a long shower can use a hundred gallons. This is an excessive amount of water, and Warren Liebold, the DEP's director of conservation, says the city would like to see this cut down to 2.5 gallons per minute.

It is entirely possible to reduce water flow without sacrificing pressure. Rakos recommends choosing a shower head that contains a pressure regulator to automatically adjust the flow of water, such as Teledyne's Water Pik. Such shower heads use no more than the specified 2.5 gallons per minute, and deliver a wholly satisfactory water pressure.

In terms of changing habits, it's helpful to remember that a ten-minute shower is often unnecessary, as is shaving while in the shower and running the water full blast. A shorter shower not only conserves water, but saves energy—the less water you use, the less you pay to heat.

Save at the Sink

You can save up to 25 percent of the water that comes out of the faucet simply by installing an aerator, which is a screen that attaches to the end of a faucet and is purchased from a hardware store for about $1. Using an aerator in both the kitchen and bathroom sinks can get the faucet usage down to between 1.5 and 2.5 gallons per minute.

Then there are the tried-and-true methods: not running water while brushing your teeth, shaving, doing dishes, cleaning vegetables and so on. In addition, if you are used to running the tap until the water comes out cold enough to drink, try keeping a container of water in the fridge instead.

Use Appliances Only When Full

Almost every household appliance that uses water could be used more efficiently. Washing machines, which account for about 25 percent of water used in the home, are a good example. Warren Liebold recommends using a front-loading machine, which uses less water than a top loader. Never run the machine without a full load, which uses about sixty gallons. And remember that you can adjust the amount of water the machine uses and the duration of the cycle, in order to pare down the water consumption to about twenty-seven gallons—a savings of over 50 percent. Similarly, a dishwasher should only be run when full, and on the shortest cycle practical.

If you want to know what impact metering will have on your water bill, you can contact firms such as Consumer's Advantage or the Vantage Group. They will evaluate your building, make suggestions, and provide an approximate estimate of your post-metering water bill. Bringing in a water consultant will enable you to pinpoint problems in your building's water consumption before the city installs the meter, giving you time to correct such problems before you begin paying for them.

Keep in mind that while replacing older fixtures for the newer, more efficient models can seem expensive, you will eventually recoup more than the original outlay in the form of a lower water bill. "Put it in the light of a return on investment," suggests John Rakos. And it's an investment not only in your water bill—but in the environment.

Major Contracting Projects

- *Architects and engineers*
- *Writing up contracts*
- *Sources of funding*

Avoid Construction Chaos: Establish and Follow Standard Procedures

By David Kuperberg and Paul Schreyer

For many years, cooperatives and condominiums struggled through construction projects like computer novices trying to figure out the latest technology. One way or another the job was completed, though frustration with contractors was often the result. In many cases, the price and work quality were suspect.

But, with the announcement of the investigation into alleged kickback deals between co-op and condo managers and building contractors, and subsequent indictments by the Manhattan district attorney, the environment has changed considerably. The investigation spotlighted the lack of controls and accountability that have been prevalent for too long. In this atmosphere, fraudulent practices proliferated with impunity. Unless proven and comprehensive procedures are developed, such as those used by most public agencies and corporate purchasers of design and construction services, the fraudulent practices will revive once the current scandal quiets down. Improved monitoring systems that some are advocating will only camouflage the problem.

Evaluating Bids

The goal is to establish objective criteria to evaluate contractor bids and the quality of work in a nonadversarial environment where the board maintains control and involvement. Lawyers versed in construction law can offer model procurement policies that can be adapted to any building.

A professional manager with experience and expertise in construction can effectively implement proper procedures and improve the flow of communications among all parties. For each project the board should determine whether an engineer or architect should be retained to assist in the design, bidding and monitoring of the work. The scope of the work, rather than the cost, should determine the selection.

There are systems and procedures that will virtually eliminate incentives for bribes and kickbacks. A little planning and good advice in setting up and monitoring the procurement contracts between the building and the contractor can often save thousands of dollars and result in quality work.

First, boards must prequalify contractors. Maintain a list of five to seven prequalified contractors per trade. In developing the list, establish objective criteria and a written questionnaire to be completed. Obtain and check references and financials and inspect previous work.

Next, formalize the bidding process. Prepare and distribute to the prequalified contractors detailed bid documents that include plans and specifications. Bidding documents set the foundation of the entire project. Once bids are received, review them carefully. For most projects, sealed competitive bidding is the best method. Be certain that all bids are comparable in scope of work and details. Be objective, not subjective, in reviewing the bids. Build in flexibility to cover those instances in which negotiated prices might be more appropriate, such as with emergency or highly specialized work.

Awarding and Customizing the Contract

After a thorough review of the bids, award the contract to the lowest responsive and responsible bidder. If necessary, do a spreadsheet to compare work to be performed and cost. Be certain you know what is included and excluded in each bid. Remember, the emphasis is on lowest *responsive and responsible* bid. The lowest dollar bid, if it doesn't meet these criteria, may cost you money in the long run.

Be sure to customize the contract. A standard form construction contract may be used, but customize it to the specific project. Rather than paying the contractor on a percentage completion basis, tie payments to easily recognized benchmarks of completion.

Be vigilant when confronted by change orders and extras, which can significantly put a project over budget. Make certain all change orders are in writing and signed by all parties, including at least one member of the board. Demand and review supportive documentation from the contractor.

The property manager, if he has expertise in construction, and the engineer or another qualified person should monitor the work frequently. Requisitions should not be approved until the work for which payment is sought is completed properly. If a problem arises, solve it immediately. Don't wait until the end of the project.

Have one member of the board of directors work closely on the project with a preset dollar range of authority to make decisions and give approvals. A businesslike decision-making process saves time and money. It also gives the board a greater oversight role in the entire project.

The board should maintain a data base of prices of completed projects for future reference. They should also perform periodic audits of completed contracts to see where improvements in procedures can be instituted and what worked well. By implementing these policies, building managers will have established procedures to follow and the board will have a much better understanding of each contract and more control over the project.

Capital Improvements: Trust the Pro's to Do It Right
By Craig Schiller, Esq.

No single task facing a cooperative or condominium board demands more professional assistance than a major capital project. While each project is different, most require the same basic approach. By employing the right professionals, the problem can be corrected in a timely, competitively priced and effective manner for the benefit of the whole building community.

For the sake of this story, let's assume that the board has been advised of repeated and serious water incursion by the occupants of the top two floors of the building. Prompt and conscientious efforts to solve individual problems have been unsuccessful in alleviating the symptoms.

Defining the Problem

The board needs to know—and is obliged to find out—if there is a problem that merits action on its part. We assume that all in-house resources (superintendent, maintenance staff and managing agent) have been exhausted, and that the board requires advice from an independent professional with an engineering background.

The board should, at this time, obtain the written report of a licensed professional as to the nature of the problem and the proposed remedy. The board should expect to pay a reasonable fee for this report. While boards tend to focus on the cost of the report, the board's time will be best spent in defining the scope of the engineer's assignment and in encouraging the engineer to spend enough time on the project to achieve a high level of confidence in his conclusions. In our hypothetical roof example, the engineer may perform a flood test with colored liquids, take core samples, remove a small cross section of the existing roof for lab analysis, perform extensive visual inspections or take whatever steps a prudent engineer would take under the circumstances.

The engineer will need to work closely with the board and the agent to obtain access to affected units. Problems caused by water incursion have a tendency to anger affected residents, and the board may expect difficulties on the access issue. Access difficulties may require the input and action of counsel to the board—and even an occasional court order. The board has a clear right to access individual units to investigate a building-wide condition needing repair (see "Gaining Legal Entry," page 168).

In this example, the existing roof is old and the engineer has recommended a complete roof replacement, since water incursion has occurred or is likely to occur in so many areas as to make repair impractical.

Much engineering work is required beyond the engineer's initial report. At this point, the board should satisfy itself that its relationship with the engineer is satisfactory. Was he responsive to the board's inquiries, clear in his presentation and capable of providing factual support for his professional conclusions? If so, the board should engage him to take the next step. (If the engineer has recommended expensive work, the board may wish to obtain the opinion of a second engineer to confirm the opinion of the first.)

Describing the Job

To nonprofessionals, all roofs may look the same, but among engineers, there are numerous types of roof systems that range in complexity and cost. A roof is a custom-made item. Thus, in order to obtain a proposed price for a new roof, the type of roof to be installed must be described in specifications for the job that will identify materials to be used and job procedures to be followed by a contractor who ultimately is selected to perform the work.

Not all job details fall within the expertise of the engineer, since business and insurance issues exist as well. Thus, when the engineering specifications are complete, the insurance requirements should be reviewed by the board's insurance advisors. In particular, the specifications should provide for enough public liability and other insurance to protect the community. Also, the advisability of payment, performance and guarantee bonds should be discussed. Care should be taken to specify a highly rated insurance carrier, since some carriers are financially stronger than others.

Counsel for the board should provide a form of construction contract for inclusion in the specifications book. The form should be one of the standard ones used in the industry to facilitate future negotiations, but should be tailored to fit the particular job being undertaken.

It might be wise to consult the board's general or real estate tax counsel and public accounting firm at this point, to ascertain whether the job may qualify for certain tax abatement benefits or whether particular language is helpful in establishing the entitlement.

When these inquiries are complete, the board should have a specification book that includes a complete job description, necessary materials and procedures, all insurance requirements and a form of proposed contract. The next task is to obtain a suitable contractor to perform the work. This requires the board or its representatives to start the interview process.

Getting Bids

A list of potential bidders for the job must be developed. The managing agent can supply the names of several, and it is strongly suggested that the board (or community members) identify at least two other bidders, from industry publications, advertisements, trade shows, word of mouth or otherwise. Generally speaking, the more independent bids obtained, the greater the board's assurance that it will obtain a fair price. Surprisingly, the most expensive bid may be four times the least expensive bid.

Should the least expensive bid be selected? Not necessarily. The lowest total job cost will not necessary result from the lowest bidder, since sloppy workmanship, extensive delays, costly errors and injuries to persons or property may result from the work of the lowest bidder (who perhaps bid the job at the lowest price because he did not understand the scope of work or planned to substitute substandard resources). To some extent, these risks are minimized by proper insurance and bonds, but the cost of delay and aggravation may never be recouped. As a general rule, the board should select the lowest qualified bidder, who, as noted, is not necessarily the lowest bidder.

Before signing the contract, the board should check at least two references supplied by the contractor on jobs that are somewhat comparable to the one at hand.

Watching the Contractor

Consideration should be given to the role of the engineer during construction before the contract between the board and the contractor is signed. Is he merely to observe the contractor's work to become generally familiar with its progress or is he to be present most of the time while work is ongoing as the board's site representative to prevent defects and deficiencies?

While site representation is more time-consuming and hence will cost the board more in engineering fees, the quality of the final construction job (that is, adherence to the job specifications) will probably be greater with closer supervision. It is unrealistic to expect the managing agent to watch the job progress every day without additional compensation.

While construction progresses, the contractor will perform installments of work and will submit periodic applications for payment for approval by the engineer and payment by the board through its agent. These occasions give the board an opportunity for periodic input and ensure that problems are corrected, disputes are resolved and work is proceeding with minimum interruption to daily building life.

After the construction is complete, certain job paperwork must be finalized in connection with final payment. This last step requires the involvement of the board, the managing agent, the board's counsel, the engineer, the contractor and the bonding company (if one was used). By following these steps and working closely with the right professionals, your building stands the best chance of completing the job satisfactorily.

Professional Advice: Need an Architect or Engineer?

By Paul Millman, PE, RA

Each spring, after winter's weather has taken its toll, many co-op board members and managing agents are asking themselves a question that goes something like this: "My building will clearly need some restoration work performed during the coming year. The parapets are leaning inward, the roof leaks and the beams supporting the sidewalk vault are visibly corroded. Should I retain an engineer or architect to prepare plans and specifications, or am I better off saving the professional fee and going directly to my favorite contractor?"

To answer this question, one must first understand the virtues attributable to a qualified engineer or architect (E/A). They are: expertise, objectivity, breadth of experience and fiduciary responsibility to the client. A fifth, and sometimes primary, virtue is that, in some cases, the involvement of an engineer or architect is a legal requirement.

Expertise

Sometimes problems are not as serious as they look, and can be corrected without substantial expense. A bulge in a wall, for example, doesn't necessarily mean imminent collapse. On the other hand, an apparently minor crack might be a symptom of significant structural damage beneath the building's skin. An experienced E/A firm will discern the difference and can objectively determine whether serious structural problems really do exist.

Once construction begins, an E/A firm can monitor the progress of the repair work, keeping it on the right track. Recently, our firm, SUPERSTRUCTURES, which provides engineering and architectural services, was called in to review a project well under way, in which a contractor had been hired to perform facade repairs that involved restoration of the underlying steel skeleton of a Riverside Drive cooperative. The contractor was well intentioned, but without proper construction documents or engineering supervision, his crews were conscientiously welding heavy steel-plate reinforcing where it was superfluous and unwittingly overlooking situations where reinforcing was essential.

With relatively little time on the job site, we were able to get the project back on track, ensuring the safety of the structure by indicating those areas still in need of reinforcing and stemming the flow of further financial waste.

Objectivity

If remedial work is required, an E/A firm can prepare contract documents that clearly delineate the scope of work to be performed, the materials to be used and the expected results. A tight set of contract documents permits competitive, "apples-to-apples" bidding among several qualified contractors. The bidding process generally results in a lower price for the work, with better terms for the building. If building management opts to stick with a particular contractor rather than go to bid, the E/A firm's contract documents can form the basis of a negotiated contract.

Breadth of Experience

Most contractors favor a relatively narrow range of repair products and methods. This is understandable because a contractor's commitment to a particular manufacturer or material entails such responsibilities as an investment in inventory, training of work crews and prequalification with manufacturers or distributors in order to use certain methods or products. On the other hand, because its labor and capital requirements are not as intensive, an E/A firm can "stock" knowledge of a broad range of repair methods and materials and can select the one most appropriate for the project at hand.

Fiduciary Responsibility

An E/A firm has a fiduciary and ethical responsibility to the client building.

Perhaps the most important specification sections in any contract are the "General Conditions," which detail such necessities as insurance and bonding requirements, temporary protection requirements and site usage restrictions. Construction documents prepared by an E/A firm invariably stipulate general conditions that are more favorable to the building than those contained in an agreement prepared by a contractor.

Also extremely important is the specification section dealing with unit prices. In bid situations, the contractor agrees in advance to unit prices for all of the tasks reasonably foreseen on the job. As a result, the project team minimizes the risk of job-stopping disagreements during the construction. Typically, specifications prepared by an E/A firm include a far more complete set of unit prices than agreements prepared by a contractor.

Legal Requirement

As mentioned, there are times when the New York City Department of Buildings (DOB) will insist on a licensed professional for certain projects. By now, most of us are familiar with Local Law 10, which requires owners of buildings taller than six stories to file a facade inspection report with the DOB every five years. The report must be prepared by a professional engineer or registered architect.

Also by law, any construction work beyond "ordinary repairs" requires a work permit in advance of construction. (Ordinary repairs are defined explicitly in the New York City Building Code Sections 27–125 and 27–126.) Generally speaking, ordinary repairs include "replacements or renewals of existing work," as opposed to modification of slabs or structural supports. Before a work permit can be obtained, plans must be prepared by a licensed professional and approved by the DOB.

What's the Answer?

Once repair specifications have been prepared by an E/A firm, most buildings invite from three to six contractors to bid on a project. In our experience, even with an extremely tight set of drawings and specifications, there is typically a spread between high and low bidder of 30 to 50 percent, with a spread between low bidder and next-to-low bidder of 15 to 20 percent.

This spread is greater than the fee a professional architect or engineer would charge on a typical project. Thus, for most projects, the participation of an E/A firm will save money for the building outright, in addition to the other benefits that the involvement of professionals brings.

On the other hand, no matter how simple a project, there is a minimum fee that an E/A firm must charge. For simple repairs, the E/A firm's expertise and objectivity are less compelling factors than for projects involving large sums of money, interaction among many building systems or serious structural issues.

For straightforward, low-budget projects (below $20,000), a building can reasonably deal directly with a trusted, qualified contractor. For projects above $20,000, or for smaller, more complex projects, retain a qualified E/A firm to inspect the areas in question, and, if required, develop repair specifications. With the inspection report and specifications in hand, select a qualified contractor through a competitive bidding process.

Given the complexity of most restoration projects taking place in the city, and considering the critical importance of preproject planning, the odds are that there will be an architect or engineer in your future.

Solving Contract Disputes: Put It in Writing at the Outset

By C. Jaye Berger, Esq.

Summer and fall are busy seasons for major building repairs. But with any capital improvement project, there is an enormous potential for problems and conflicts to arise both during and after the fact. Who is responsible when postconstruction problems arise? It's important to determine the answer and put it in writing before the job begins. All too often, lack of knowledge about the construction industry's customs and practices can lead to a day—or a month—in court. Fortunately, there are several measures you can take to avoid disputes.

Preproject Planning

In my experience as a lawyer specializing in building construction, the vast majority of disputes can be traced back to poorly drafted or nonexistent contracts. If the contract does not make clear what it does and does not include, then disputes will inevitably arise when the contractor hands in his first change order for additional work and fees.

It is also important to spell out the parameters of the project itself. For example, suppose a waterproofing contractor is hired to replace bricks, do pointing and reset lintels, but has provided no drawings documenting what he will be doing. When the co-op has a leak, there will be no way to establish whether it was the contractor's responsibility or the result of the aging of the building. It is wise to invest in having an architect or engineer prepare plans for the contractor before any work is started.

Payment provisions should also be spelled out beforehand. Otherwise, a subcontractor may believe that he should be paid when his work is done, but the co-op may want to hold the final payment until all trades have completed their work. There have been situations in which mistrust develops and the contractor becomes fearful that he may not be paid when he finishes his work. At that point, attorneys must be brought in to negotiate a resolution.

Remember that when there is a dispute as to payment, it is the contractor's prerogative to file a mechanic's lien. If the co-op is refinancing its mortgage, this can prove to be problematic. Therefore, it is in the board's best interest to spell out the terms of payment beforehand.

Also, be aware that there is no such thing as a standard construction contract. While many provisions apply to most projects, there are also different provisions required for each project. Often when printed agreements and riders are used, no one bothers to check and see if there are any conflicts in the provisions or if any provisions overlap.

The co-op must appoint a representative who has the authority to make decisions on a daily basis. If the contractor has to wait days for a decision or a board meeting, the result will be expensive delays and cost overruns. The co-op should also have either a building manager, construction manager, architect or engineer to periodically check on the contractor's work and progress. Remember, once the work is done, it is very expensive to rip it out and redo it.

When a Dispute Arises

If either side initiates a lawsuit in court, it is important to have legal counsel knowledgeable in this area of the law. Many general attorneys do not have the expertise or access to the expert consultants needed to assess the problem and assist them in making a fair settlement or in winning a trial.

Arbitration is the method of settlement that I usually recommend for resolving construction disputes. However, it must be specifically stated in the signed contract that conflicts will be resolved through arbitration or else both parties must consent.

Major contract work is one of the realities of owning a building. It should be a top priority to protect the building residents from becoming entangled in a battle over a construction project flaw. By working with professionals throughout the project, putting everything in writing and anticipating problems, the board and manager can minimize potential conflicts.

Alternative Funding Sources: Financing Capital Improvements

By Chris Luongo

When the brickwork begins to crumble, the boiler sputters to a stop or the roof springs a leak, many co-ops and condos that are barely able to stay financially afloat can turn to various public and private programs for support. By taking advantage of long-term payment plans, tax rebates and other initiatives, boards can proceed with needed capital improvement projects without having to dig deeply into their reserve funds or pass maintenance increases or assessments on to building residents.

Oskar Brecher, managing director of American Landmark Management Corporation, says that funding initiatives have become "an important catalyst" in keeping his buildings operating smoothly and their structures in decent shape. "Without these initiatives," he says, "many projects simply wouldn't take place at all."

Vincent Occhipinti, vice-president of management at Elm Management, says that he too is always on the lookout for funding sources that can help his buildings through necessary capital improvement projects, and will frequently organize seminars that bring building boards up to date on the latest financing or tax-abatement program, as well as energy and water-saving initiatives offered by city agencies. "I pass information along to the managing agents and they in turn pass it on to the boards," Occhipinti says, explaining how with some boards, it can be particularly difficult to convince them that a program is worthwhile in the long run, especially if there is no immediate return.

Water-Saving Initiatives

One such aid that Occhipinti has had little trouble pitching to his clients is the New York City Department of Environmental Protection's (DEP) water-conservation survey. Within weeks after reviewing the survey—which, since 1991 has been offered to one- to three-family homes and has now been expanded to include multifamily dwellings—a number of Occhipinti's buildings signed up to participate.

The survey, which is designed to help reduce water and sewer bills, is conducted door to door at participating co-ops and condos by an approved contractor who will then install free water-saving showerheads, faucet aerators and toilet water-saving devices. The contractor will also check for leaks and provide an estimate of the water/sewer bill savings if the leaks are repaired. Rick Gunthorpe, who manages the DEP's water audit program, explains that the survey's aim is not to issue notices of violation, "but to do whatever we can to save water and reduce your bills."

The DEP's toilet rebate program is also designed to reduce water consumption. Buildings that qualify can receive cash rebates of up to $240 for old toilets that are replaced with 1.6-gallon-per-flush models and old shower heads that are replaced with water-saving designs. To qualify for the rebate, at least 70 percent of the toilets in a building must be replaced with low-consumption models.

According to former DEP commissioner Albert F. Appleton, the goal of the three-year, $270 million program is to reduce city-wide water use by about 90 million gallons per day. Reaching this goal will require the replacement of up to 1.5 million toilets in the next three years, he says.

"Quite simply, this is an environmentally responsible program that will conserve our most precious natural resource—our drinking water—and save money for everyone involved," Appleton says. He points out that the clincher for residents is that once they replace their old toilets and showerheads with more efficient models, their water and sewer bills are likely to drop by 20 to 35 percent.

Energy-Saving Initiatives

With energy costs also consuming a major portion of a building's operating budget, buildings should consider the State Energy Office's Energy Investment Loan Program (EILP), which offers low-interest-rate loans for energy-saving capital improvements. Funded by penalties paid by oil companies for violating federal pricing regulations or contributing to environmental disasters such as the one involving the *Exxon Valdez*, the program pays interest subsidies on loans made for the installation of energy-efficiency projects, including new boilers, windows, insulation, lighting, energy-management systems and process equipment. Buildings that qualify for a subsidized loan are reimbursed by the state for any interest payments above the EILP rates—currently 2.5 percent for five-year loans and 5 percent for ten-year loans of up to $500,000.

State energy commissioner Francis J. Murray says that more than $15.5 million in EILP subsidies has been approved for $66.3 million in energy-efficiency projects across New York, which save more than $10.7 million annually in energy costs. "Improving the energy efficiency of multifamily buildings can cut costs and increase comfort for tenants," Murray says. "This program makes investing in efficiency projects more affordable."

The Energy Office recently approved $267,058 to thirteen New York City multifamily buildings for energy-saving improvements. They include a $14,689 subsidy to the 192 East 8th Street Housing Corp. for a $56,000 project to install a multi-fuel heating system, water heaters, heat timers and a fuel computer; $41,398 to a condo on East 72nd Street to install an on-site boiler to replace purchased steam and $115,579 to a co-op in Rego Park, Queens, for a $640,000 project to install six high-efficiency boilers.

J-51 Extended to 1999

Another means of generating funds for building improvements on windows, elevators, electrical wiring, roofs, plumbing and other areas is through the city's J-51 Program, which offers tax abatements and tax exemptions to residential buildings that undergo renovation or major capital improvements. Designed to encourage the rehabilitation and upgrade of multiple dwellings, J-51 benefits have been extended to include projects completed between January 1, 1994, and December 31, 1999, and new laws have been passed making it easier for co-ops and condos to obtain financing.

One of the major changes was the liberalization of the eligibility provisions for co-ops and condos that complete qualifying work more than three years after their initial closing date. According to real estate consultant Meir Mishkoff of Rottenstein & Golowa, the new bill eliminates the requirement that co-ops and condos replace a major building-wide system in order to receive benefits.

"Before, you could be spending hundreds of thousands on brickwork and still not be eligible," Mishkoff says. "Some cases were so unfair, and so those rules have been thrown out."

The new law also raises the assessed valuation cap for co-ops and condos to $40,000 per unit regardless of the percentage of units sold in the three years preceding commencement of construction. And it specifically allows asbestos abatement as an eligible item of work for older co-ops.

Private Financing

With numerous co-ops unable to afford the major renovations and restorations their property requires, a couple of exterior maintenance firms are providing financing for roofing, waterproofing and restoration work, and they are seeing a growing demand for this service. Since Sentry Contracting began offering financing two years ago, it has helped co-ops through some twenty projects by setting up a payment plan—at little or no interest—to coincide with the individual building's budget. Sentry's director of sales and marketing, Linda Peters, says that without having the option of some sort of financing, co-ops wind up doing patchwork as each new problem occurs, and pushing major improvement jobs off to the next season, which can wind up costing more money in the long run.

"Several years ago co-ops seemed to be rolling in money," Peters says. "But the times have changed for everybody. Buildings just don't have access to the same funds."

According to Vana Post, president of Allied Renovation Corporation, since her company set up a financing program for building renovations three years ago, it has arranged nearly $8 million in financing for two dozen co-ops. She says that given today's financial constraints on buildings, she anticipates that other contractors, such as boiler companies, will soon be offering some sort of financing as well.

"We're looking at each project as a long-term investment," Post says. "Many buildings are nowhere near capable of paying something like $600,000 for a project without substantially raising the maintenance. So we said, 'Let's do the work and you can pay us later,' and this is much more palatable to them."

After learning of the financing program, the co-op board of Roslyn Gardens, a 402-unit Long Island co-op, and its managing agent, Michael Samuel, of Kreisel Management, turned to Allied for over a million dollars in financing and was able to undertake roof jobs on all twenty-five of its buildings after providing a 10 percent downpayment. "Without some sort of financing, we would have had to put the burden on the co-op," says Samuel. "This makes things much easier. It's the wave of the future."

Facing Sponsor Default

- *Co-op defaults*
- *Monitoring the sponsor*
- *Workout alternatives*

A Growing Problem: The State of Sponsor Default

By Sam Adler

Since the city's default problems peaked in mid-1991, "The number of buildings with default problems has stayed constant. While a number have been resolved, new ones have come to light," says Frederick K. Mehlman, former chief of the attorney general's Real Estate Finance Bureau. These scenarios involve everything from defaults on maintenance to reserve fund commitments, underlying mortgages or major capital improvement work that has been halted in the middle for lack of funds. "The most serious problems we have seen are when a sponsor holds a wrap mortgage on a building and is responsible for making the underlying mortgage payments and has not made them," adds Mehlman.

Attorney Richard Nardi, who specializes in representing banks with problem underlying mortgage loans, has dealt with some of these worst-case scenarios, and says many times the sponsor controls the management company, and shareholders often first learn of the problem when they're contacted by the bank. "There are a fair amount of these around. I've worked on four or five, and I'm just one of many," he says.

If troubled sponsors are no more numerous—a contention most in the real estate community dispute—their plight is certainly more desperate. Recently, a foreclosure proceeding on an underlying mortgage went to judgment—the first such instance of shareholders losing their equity in their apartments. And there are a slew of pending foreclosures. "Freddie Mac alone probably has twenty," Mehlman says.

Newer Conversions More Vulnerable

Many of the buildings experiencing sponsor defaults were converted in the late 1980s, says Mehlman, a time when many plans were approved with as few as 15 percent of the units sold. Such buildings also tended to carry a lot of debt: A conversion in the early 1980s might have carried $1 in debt to $3 in equity; in latter-day conversions a 1:1 ratio was more typical. In addition, buildings converted in the last few years tended to be in worse physical condition than earlier-converted buildings. As a result, their sponsors obligated themselves to undertake more repairs than earlier sponsors had, and they were more likely than their forebears to be hit with maintenance increases on their unsold shares.

Nardi says the most common default scenario is in a noneviction conversion in which the sponsor is left holding a majority of shares. When the rental income fails to cover his maintenance costs, the sponsor has to cover the difference. In today's soft market, this may go on for years, and eventually the sponsor may run out of money. So he doesn't pay his maintenance, leaving the building unable to cover its obligations.

In the event of a sponsor default, or the threat of one, the first step shareholders should take is to get an independent managing agent in place to control the purse strings, according to attorney David Berkey of Gallet, Dreyer and Berkey. He notes that if a sponsor is not making payments on the underlying mortgage, he is probably not making escrow payment for taxes and the building could also face tax delinquency.

Next, it is important to remove the defaulting sponsor from the board of directors, notes Berkey. Shareholders can accomplish this by suing the sponsor for breach of fiduciary duty. Usually sponsors relinquish their seats to avoid such a suit, or give the seats up at the insistence of the banks holding the underlying mortgages.

Negotiating a Workout

Workouts can be accomplished in various ways. The most common among co-ops involves a reduction in the interest rate currently being paid on the underlying mortgage. The difference is then tacked onto the principal, which is payable later. Another possibility, although far less common, is forgiveness by the bank of part of the loan obligation.

In a workout situation, banks expect that shareholders will either take over the sponsor's shares or enforce their rights against the sponsor, by collecting rent directly from tenants and then going after the sponsor for the unpaid balance of his maintenance obligations.

According to court decisions, if a sponsor pledges his shares as collateral against a loan, the bank can sell his shares without going to court in the event of a default. The bank simply puts a notice in the newspaper that the shares are for sale. Known as a Uniform Commercial Code (UCC) sale, this method is now being used by co-ops when sponsors default on their maintenance obligations. If the sponsor defaults on an obligation other than maintenance, such as a promise to do a window replacement, the co-op must bring a plenary suit, which is a more lengthy proceeding.

Of course, many sponsor default problems are resolved by the sponsor voluntarily relinquishing his shares, whereupon the co-op sells them, often at auction, to a financially responsible party or parties and applies the proceeds to the arrears.

In the meantime, buildings often deal with a negative cash-flow situation by entering into exclusive contracts with vendors in exchange for the vendor holding a note, says JoAnn Levine of Gateway Community Restoration Corp., a nonprofit group that helps tenant-shareholders cope with sponsor default situations. Such vendors also usually charge more for their services, she adds.

Help from the Attorney General

One way of bringing pressure to bear on a sponsor is to file a complaint with the attorney general's office. A co-op can do this if it suspects there was a failure of disclosure in the offering plan. Under the Martin Act, the attorney general is charged with prosecuting fraud connected with the offering plan.

But Berkey warns that the attorney general's office "doesn't have the resources to investigate and prosecute all the buildings suffering problems." Jimmy Lanza, a tenant-shareholder in a Queens co-op where the sponsor didn't pay a dime of maintenance for six months, says the attorney general's office was a "major disappointment."

"I think many of the problems afflicting our building existed because the attorney general's office hadn't read the plans closely enough," Lanza says, adding that when it comes to enforcement, the office is a paper tiger. "You get a workout, but the sponsor gets off the hook," he says, noting that in the case of his building, the sponsor retained 120 rent-stabilized apartments.

Mehlman counters that the attorney general's emphasis on negotiation rather than confrontation is the appropriate one. "Suing a sponsor won't necessarily get the building its fee. Jimmy might have been disappointed at why we haven't acted against the fraudulent conduct. We think our priorities are right. We think it's better to get the parties talking," he says.

Failure to achieve a workout can have dire consequences for shareholders who can lose their ownership interests if a bank forecloses. Fortunately, foreclosures are rare. Nardi says he has twice instituted foreclosure proceedings and in both cases the problems were ironed out before judgment. As of March 1995, there have been a total of three co-op foreclosures in the state of New York that resulted in the buildings' reverting back to rental apartments.

Influencing the Bank

One way a building can keep arrears on the underlying mortgage to a minimum in the event of sponsor default is to find out if the sponsor has borrowed on his shares and then go to the lender with the following ultimatum: Unless you satisfy the sponsor's maintenance obligations, we're going to sell your collateral right out from under you. (Under the law, the co-op corporation has a first lien on any shares in the co-op in the event of a default on maintenance.)

In addition to litigation and negotiation, a third way out of the sponsor default mess may be legislation. After hearing her share of horror stories, Queens borough president Claire Shulman has been pushing for passage of numerous bills to help resident shareholders. One bill, signed into law in November 1991, allows co-ops and condos to collect directly from nonpurchasing tenants rents that would otherwise be paid to the sponsor, if the sponsor is more than thirty days late on maintenance, assessments or other fees.

A New Trend: Co-ops Declare Bankruptcy to Prevent Foreclosure
By Laura Rowley

Since January 1991, at least four cooperatives in New York City have filed for bankruptcy, seeking Chapter 11 protection from their creditors as a result of sponsor defaults. While a January filing by a Washington Heights co-op has been the most highly publicized, co-ops in Queens and Brooklyn filed well over a year ago.

The rash of bankruptcies is the latest development in the sponsor default debacle that began at the end of 1989. Sponsors who converted properties as the real estate market collapsed found themselves paying maintenance on up to 85 percent of the units, which often drew regulated rents far below their obligations. According to the attorney general, more than five hundred buildings citywide face some kind of sponsor default, on maintenance or other obligations.

Bankruptcy appears to be the newest defense of last resort. On February 11, Sunnyside Commons, a co-op complex in Queens, had its reorganization plan approved by the United States Bankruptcy Court for the Southern District of New York. Judging from that plan, it appears that bankruptcy is not only a necessary evil but a viable way for shareholders to save their co-ops. "Shareholders faced with foreclosure have no choice but to declare bankruptcy, or their homes will be wiped out," declares Michael Beck, head of the New York real estate department of the law firm Loeb and Loeb.

Last year, a foreclosure on an East 61st Street co-op resulted in a complete loss of equity for the shareholders when the Supreme Court of New York County ruled that they would revert to rent-regulated tenants. But for the few affluent shareholders involved, it was cheaper to walk away than to file for bankruptcy.

A Bankruptcy Case Study

The case of the Duncraggen in Washington Heights is just one example of how the recession has twisted the promise of home ownership into a nightmare of default and bankruptcy. After eighteen months of trying to negotiate a workout of its $2.2 million mortgage with the lender, CrossLand Savings F.S.B., the Duncraggen filed Chapter 11 in federal bankruptcy court in Manhattan on January 31, 1991.

The story began in the fall of 1989, when the prewar building was converted by Duncraggen Associates, and twenty out of seventy-two units were purchased. The six-story apartment house represented a spectacular deal to the mostly young, middle-class couples and families who lived there. The large one- and two-bedroom homes offered views of the Hudson River, a longtime staff that maintained the building's well-worn charm and a gentrifying neighborhood, only fifteen minutes from midtown on the A train. A two-bedroom unit went for $46,000 to insiders—a bargain even in this market—with an appraised value of $80,000. Many shareholders got 100 percent financing with no money down.

"I've lived in the building eight years, and I came to the neighborhood because you could get a nice value without getting in over your head," says Mark Liberman, vice-president of the board and an actor/bartender who shares a two-bedroom with his wife, three-year-old son and seven-month-old daughter.

By the fall of 1990, though, the picture had begun to change. The sponsor had fallen behind on maintenance because nine vacant apartments sat on the market for months with no takers, and the balance of the unsold units contained rent-regulated tenants whose rents fell far short of the maintenance.

When the heating season began that fall, the board knew it couldn't pay both the fuel bill and the mortgage. "When I first started to feel that there was a problem with the co-op, I had big anxieties, it was terrible," Liberman recalls. "I didn't know what the law was. Was I going to lose my home and all my equity?" Liberman says the board tried to talk to the loan officer, who said he could not discuss the matter until the co-op was in arrears.

Attempting a Workout

In September 1990, the board held a meeting with Ronni Arougheti, executive vice-president and in-house counsel of Heron Management, the building's agent, and Allen Turek, the attorney who had represented the tenants' association during the conversion, as well as the sponsor and his attorneys. Shortly thereafter, the sponsor signed an agreement allowing the co-op to collect income from his units and pledging his shares to any future workout. The board rented out the vacancies in excess of the maintenance, which helped cover some bills, but soon stopped paying the mortgage.

"This was not your typical problem with a sponsor who says, 'I'm taking the rent, to hell with you,'" says Turek, a partner with Schiff, Turek, Kirschenbaum, O'Connell, LLP. "The sponsor was very mature and responsible about it." Because of the amicable relationship, the board chose to avoid the legal cost of canceling the sponsor's shares and auctioning them off, moves that also would have incurred a potential capital gains tax liability.

On December 19, 1990, the board and its officials met with the loan officer and attorneys at CrossLand. "I showed them a deal I had worked out with another bank for another co-op, because it was a very good deal on both sides," says Arougheti. She says the bank was encouraging, eventually requesting financial statements, an appraisal and even visiting the building—all steps toward a workout.

But CrossLand Savings was drowning in its own financial morass; the Duncraggen's mortgage was a drop in an ocean of millions in bad real estate loans. In July 1991, both the Federal Deposit Insurance Corporation (FDIC) and the Office of Thrift Supervision (OTS) were investigating the bank, and seeking a buyer for the troubled institution. CrossLand never came back to the table with a proposal. Instead, in February 1991, it instituted foreclosure proceedings.

Turek says he immediately contacted the bank officials, who said the bank's servicing agent—not the bank itself—had ordered the move; in other words, "the computer told the attorneys for the bank to start the foreclosure," Turek explains, adding that he was told the proceeding would be discontinued.

Letters were exchanged but nothing concrete happened until November 1991, when the bank made a motion for a receiver—again, a step toward foreclosure. "Receivership can be a death blow to a building," explains Turek, because the board loses control over its budget, bill collection, legal expenses and even management.

The board, Arougheti and Turek met in December 1991 at the offices of the bank's attorney, who agreed to adjourn the receivership motion until January 10, 1992. It was adjourned again until January 24—the final date allowed by the judge. The board convened on January 15, and voted to file bankruptcy if CrossLand would not negotiate a workout.

Bank Failure Intervenes

On January 24, CrossLand Savings was declared insolvent, taken over by the federal government and renamed CrossLand Federal Savings. On January 29, the bank notified Turek that it was going ahead with the foreclosure. Two days later, the Duncraggen filed Chapter 11. Aside from the CrossLand mortgage, the co-op's debts totaled about $170,000, most of it in city taxes, with less than $50,000 due to heating, utility and window companies.

"I was shocked," says Arougheti. "We had proved to the bank—by their own formula—that if they foreclosed, they were going to take an enormous hit on their loan. They knew they were going to get their legs chopped out from under them the minute we filed bankruptcy, so why didn't they sit down with us?"

Bruce Williams, the loan officer for CrossLand, and Antonia Donohue of Cullen & Dykman, who had been the attorney for CrossLand in December, both refused to comment and referred questions to John E. Gunther, in-house counsel for CrossLand. "The matter is being reviewed by the bank," says Gunther, adding that he planned to meet with Turek at the end of February.

Some say that the Washington Heights co-op got caught up in the bank's misfortunes. "When the FDIC takes over, the regulators' first reaction is to say no to everything and go ahead and liquidate," says Sheldon Gartenstein, vice-president of the National Cooperative Bank, one of the nation's largest lenders to real estate co-ops. "Their forte is not negotiation. It's bad for the co-op because the lender becomes a regulator who wants the item resolved."

A Hopeful Future

The Duncraggen has 120 days, possibly longer, to come up with a plan of reorganization. The co-op is taking a major gamble in declaring bankruptcy because the action puts the individual owners' mortgage loans at risk, since their collateral—shares in the co-op—has been put in jeopardy, according to Ronald Gold, a partner with Wagner, David and Gold. "Banks could call in those individual notes," he says, but points out "if the banks are still getting paid on those mortgages, they won't pull the plug."

Arougheti says the building's services were never disrupted by the mortgage problem, and vendors remain willing to work with the co-op because under bankruptcy it must pay all bills on a going-forward basis. But the owners cannot sell or refinance for a year, possibly longer. In the meantime, at least two shareholders have defaulted on maintenance because of financial problems unrelated to the bankruptcy.

However, the outcome of the Sunnyside Commons bankruptcy gives the Duncraggen shareholders reason to hope. In that case, the sponsor, Brett Lurie of BKL Management, had defaulted on a loan from Great Neck–based BRT Realty Trust. When BRT moved to foreclose on the shares, the sponsor filed Chapter 11 on behalf of the co-op. Under the reorganization plan, BRT gave the co-op a slight reduction on the mortgage interest rate and cut the principal from $11.5 million to $9.4 million, along with waiving two years of back interest, in exchange for all 271 unsold units, according to court papers. The maturity date of the mortgage was also extended for a total of ten years. "The shareholders made out very well at Sunnyside—their maintenances didn't even go up," notes Michael Beck, who was the attorney for the bankruptcy examiner. "It's as if the bankruptcy never occurred."

There remains the question of the long-term stigma bankruptcy will have on a co-op's value, but Beck is optimistic: "Having the stigma of bankruptcy isn't the best thing for real estate values, but when the market improves, people have very short memories."

Keeping an Eye on Sponsors: The Law Mandates Disclosure

By Alvin I. Apfelberg, Esq.

Today's tight times require that co-op and condo boards keep an eye on their building sponsors, especially those who own a substantial number of units and continue to manage the property. Invariably, during a conversion, the sponsor prepares and files sales-offering documents designed to maximize his own profits and retain sponsor control of the property as long as legally permissible. At times, unprincipled developers retain power beyond permissible limits via voting control, sweetheart contracts, favoritism, resident apathy or just plain dirty dealing.

Honest and solvent developers unaccustomed to disclosing building business affairs must be taught the new language of cooperative efforts. The board and sponsor should read aloud the dictionary definition of "fiduciary" and chant the definition whenever action is contemplated. Conflicts of interest, both real and questionable, should be disclosed. If the board decides not to take action, all members must abide by that decision. If there is a disagreement, the building's attorney should decide. Governing documents, including by-laws, house rules and proprietary leases, should be read, understood and explained to the sponsor. If interpretations of those documents differ, arrange a conference call with the board, sponsor and building attorney for a legal opinion. If the sponsor requests a second opinion, get it.

If the board handles issues in a professional and open manner, a stubborn sponsor will learn that a refusal to cooperate may lead to costly litigation and legal fees. Sponsors who refuse access to books of account when officially requested by the board can be compelled to turn over their records by the court or the Real Estate Licensing Division of the State Education Department. If there are fraudulent practices, the attorney general can intervene.

Demonstrate Fiscal Responsibility

One way to get the sponsor to cooperate with the board is to let him know that both parties share similar financial goals for the building—that is, cost-effective operations and positive cash flow. In most cases, sponsors will open up to the board when fiscal responsibility is demonstrated. Silence may be replaced by expressions of gratitude when resident owners assist a financially responsible sponsor in promoting unit sales. Brisk arm's-length sales indicate that a building is respected and valuable, and mark the beginning of the end of sponsor control.

Sponsors who are honest but debt ridden and have major financial interests in a building pose a significant threat to the welfare of inhabitants. Sponsors who are juggling debt don't usually advertise their plight. Boards and their representatives must ferret out signs of financial distress on the part of the sponsor. Maintenance arrearage, unanswered phone calls and faxes, reduced support staff, nonappearance at board meetings, complaints by renters of a decrease in services and inquiries by creditors or government authorities signal sponsor troubles.

Take Preventive Action

Discussions held by the board with a financially troubled sponsor should be followed up by immediate protective action. Counsel's guidance here is critical. Confrontation, debt workout or litigation in most instances opens up a sponsor's sealed lips, because by this stage, counsel or others have most likely discovered the whereabouts of the sponsor's assets. Banks, government agencies, creditors, trustees or court appointees may join the workout seeking their own financial redress. Boards and their representatives now walk a fine line between keeping the sponsor afloat, shielding the building from foreclosure and protecting apartment values from being savaged by auctions. Status reports from the board to shareholders or unit owners at this stage are crucial.

Finally, there are those "bad apple" sponsors who have taken building funds. Boards must pursue these malfeasors relentlessly through the courts, the attorney general's office and the criminal justice system. Unfortunately, these bad apples respond most satisfactorily to the prospect of financial ruin or jail time. In this type of scenario, boards must bail out the building, restore the faith of residents and try to devise a course of action that maintains both asset value and quality of life.

Boards must be their own best managers in today's climate. Each step that a board takes to help itself saves time and money, and assists professionals in achieving the goal of maintaining the building's equilibrium, until better times come.

White Knight to the Rescue: Investor Plays Hero to Co-op in Distress

By Allen M. Turek, Esq.

In recent years, boards of directors of financially distressed cooperatives have often wished for a white knight to ride to the rescue and save their buildings from foreclosure. The scenario, reminiscent of an Arthurian fable, has the cooperative besieged by the bank or other holder of the nonperforming underlying mortgage. More often than not, the cooperative is in default on its mortgage because its sponsor, or another investor holding a significant number of unsold shares, is in arrears of its maintenance obligations to the cooperative. Sometimes the problem is compounded by an urgent need for an infusion of money to fund necessary capital repairs or replacements. In other instances, the property owes a significant amount of past due real estate taxes. The situation begins to take on the look of hopelessness with the mortgage lender seriously considering a foreclosure to stanch its losses and the apartment corporation contemplating a bankruptcy filing to save its equity in the property.

As in the medieval fable, when all hope is about to be abandoned, in charges the white knight on his steed. Guided by the purest of intentions and armed with cash instead of a lance, the white knight acquires the underlying mortgage at a discount and, in replacing the original lender, takes a more benevolent approach to the cooperative's financial shortcomings.

Not All Knights Are White

While many lenders appear to be happy to unload nonperforming loans at a discount rather than face the uncertainty of a foreclosure proceeding, cooperatives have become wary of embracing the first would-be savior who arrives on the scene dressed in shining armor. The more sophisticated boards are thinking twice about what they are about to get themselves into, preferring to perform their due diligence in investigating their would-be white knights and closely examining their offers.

While the mortgage lender's concerns are usually limited to how much the white knight is willing to pay to acquire the non-performing loan, the issues concerning the cooperative are more intricate and far-reaching. Most cooperatives are loath to replace one sponsor with just another investor; what's worse is the fear of having the mortgage held by someone who might also have control over the board of directors by virtue of owning a majority of shares.

In a recent transaction, the board of directors of 302 96th Street Owners Corp., a Brooklyn cooperative, was able to significantly rewrite the script for its own rescue by negotiating a unique workout between the holder of the underlying mortgage and the white knight of its choice.

In this instance, the Resolution Trust Corporation (RTC), acting through a subsidiary, owned the $4 million underlying building mortgage as well as the unsold apartments (representing 65 percent of the total number of apartments) in the cooperative. The cooperative had not made a mortgage payment in over eighteen months while the RTC, as the owner of the unsold units, had not made any maintenance payments for over a year. As is often the case in these situations, the maintenance charges on the unsold units were significantly greater than the rents payable by the rent-regulated tenants of the unsold apartments. To make matters worse, the cooperative was in the middle of a real property transfer (RPT) tax audit to see if the transfer taxes had been paid and calculated properly. On top of that, the building needed substantial exterior brickwork.

Get a Long-Term Commitment

While a less sophisticated cooperative might have jumped at the first opportunity to have its mortgage acquired by a white knight on any terms so long as a foreclosure was averted, Elizabeth Bulous, president, and Randy Starr, treasurer of the board at 302 96th Street Owners Corp., moved with caution and at a deliberate pace. First they were concerned whether their white knight had sufficient financial staying power. "In all of our discussions [about locating a white knight] our one nonnegotiable demand was that he or she had to have deep pockets to sustain them on a long-term basis," notes Bulous. Having watched the apartment corporation's own financial strength diminish as the sponsor's fortunes took a turn for the worse, Bulous was not eager to enter into a relationship with a financially unsecured investor. In this regard, the apartment corporation shared a common goal with the RTC.

The white knight, Somerset Investors Corporation, located in Great Neck, New York, proved to have sufficient financial strength to satisfy the RTC and the cooperative. The RTC and the cooperative were both impressed by Jules Reich, the president of Somerset. Reich has a proven track record with extensive experience in cooperative housing, including conversion, renovations and sales as well as management of similar residential properties. Bulous agreed to meet with the RTC and Somerset to negotiate the financial terms of the transaction. The cooperative's active participation proved to be pivotal to the success of the entire workout since Somerset was not prepared to acquire the underlying mortgage unless it was assured that the cooperative would be financially healthy at the conclusion of the transaction.

"From our perspective it was only logical to equate the value of the apartments with the security of the underlying mortgage," comments Reich. "If our purchase of the underlying mortgage was to have any value, we had to make sure that the cooperative was financially secure and able to carry its debt."

It also helped that both Somerset and the apartment corporation were represented by counsel specializing in the issues concerning cooperatives in financing restructuring. My law firm, Schiff, Turek, Kirschenbaum, was representing Somerset, and the apartment corporation was represented by Dennis H. Greenstein, Esq. of Haas, Greenstein, Cohen, Gerstein & Starr, P.C., both firms located in Manhattan.

A Mutually Beneficial Relationship

After in-depth negotiations between RTC, Somerset and the cooperative, it was agreed that the $4 million mortgage with accrued interest charges of an additional $400,000 would be acquired by Somerset for less than half of its original face value and RTC agreed to surrender its unsold shares to the cooperative. In turn, Somerset negotiated a modification agreement with the cooperative that included a significant reduction in the principal indebtedness of the mortgage and the annual interest rate as well as an extension of the mortgage term. Finally, the cooperative assigned most of the unsold shares to Somerset, who agreed to assume the responsibilities of owning the unsold apartments.

Working together, the white knight and the cooperative were able to reduce the annual debt service and thereby the monthly maintenance charges so that the unsold apartments took on a positive value of their own. Somerset as lender was given the incentive to keep the cooperative's debt service at a minimum so that not only would the value of the mortgage security interest be maintained, but Somerset's equity in the unsold apartments would appreciate in time. Furthermore, care was taken to structure the workout so as to avoid any risk of losing the shareholders' tax deduction by violating the so-called "80/20 rule" of the Internal Revenue Code.

To make it a perfect financial match, Greenstein and I consulted with special tax counsel to structure the transaction so that a minimum of taxes became due on the federal, state and city levels. Tax attorney David Buss of Varet & Fink attributes his success in minimizing the tax consequences to his involvement at the initial stages of negotiations. "It always makes my job easier when I am brought into a transaction at an early stage," notes Buss. "That way, I can steer the negotiations away from the tax danger areas, without having a major impact upon the substance of the transaction."

Retaining Board Control

But this cooperative was not satisfied with simply negotiating its own financial recovery. Working in a spirit of common cause, the white knight was encouraged to trust the cooperative's present board of directors to continue to control the affairs of the apartment corporation. Negotiations between Somerset and the apartment corporation took a decisive turn when Somerset volunteered to yield control of the board of directors to the resident shareholders, even though Somerset would be the cooperative's majority shareholder for some time.

In response to the building's need for an infusion of funds to pay for necessary capital repairs and to replenish its reserve fund, Somerset assigned to the cooperative an equity position in the proceeds from the sale of some of the unsold apartments. Finally, in order to allay the fears of the resident shareholders that Somerset might dump its apartments on the market and thereby devalue their own apartments, Somerset assured the resident shareholders that its immediate intention was to hold the apartments as an investment and further agreed to a schedule governing when its apartments could be sold and setting a minimum price for each apartment. Greenstein commented that "Anytime a troubled cooperative considers the sale of a block of apartments to a single purchaser, there is a nagging fear in the back of their minds that the investor might be tempted at some time to sell the apartments at a deep discount and thereby bring down the value of all the apartments."

For board president Bulous, it has been quite an extraordinary experience: "I remember the night when we held the shareholder meeting to introduce Jules [Reich] to the shareholders of the building. Even though I was an active participant in the day-to-day negotiations, I found myself getting caught up in the excitement of hearing how our building was brought back from the brink of disaster."

For his part, Reich appears to be enjoying his white knight status among the residents of the building. "I'm there at least once a week to check on renovations or our rental program," he says. "Without fail, I run into one of the residents who breaks out into a smile or extends a hand in greeting, as if welcoming an old friend. I've been in residential real estate for over twenty years but I've never had this type of reaction before. Frankly, it's just great the way these people have accepted me into their community."

What was remarkable about this white knight was Somerset's willingness to enter into a relationship with the apartment corporation based upon trust and mutual dependency. If there is a moral to be learned from this modern knight's tale, it is that the cooperative, as damsel in distress, should seriously evaluate her hero and the terms of his offer, before riding off to live happily ever after.

Law and Governance

• *Shareholders' rights*
• *Governing documents*
• *Board control*

Shareholders' Rights: How Far Can House Rules Go?

By Sam Adler

House rules. You can't live with 'em, you can't live without 'em. They can be the mortar that keeps a building together or the dynamite that threatens to explode the cohesiveness of the residential community. Unlike by-laws, which govern internal management of a building's affairs and other operational and administrative matters, house rules govern residents' conduct, usually prohibiting illegal, objectionable or antisocial behavior.

According to Neil Kreisel, president of Kreisel Management, an agency managing some thirty thousand units, many shareholders still have a "tenant" mentality and view the board as a "landlord" when it tries to enforce rules that are, in most cases, in the best interest of the building. "They see the board as the enemy because they have to put the dog on a leash or pay a sublet fee or move only between the hours of 9:30 A.M. and 4:30 P.M.," says Kreisel. "There seems to be a dichotomy between the board, which is charged with enforcing the rules, and the tenant-shareholder, who thinks the rules are there to harass rather than to protect."

Major house rules are usually covered in the by-laws or proprietary lease. For example, rules prohibiting the use of heavy appliances, such as washing machines, are intended to prevent wear and tear on a building's infrastructure and are commonly included in by-laws or proprietary leases. Ditto for subletting rules. In fact, New York's highest court ruled that a transfer fee or flip tax is of too much concern to tenants to be only a house rule, ordering boards to put the matter to a vote of their shareholders for inclusion in the proprietary lease.

There are several kinds of controversy related to house rules: the shareholder who flagrantly violates them, driving a neighbor crazy; the board that enacts too many rules, driving everyone crazy and the board that enacts too few house rules, resulting in anarchy. Finally, there is the board that refuses to enforce the rules because it either doesn't believe a complaint or doesn't want to spend the money to hire an attorney to deal with the situation.

Enforcing the Rules

Enforcing a house rule against a renegade tenant can be dealt with in a number of ways. The first is to bring an eviction proceeding in housing court. This action is based on a clause in the proprietary lease stating that a violation of house rules constitutes "just cause." But there is no guarantee of success, because even if a violation is substantiated, housing courts are loathe to evict.

According to Alvin I. Apfelberg, a real estate attorney, courts have adopted a rule of thumb that if a house rule isn't important enough to have been adopted into the proprietary lease (an act requiring a two-thirds majority of all shareholders), its violation doesn't warrant eviction. He suggests that house rules make specific reference to the default provision in the proprietary lease, which should state under what conditions breaking a house rule will result in eviction.

Moreover, some lawyers say housing court is an avenue to be avoided altogether, because eviction is a draconian remedy as well as a long, drawn-out process requiring notice of default, time to cure, several court appearances and so forth. In addition, it's not even an option in the case of a condo owner. "No one can throw a unit owner out of his property. You can fine them and put a lien on their property, but you can't throw them out," says Apfelberg.

An alternative, albeit more costly, route is to seek a declaratory judgment and injunction from the state Supreme Court. Instead of asking for possession the way one would in housing court, a board is saying that the co-op has house rules, this individual is violating them and thus the court should declare the house rule to be fair and enjoin the errant resident from violating it again.

If the co-op wins and the house rule is upheld, a subsequent violation by the tenant would violate the court order and the tenant could be held in contempt of court and thrown in jail. Moreover, the viability of the house rule would not have to be relitigated in an injunction proceeding against another tenant.

A simpler enforcement tool is to notify the bank holding the offending shareholder's mortgage that the shareholder is in violation of the proprietary lease and the board is considering terminating it. This will usually result in the bank putting pressure on the shareholder, that is, threatening to foreclose. While the tenant may thumb his nose at the board, he might be fearful enough of the financial repercussions to comply.

Most attorneys do not recommend imposing fines against shareholders who flout the rules, because it can become a situation in which wealthy tenants have more rights than less affluent ones, because the wealthy ones can simply pay fees for sending the maintenance check late or for having a dog. Instead, by-laws can be amended to provide for binding arbitration of disputes between the board and shareholders relating to the proprietary lease, the house rules or the by-laws. An arbitration decision can be turned into a judgment of the court immediately.

Over-Lenient Boards

Often the problem is not too many rules, however, but rules that are not enforced. According to Kreisel, the rule that residents most often say boards ignore is the rule against excessive noise, usually involving a too-loud stereo, barking dog or musical instrument. Kreisel says boards are less to blame for failing to enforce house rules than for failing to communicate why the rule was created. "If people understood the reason for a rule, there would be more adherence," he says.

Managing agents sometimes wind up being the monkey in the middle, says Kreisel. "If the board doesn't want to enforce a rule, we have to obey the board. But tenants often think it's a case of the managing agent not following up their complaint," he says. "In such cases, tenants should write a letter to the board to ascertain whether the managing agent was not being responsive."

On the other hand, sometimes rules need to be adjusted or loosened to accommodate change, even though some shareholders might object. With the real estate market in the pits, shareholders everywhere are violating rules limiting sublets, Kreisel notes. In many cases, boards have remained uncompromising instead of amending the sublet rule, with the result that "people sublet without permission, and you wind up with people you don't know living in the building," he says.

Surprisingly, even fashion can affect whether or not a rule is enforced. As oak, beech, bleached wood and other bare floors have become fashionable, the common rule requiring that 80 percent of an apartment be carpeted has fallen on hard times. Boards may be unwilling to hire an attorney to get a shareholder to comply, to the chagrin of the tenants living below the hardwood floors.

Along with unenforced rules, extremely liberal house rules can create a living hell for residents. Audrey Kesten, who lives in a Gramercy Park co-op, says her building allows construction seven days a week. When tenants complained, "the directors said, 'This is a working building. When will these people ever get anything done?'" Kesten notes. "We were after them for at least no work on Sundays and holidays. But we didn't have enough votes to call a special meeting on the issue or vote out the board."

Changing the Rules

Kesten's situation points up the difficulty of getting change in a building where residents are apathetic or the complainers constitute a minority. Steven Gold, an attorney with Wagner Davis and Gold, suggests that unhappy shareholders avoid litigating with their neighbors. "Petition the board with a letter, asking them to address the issue directly," he says. "Start with the presumption that if there is a rule, there's a good reason for it, and if not, the board should be willing to change it. Don't call in a lawyer and tear the building apart."

If a letter gets no results, make a strong showing with other shareholders at a meeting—either an open board meeting or the annual meeting—and ask the board for a clear explanation of why the rule is being imposed and the underlying logic. If this doesn't help, at the next election present your own slate of candidates who would be willing to change the offensive rule—make it a campaign issue, Gold suggests.

Another recourse is to call a special meeting of the shareholders or unit owners, which typically requires 25 percent of the outstanding shares; the purpose of the meeting would be to propose and pass a resolution to rescind or modify the house rule. While the majority rules here, the resolution is not binding on the board. The shareholders cannot compel a recalcitrant board to change a house rule, Gold warns. "But if a majority of shareholders at a special meeting voted down a rule, the board would be foolish to ignore it," he adds.

There are a few extreme recourses as well. If the offensive rule is in the proprietary lease, this can be amended if 75 percent of outstanding shares vote in favor. But most house rules don't generate that kind of hostility. "I've never seen a building get 75 percent to amend the proprietary lease," Gold says. The proprietary lease also provides for the recall of directors, but that also requires a high percentage of the shareholders to agree, an almost impossible task when there has not been impropriety of the highest order. "I'd recommend going to the annual meeting, getting the directors to commit to changing the rules or getting your own slate," says Gold.

Finally, you may just have to live with the building you've chosen. Which only points out the absolute necessity of looking at a building's house rules and deciding if you can live with them *before* you buy.

Effective Rule-Making: Do It Right to Avoid Lawsuits

By Bruce A. Cholst, Esq.

Board power to impose rules and regulations upon community residents is the quintessential feature of cooperative and condominium living. The exercise of this power, however, has frequently resulted in acrimony and costly litigation. These tensions and costs might well be reduced through more effective rule-making.

The key to more effective rule-making is a better understanding of the source and scope of board power to regulate community life. Such an enhanced awareness would assist board members in insulating their regulations from legal challenge, thus reducing the prospect of litigation. By the same token, greater familiarity with their rights and obligations might foster an atmosphere of voluntary compliance among residents.

Source of Board Power

Contrary to popular belief, the ultimate source of a board's rule-making power is not the "business judgment rule," as applied in the 1991 landmark case of *Levandusky v. One Fifth Avenue Apartment Corp.* Rather, a board derives its authority to regulate almost entirely from the building's governing documents. In condominiums, the relevant governing documents are the declaration and by-laws. In cooperatives, the relevant governing documents are the certificate of incorporation, by-laws and proprietary lease. Unless the language of these documents expressly or implicitly permits such regulation, it will not survive judicial challenge.

Two recent cases concerning co-op boards' power to impose sublet fees illustrate the significance of governing documents as defining instruments of boards' regulatory authority. In the first case, the co-op's by-laws authorized the board to "fix a reasonable [sublet] fee to cover actual expenses and attorney fees of the corporation [and] a service fee." The board assessed a sublet fee equal to 30 percent of the annual maintenance charge of the applicable unit, payable in advance as a condition to approval of the sublet. A shareholder found someone willing to rent his apartment for an amount equal to his mortgage, maintenance and insurance costs. However, he was unable to afford the co-op's up-front sublet fee. Since the board refused to waive its fee, the shareholder was forced to abandon his prospective sublet arrangement. The shareholder subsequently defaulted on his mortgage and lost his unit at foreclosure. He then sued the co-op for monetary damages, alleging that its sublet fee was illegal. A lower court dismissed this suit on the ground that co-op boards' power to regulate subletting has long been established, and imposition of a sublet fee is a valid exercise of such power.

An appellate court, however, viewed the matter differently. The appellate tribunal observed that this particular co-op's authority to regulate subletting is limited by the requirement in its by-laws that any fee bear a "reasonable" relationship to actual expenses of the transaction. The case was therefore reinstated and set down for trial on the issue of whether the up-front 30 percent sublet fee is "reasonable" to cover actual expenses, attorney fees and a service fee, as stipulated in the by-laws.

In the second case, a sublet fee of one-third of maintenance was stricken down because the court could not divine any authorization in either the by-laws or the proprietary lease to impose a sublet fee. The court rejected the co-op's contention that its unrestricted right to reject a proposed sublet arrangement (which was specified in the proprietary lease) implicitly empowered it to impose conditions such as payment of the fee, upon its approval of the deal.

Condominium by-laws and co-op proprietary leases usually give the board power to enact house rules without unit owner or shareholder approval that govern use of dwelling units and communal areas. Boards, however, must take special care to insure that their house rules do not sweep so broadly that they can be construed as attempts to amend the by-laws or proprietary lease. When this happens, courts will require that the house rule in question be ratified by unit owners or shareholders, since amendment of an association's governing documents almost always requires such approval. The overwhelming majority of governing document provisions cannot be amended without the consent of at least two-thirds of the association's outstanding shares or common interests.

Changing Governing Documents

Two types of board-enacted house rules are most frequently construed as impermissible attempts to amend co-op proprietary leases and condo by-laws. The first category consists of those house rules that specifically alter the terms of existing governing document provisions. Obviously, such an alteration constitutes an amendment to the governing document. The second category consists of those house rules whose effect is to alter the existing financial obligations of a shareholder or unit owner to the association (that is, imposition of a flip tax, late fee or home owner's insurance requirement). Since one of the primary functions of by-laws and proprietary leases is to define the unit owner and shareholder's financial obligations to the association, any changes with respect to such responsibilities generally require an amendment to these documents.

Since the distinction between permissible house rule revision and impermissible governing document amendment (without shareholder or unit owner ratification) is often difficult to discern, it is always a good idea to consult counsel before altering existing house rules.

If a co-op's by-laws or proprietary lease stipulate that the board cannot unreasonably withhold its consent to a sublet arrangement and the board wishes to assert absolute control over the sublet process, it can sponsor and lobby for passage of an amendment to the governing documents giving it such authority. Conversely, if the board presently enjoys unfettered control over the sublet process and for whatever reason wishes to limit its own authority, it can sponsor and lobby for passage of an amendment to that effect.

Most by-laws contain a procedure that permits residents to call a special meeting of shareholders or unit owners at which a vote on a proposed amendment can be taken. Thus, resident-initiated proposals to limit or expand rule-making power can be considered even over board opposition.

Legal Limitations on Boards

Even when a particular exercise of regulatory power is authorized in a building's governing documents, there are instances in which it will not be enforced by the courts. For example, rules that are illegal on their face (such as patently discriminatory regulations or those that are in violation of some statute or ordinance) will be stricken if challenged. Moreover, regulations that are shown to be motivated by board members' self-interest, vindictiveness or other bad-faith purpose will not be enforceable, even though they might be authorized by the governing documents and legal on their face.

Finally, rules that are authorized in the governing documents, legal on their face and not motivated by a transparently bad-faith purpose are nevertheless vulnerable to legal challenge when they are enforced in a selective fashion.

Business Judgment Rule

The *Levandusky* decision, cited above, states that the "business judgment rule" can be cited as justification for avoiding judicial interference with a board's rule-making authority, provided that the regulation is authorized by the association's governing documents and is otherwise legal, is conceived in good faith for a legitimate purpose and is applied in a manner consistent with the board's fiduciary duties to community residents. Shareholder Ronald Levandusky had submitted plans for a proposed kitchen renovation to his co-op board for its approval. After the board consented to the renovation, Levandusky indicated for the first time that he wished to move a steam riser into the kitchen as part of the renovation. Relying upon its engineer's advice, the board refused to permit relocation of the steam riser and by resolution reaffirmed its building-wide policy of prohibiting renovations that encompass relocation of risers.

Nevertheless, Levandusky proceeded to remove the riser—apparently without inflicting structural damage to the building's physical plant. The co-op ordered a halt to the renovation, and Levandusky sued to have the board's "stop work" order set aside.

The Court of Appeals, explicitly rejecting Levandusky's argument that the board policy against removal of risers was irrational since he had proved the procedure could be done without damage to the building, refused to interfere with the board's administration of apartment renovations. In so ruling, the court stated: "We conclude that these goals (striking a balance between minimal interference with board's management function and protecting individual residents against possibly abusive board action) are best served by a standard of board review…analogous to the business judgment rule applied by courts to determine challenges to decisions made by corporate directors…So long as the corporation's directors have not breached their fiduciary obligation…the exercise (of their powers)…may not be questioned although the results show what they did was unwise.…

"For present purposes we need not…determine the entire range of fiduciary duties of a cooperative board other than to note that the board owes its duty of loyalty to the cooperative—that is, it must act for the benefit of the residents collectively. So long as the board acts for the benefit of the cooperative, within the scope of its authority and in good faith, courts will not substitute their judgment for the board's. Stated somewhat differently, unless a resident challenging board action is able to demonstrate a breach of this duty, judicial review is not available.

"The business judgment rule protects the board's business decisions…from indiscriminate attack. At the same time, it permits review of improper decisions as when the challenger demonstrates that the board's action has no legitimate relationship to the welfare of the cooperative, deliberately singles out individuals for harmful treatment, is taken without notice or consideration of the relevant facts or is beyond the scope of the board's authority."

The court concluded that the board's policy of prohibiting removal of risers was conceived in good faith on the basis of its engineer's recommendation, for a valid corporate purpose (avoiding the prospect of structural damage), and was not arbitrarily enforced against Levandusky. It therefore refused to second-guess the wisdom of the policy, irrespective of the fact that Levandusky's removal of the riser did not actually result in damage.

Thus, the business judgment rule is not a sword for the affirmative enforcement of board policies. Rather, it is a shield with which to fend off unwanted judicial interference with community life. The shield, however, can be deployed only when board regulation conforms to the guidelines elucidated in the *Levandusky* decision.

Every board must be aware of the potential pitfalls in enacting and enforcing association policies. Counsel should be consulted with respect to any questionable policies to assure that they are properly insulated from legal challenge.

Not Written in Stone: Changing Governing Documents

By Bruce A. Cholst, Esq.

As annual meeting season approaches, many cooperative and condominium boards are considering proprietary lease and by-law amendments to facilitate operations and enhance the quality of life in their buildings. Governing documents can be modified to achieve such objectives, but it's important for boards to know exactly how to do so legally and smoothly. Because planning and preparation for such changes will take several weeks, consideration of their applicability to your building should begin well in advance of the next annual meeting.

Late Fee Provisions

Late fees are commonly relied upon as a method for inducing timely payment of maintenance or common charges. However, many late fee provisions are vulnerable to legal challenge, either because of the manner in which they were implemented or because they are excessive by prevailing judicial standards.

The vast majority of courts have held that late charges can only be enacted by means of a proprietary lease or condominium by-law amendment, since those instruments define a shareholder or unit owner's financial obligations to the association. Thus, those boards that have imposed late fees through house rules or by mere resolution should consider validating the procedure by enacting a proprietary lease or condominium by-law amendment.

Generally speaking, courts have upheld late charges that are deemed to be "reasonable" and invalidated those that are considered "excessive," even if they were enacted by means of a lease or condominium by-law amendment. Unfortunately, there is no judicial consensus as to what constitutes a "reasonable" late fee. However, in the course of striking down a 5-percent-per-month late charge as excessive, at least one appellate court compared the 60 percent annualized rate of this penalty to the 25-percent-per-annum criminal usury standard. This would imply that a late charge in the neighborhood of 2 percent per month (24 percent per year) might be considered "reasonable." (Such a penalty would also be consistent with proprietary lease or condominium by-law provisions that authorize imposition of late fees equal to "the highest legal rate of interest"). In any event, it is clear that cumulative late fees (that is, charges of $25 the first month, $50 the second month, $100 the third month and so on) would be deemed unreasonable on their face, since they present the prospect of indefinite acceleration, ultimately exceeding the threshold of "reasonableness," however imprecisely that term may be defined by the courts.

Boards may wish to analyze the amount and structure of their late fees, and amend the provisions as appropriate to insulate them from legal challenge. Those boards that have not yet enacted late fees may wish to do so in accordance with the guidelines described above.

Mandatory Insurance Provisions

Mandatory maintenance of liability insurance provides shareholders and unit owners with funds for personal injury or property damage to third parties arising from their negligence. Mandatory maintenance of property insurance provides them with a means of reimbursement for damage to their own personal property. Such coverage protects not only the owners but also the building, inasmuch as it prevents accidents or casualties from putting a financial strain on residents, which might conceivably impede their ability to remain current on maintenance or common charge payments. Appropriately modest coverage limits can blunt resistance to this proposal. Since this measure affects residents in an economic sense, its enactment requires a proprietary lease or condominium by-law amendment.

Alterations

A significant number of cooperative proprietary leases permit board regulation only with respect to "structural alterations" (those that infringe on building systems). However, many kinds of alterations are potentially noisy, disruptive and/or dangerous to the building residents even though they may not be "structural" in a technical sense. Co-op boards may wish to consider a lease amendment that would make all alterations (except for decorative work) subject to their approval and scrutiny. The amendment should require each shareholder to execute an alteration agreement with the co-op after board approval is obtained but prior to commencement of the work, which specifically delineates the scope of the alteration and the conditions under which it is to be performed. The board would thus be able to regulate alterations in a manner it deems to best preserve the quality of life in the community. It should be noted, however, that holders of unsold shares would almost certainly be exempt from compliance with such an amendment.

Decreasing Quorum Requirements

Most by-laws require the presence (in person or by proxy) of a majority of shareholders or owners in order to obtain a quorum at a shareholder or unit owner meeting. Failure to satisfy the quorum requirement will preclude the conduct of any official business (including the holding of board elections) and necessitate an adjournment of the gathering.

Notwithstanding their best efforts to generate attendance at these meetings, an inordinate number of boards encounter difficulty in amassing a quorum. Associations that habitually encounter this problem may consider a by-law amendment reducing the quorum requirement to one-third of the outstanding shares or common interests. (State law precludes a lesser quorum requirement.)

By-Laws and Lease Provisions

Most governing documents fail to take into account such technological innovations as fax machines and conference call facilities, or advances in delivery methods like Express Mail and courier services. For example, very few by-laws permit board members to participate in meetings via conference call or recognize the validity of proxies tendered by fax. Moreover, most proprietary leases and by-laws require notices to be furnished by registered, certified or first-class mail, while they could often be more efficiently and effectively delivered by fax, Express Mail or courier service. Amendments of this nature can greatly facilitate a board's management function.

Limiting Board Members' Liability

In 1987, the state Legislature greatly liberalized existing law to permit elimination of corporate directors' personal liability to the corporation and its shareholders for negligence in their exercise of business judgment on behalf of the corporation. (Exculpation of liability for acts performed in bad faith or intentional misconduct is still prohibited.) The Legislature also permitted corporations to facilitate the process by which their board members are reimbursed for personal judgments and litigation expenses incurred by them under certain circumstances during the performance of their official duties. The exculpation from personal liability for negligence requires an amendment to the certificate of incorporation, whereas facilitation of the indemnification process is accomplished through amendment to the corporate by-laws.

Inexplicably, a substantial number of cooperatives have still not afforded their board members this enhanced protection. Enactment of these measures would doubtless attract a larger pool of qualified individuals who have heretofore been reluctant to serve as board members for fear of exposing themselves to the risk of litigation.

Examining Books and Records: When Do Owners Have the Right?

By Bruce A. Cholst, Esq. and Peter I. Livingston, Esq.

Scenario: A hostile shareholder or unit owner suddenly demands an inspection of the board's books and records. Since the board is not guilty of financial impropriety or the squandering of funds, it has nothing to hide. Nevertheless, the board does not wish to deliver ammunition that can be used to sew discord within the residential community.

Question: Can the board lawfully refuse the request for an inspection of its books and records?

Answer: It depends.

Under common law, "books and records" generally applies to all documents pertaining to the board's business affairs, including the cooperative's certificate of incorporation or the condominium's declaration, list of shareholders or unit owners, various contracts, transfer records, tenant files, minutes of board and shareholder proceedings, financial statements, bank and brokerage statements, records pertaining to receivables and payables, books of account (for example, receipt and disbursement ledgers, purchase orders and invoices) and insurance records.

Since the rights of a condominium's unit owners to inspect their association's books and records may be much more limited than those of cooperative shareholders, they are discussed separately.

Cooperators' Rights

Corporate shareholders in general are afforded certain rights, both by statute and under common law, to inspect books and records of companies in which they own an equity interest. A cooperator's right of access to building documents therefore derives primarily from his legal status as a shareholder in the apartment corporation.

The statutory right of inspection is rather limited in scope insofar as it relates to only three kinds of documents: financial statements, shareholder lists and minutes of shareholder (as opposed to board) meetings. Moreover, shareholders seeking access to any of these documents are required under the statute to meet certain threshold requirements.

Shareholders owning at least 5 percent of the company's stock, or those who have been stockholders of record for at least six months, irrespective of the extent of their equity interest in the company, have an absolute right, upon written request, to obtain the preceding fiscal year's financials, as well as the most recent interim financials to the extent that these have been distributed to the shareholders. Most co-op by-laws require that year-end financials be distributed to all shareholders as a matter of course within four months of the fiscal year end.

Shareholders meeting the same threshold eligibility requirements, or their authorized agents, have the right, upon written demand with five days' notice, to inspect and make copies of the shareholders' list and minutes of shareholder proceedings. Such an inspection, however, may be denied in the absence of a sworn statement that the review is desired only for purposes relating to the business of the corporation and that neither the shareholder nor his authorized agent (if applicable) has participated in the sale of a shareholders' list for any corporation over the past five years.

Thus, if a board wishes to adopt a hard line toward a request for access to these documents, it should first check to see that the demand was actually initiated by a shareholder of record (as opposed to a nonowning spouse, relative, subtenant and so forth) and that the shareholder meets the threshold eligibility requirements.

Under common law, shareholders are given a much broader right of review (that is, access to the entire gamut of books and records), but this prerogative is subject to two major caveats: that the inspection demand be initiated in "good faith" and that its purpose be related to the shareholder's interest in protecting his investment in the corporation rather than advancement of his own private agenda.

In the leading court decision on inspection of corporate books and records, the court described "good faith" as "an intangible and abstract quality with no technical meaning or statutory definition. It encompasses, among other things, an honest intent, the absence of malice, the absence of a design to defraud or to seek an unconscionable advantage. An individual's personal good faith is a concept of his own mind and inner spirit, and therefore may not be conclusively determined by his protestations alone. The existence of good faith as a substantive fact therefore necessitates an examination and evaluation of external manifestations as well. This may be evidenced by facts and surrounding circumstances existing prior and subsequent to the application for the relief sought in a proceeding of this type."

Since a shareholder's good faith in seeking a review of corporate documents is presumed, the burden of proving bad faith motive is upon management. Proof of bad-faith motive will almost always hinge upon the introduction of circumstantial evidence from which a court can infer that the shareholder's reason for demanding an inspection is for a purpose other than monitoring his investment.

The mere existence of hostility between the shareholder and corporate management or litigation will ordinarily not be sufficient in and of itself to establish bad faith. However, a long history of discord and controversy can be cited as circumstantial evidence that the inspection request is motivated by a desire to harass or some other improper purpose. In order to refute a petitioning shareholder's allegations of good faith, the board must be able to document each and every aspect of its relationship with the shareholder.

Two recent cases entailing co-op shareholders' assertions of their common-law right of inspection offer some insight into how courts view the issue of good faith. In the first, the shareholder had commenced three separate civil suits against the co-op and initiated two criminal complaints against its board president (none of which was resolved in his favor), all following the board's refusal to permit the sale of his apartment. Although corporate mismanagement was cited as a pretext for the inspection request, the court noted that the shareholder "failed to make a prima facie showing of need for the information sought."

In this regard, the court observed that the petitioning shareholder received the co-op's financial statements and attended shareholder meetings at which the apartment corporation's financial condition was discussed. After describing the preexisting litigation in detail, the court concluded that the application for an inspection of books and records "was not made in good faith."

In the second case, the petitioning shareholder cited an accountant's audit that suggested possible financial improprieties by a prior board as grounds for her request to probe books and records relating to the tenure of the incumbent board. In opposition to the request, the co-op cited as evidence of bad faith a ten-year history of acrimony between the shareholder and her husband and successive boards, which included documentation of harassment, intimidation, and the public utterance of false statements about board members, as well as the initiation of several unsuccessful lawsuits against the co-op and individual board members. After acknowledging the shareholder's "past incidents of apparent bad faith," the court concluded that they were "insufficient to raise a question of fact as to the lack of bona fides here."

In all probability, the distinguishing factor between these two cases is that in the former, the shareholder was unable to present any discernible basis for his suspicion of mismanagement, whereas in the latter, tangible evidence of possible improprieties by a prior board was adduced, thus raising a colorable basis for the shareholder's review despite her "past incidents of apparent bad faith."

A shareholder's common-law right to inspect corporate books and records can also be defeated by showing that the purpose is to advance his or her own private agenda. For example, where the shareholder seeks to scour corporate documents in order to obtain a shareholder list for his or her own commercial use, gather evidence to fuel a private vendetta against a fellow stockholder or facilitate prosecution of a claim against officers or board members in their individual capacities (as opposed to suing the corporation for official wrongdoing), the review can be denied.

Some co-op proprietary leases and by-laws specifically give the shareholder a right to review the apartment corporation's "books of account." Where such provisions exist, the shareholder may well have an independent contractual right to inspection in addition to his limited statutory and common-law rights. However, the well-established legal principle that every contract carries an implied covenant of good faith might be asserted, which would permit introduction of evidence of the shareholder's bad faith to possibly defeat his right to an inspection.

Condominium Unit Owners' Rights

As previously indicated, a cooperator's statutory and common-law right of inspection is predicated almost entirely on his status as a shareholder of the apartment corporation. Since condominium unit owners are not corporate shareholders, it is clear that they do not have standing to avail themselves of the same legal rights to review association documents as are enjoyed by their cooperator counterparts. Although there are no reported cases on the subject, it may well be that condominium unit owners are limited to those rights of inspection expressly set forth in their associations' by-laws. These rights are typically narrow.

Appropriate Board Response

Upon its receipt of a request for inspection of corporate documents, the board should attempt to elicit from the shareholder or unit owner a written statement as to the reason for the review. In addition to possibly providing evidence of bad-faith motive or other impermissible purposes for conducting the inspection, which could facilitate a hard-line approach, such a statement will assist the board in gauging its response to the request. For example, it might become apparent that the shareholder or unit owner's curiosity can be satisfied through the release of a limited number of documents, the exposure of which would not be inimical to the board's interests. Moreover, particularly sensitive or confidential aspects of specific documents can be redacted while giving the shareholder or unit owner the gist of what he seeks. Accommodations of this nature often go a long way toward calming the suspicion of hostile shareholders and unit owners, thus avoiding unnecessary litigation.

Requests for inspection of building documents are usually manifestations of deep-seated suspicion or resentment over board policies. Such sentiments are often defused through an attempt at accommodation. This type of approach, however, can prove disastrous where sensitive or confidential information is inadvertently leaked to unscrupulous shareholders or unit owners. By the same token, when the conciliatory approach fails, or when for whatever reason a hard-line stance is favored from the beginning, boards should be aware that there are numerous legal pitfalls in denying access to documents. In either case, counsel should be consulted every step of the way.

Gaining Legal Entry: Co-op Owners Must Allow Board In

By David A. Goldstein, Esq.

In a co-op setting, where each resident is a shareholder and the board of directors has the responsibility of managing and maintaining the building on behalf of all shareholders, questions sometimes arise about the authority of the board with respect to individual apartments. Does a shareholder have total control over the apartment in which he or she lives? Or do the rights of the co-op and its board of directors sometimes take precedence over the individual's wishes?

A recent court decision involving a Queens co-op is a case in point. This case reaffirmed that co-op boards do have the right to access individual units to make necessary repairs—whether or not the particular shareholder consents. The case involved the attempts by a co-op to have an exterminator work in a particular apartment. The extermination process required tearing up a floor in the apartment and placing chemicals at that location.

The shareholders argued that they would have to relocate for several days while this work was taking place. Therefore, they claimed that they should be entitled to financial compensation in return for their cooperation. In addition, they said that they were concerned about the possible effects on their family of the use of the exterminator's chemicals.

My law firm represented the co-op board in this case, and in our arguments, we pointed out that in state and city law, the proprietary lease and the co-op's house rules require shareholders or tenants to provide access to the building management in order to make necessary repairs and perform functions like extermination. We pointed out that the apartment residents in question, as stockholders, are part owners of the structure in which they live, and should realize that one of the responsibilities of cooperative ownership is to share, with their neighbors, in the proper upkeep of the building. We also argued that the shareholders in this case were not entitled to the monetary compensation they had requested. The court agreed.

In its decision, the court ruled that the shareholders had "not provided to the court any legal authority requiring payment." On the issue of the use of potentially harmful chemicals, the court simply ordered the building to comply with all appropriate laws and regulations related to extermination, and allowed the building management access to the apartment "continuing until the treatment is completed."

The case, *Sunnyside Towers Owners Corp. v. John A. O'Sullivan and Margaret O'Sullivan,* was decided in Queens Supreme Court by Justice John A. Milano. It shows that owning shares in a co-op obliges the shareholder to abide by the by-laws designed to protect and benefit the entire building. This decision reaffirms that individual shareholders cannot unilaterally take exception to rules that allow the co-op board and management to serve the entire corporation and all of its shareholders.

"Owning" Outdoor Space: Board Control of Terraces and Roofs
By Bruce A. Cholst, Esq.

Terraces, rooftops and ground-floor gardens are perhaps the most coveted amenities among New York apartment dwellers. Unfortunately, they are also an all too common source of litigation in co-op buildings. The reason is that while standard proprietary lease provisions define certain parameters, they do not adequately address the rights of shareholders to use adjacent outdoor space or their responsibility for maintenance and repairs. Courts are therefore repeatedly called upon to fill the void.

Use Restrictions

Many shareholders are unaware of the extent of a board's power to restrict or regulate their use and enjoyment of terrace, roof and garden areas that adjoin their apartments. This power is expressly delineated in most proprietary leases, which contain explicit-use prohibitions, permit the imposition of additional restrictions on an ad hoc basis by means of house rule, reserve for the co-op board right of entry upon these areas for the purpose of making repairs and permit the board to veto or limit proposed construction within this space. Virtually every proprietary lease explicitly prohibits cooking in these areas under any circumstances, and proscribes the installation of plants, fences, structures and lattices or the painting of walls without written board approval.

Shareholders' use of this space is also routinely made subject to "such other regulations as may from time to time be prescribed by the directors" in the form of house rules, the violation of which is deemed a lease default. The board's power to promulgate house rules of this nature, so long as they are enacted in good faith for a valid corporate purpose and enforced in a nondiscriminatory, disinterested fashion, has consistently been upheld by the courts.

Boards commonly enact house rules to regulate the size, height and location of plants on terraces and penthouse roofs. Although these safeguards are necessary to protect the terrace and roof surface areas from structural damage that invariably results in water leakage to adjoining apartments, they are often challenged by shareholders with elaborately constructed roof gardens, who protest the intrusion upon their lifestyle. Recognizing that house rules of this nature are designed to preserve corporate property, courts have uniformly sustained those regulations as a valid exercise of board power, and compelled the removal of shareholder plantings that violate such guidelines.

No Exclusive Haven

Although terrace, penthouse and garden-apartment owners regard their enclaves as havens of privacy, their right to use and occupy these areas is hardly an exclusive one. Virtually every proprietary lease grants the co-op a right of entry for the purpose of making repairs within that area or reaching adjoining communal space to effectuate repairs or install equipment there.

In two recent decisions, courts have upheld the rights of co-ops to temporarily appropriate terrace space for the purpose of effectuating capital repairs, rejecting shareholders' claims that such a limited encroachment constitutes a breach of warranty of habitability or a partial eviction. In one case, the co-op used the terrace to hang and store scaffolding over a four-month period while roof work was being performed. In the other case, the terrace was used by contractors during a repair project involving the parapet walls. It should be noted, however, that in both of these cases, the co-ops demonstrated the absolute necessity of the repair work and the indispensability of the terrace as an accessory to its implementation. Both courts also noted the co-ops' diligent efforts to avoid inconvenience to the shareholders and keep them apprised of the construction's progress. It seems clear that courts will not countenance a wanton appropriation of terrace space for performance of nonessential building repairs, particularly where the board makes no attempt to mitigate inconvenience to the affected shareholder.

Proprietary leases routinely give co-ops the right to remove structures installed by shareholders on terrace, roof and garden areas when necessary to effectuate building repairs, and to charge the cost of their restorations to shareholders.

The power of boards to review, regulate or prohibit structural alterations such as the construction of glass enclosures, greenhouses and roof gardens constitutes another substantial limitation upon shareholders' use of their outdoor space. Although many leases provide that board approval of such alterations may not be unreasonably withheld or delayed, courts have explicitly sustained a co-op's right to severely restrict or proscribe these kinds of structures where such a prohibition is undertaken in good faith, for a valid corporate purpose and is not enforced in a discriminatory manner.

Boards are well advised to reject plans for the installation of grandiose structures on terraces, penthouse roofs and in gardens, since the corporation is responsible for repairing water damage to adjoining apartments. At the very least, boards should exercise the right to retain (at shareholder expense) engineers or architects to review the proposed plans and legal counsel to draft an alteration agreement with appropriate safeguards, such as indemnification for the cost of repairing any damage attributable to the construction.

Repairs

While most proprietary leases require shareholders to keep their outdoor spaces free of snow, ice, leaves and debris, and to maintain the screens and drain boxes on terraces, repair of exterior structures and surface areas is largely the co-op's responsibility. Abrogation of this responsibility exposes the co-op to liability for breach of warranty of habitability. This is particularly true when the structural disrepair causes water damage to adjoining apartments or presents a safety hazard to residents.

Courts have, however, afforded boards broad discretion in determining the precise nature, scope and quality of the work to be undertaken. Thus, boards are free to utilize lesser-quality materials, do patch work rather than replacement and employ a superintendent rather than a professional contractor in the interest of cost control, even over shareholder objections. (Of course, boards may wish to avert controversy by offering to perform repairs in a manner acceptable to shareholders with the shareholders bearing the additional cost.)

As previously indicated, boards can shift responsibility for the repairs of and damage caused by structures installed by the shareholder to the shareholder through the device of an alteration agreement. However, under no circumstances should the board delay making repairs because of a dispute with the shareholder over financial responsibility, because in so doing it risks breaching its warranty of habitability. Rather, the co-op should complete the repair expeditiously and then pursue whatever remedies it might have against the shareholder.

Boundary Disputes

Occasionally disputes arise as to whether a shareholder has the right to occupy an adjacent terrace, rooftop or garden. The controversy usually surfaces when a shareholder takes possession of an area and the co-op concludes that he is encroaching upon common property. Can the co-op oust him from this space? It depends.

If the shareholder has openly and continuously occupied the disputed area, under an implicit claim of right to do so, for a period of at least ten years, he may be deemed to have acquired an easement by prescription, which will permit him to remain there indefinitely, even if the proprietary lease language or other documentary evidence indicates that the space was not explicitly leased to him in the first place.

Assuming the shareholder has not met the strict criteria for an easement by prescription, courts will engage in a three-tier analysis to determine his right to remain in the disputed area. First, they will look to the proprietary lease for guidance. In most cases, however, the proprietary lease language is ambiguous as to the extent of roof or garden space allocated to the shareholder, merely stating that "if" the area in question is "appurtenant to the apartment" the shareholder has exclusive use thereof. Next, courts will review other objective criteria, such as the share allocation scheme, the building's floor plans, the contract of exchange and other conversion documents, to ascertain whether the space at issue was intended to constitute part of the shareholder's leasehold.

Whenever these documents fail to shed light on the controversy, courts will review the conduct of the parties to determine their respective rights relative to the disputed space. If the board has failed to challenge a shareholder's open occupancy of an area believed to constitute communal property for a long period of time (even if not the ten years required to establish an easement by prescription), the court will probably permit him to remain there. This is particularly true if the shareholder was led to believe from the beginning that the space was his to use, and was permitted to install plants or structures without board intervention. It is therefore imperative that boards immediately challenge a shareholder's use of an area believed to constitute common property; the longer the delay, the less likely they are to be able to successfully oust the shareholder from this space.

When boards voluntarily permit shareholders to use space that is arguably common property, they should insist upon an upward reallocation of his share interest in order to permit the collection of increased maintenance in perpetuity. Failure to take this precaution exposes the board to claims by other shareholders of corporate waste or breach of fiduciary duty.

Fundamentals of Subletting: A Reasonable Policy Gets Best Results

By Robert D. Tierman, Esq.

The subletting of co-op apartments is a controversial topic that pits boards seeking to preserve the quality of life and financial well-being of their buildings against shareholders desperate to rent their apartments because they cannot sell them at acceptable prices. As owners, shareholders feel entitled to allow others to use and occupy their apartments provided the occupants adhere to the co-op's rules. As landlords' representatives, boards feel duty-bound to regulate activity in the best interests of all shareholders.

There is no absolutely proper way to deal with subletting. However, there are certain fundamentals—practical, moral and legal—that should aid boards in establishing fair and effective sublet policies and shareholders in evaluating those policies. These fundamentals reflect practical realities mixed with legal standards that evolve regularly as conflicts over subletting are increasingly resolved in the courts.

A Board Decision

Most proprietary leases give boards authority to grant, deny or condition consent to sublet applications for any or no reason. The right to condition consent provides the basis for boards to establish sublet policies. Because there are so many variables to a policy (length of term, number of successive terms, limits on total units sublet, fees, conditions under which subletting will be permitted), it is not practical or wise to have shareholders vote on a precise policy. If the vote is negative on one or more policies proposed, the board will be left with no policy. A board may consider holding an informational meeting at which shareholders can comment and board members can hear their views. However, the board should then make the ultimate decision.

Most co-ops' governing documents are alike but few are identical. Boards and shareholders should begin their consideration of subletting with a thorough review of their governing documents. Along with these, boards are subject to legal standards. Refusal of an application cannot be based on unlawful discrimination (concerning race or religion, for example). A board cannot act in bad faith (treating one shareholder differently from others) or engage in self-dealing (where the decision affects the self-interest of a director voting whether to approve or disapprove an application).

If a board can grant or deny applications to sublet for any or no reason, it seems logical that it can announce that no subletting will be permitted. However, boards should be reluctant to refuse to allow a hardship appeal.

Risks of Subletting: Myth and Reality

A liberal subletting policy may seem reasonable, especially when weighed against the hardship that shareholders may suffer if not allowed to sublet. However, there are negative aspects to subletting that boards must consider, some of which can be easily mitigated.

Myth: Subtenants don't treat a co-op's property with the same care as a shareholder.

Reality: In fact, this is more likely to affect the shareholder who is subletting than the co-op as a whole since much of the extra wear and tear takes place inside the sublet apartment. Effective adoption and enforcement of house rules and insurance requirements should take care of most dangers to the co-op's common areas.

Myth: Subtenants pose additional security risks in co-op buildings.

Reality: This need not be the case. Subtenants have as big a stake as other residents in not being attacked or robbed in their buildings. Careful screening of prospective subtenants should prevent the possibility that the premises are left less safe after a shareholder moves out and a subtenant moves in.

Myth: It is more difficult for a board to regulate the behavior of subtenants than shareholders.

Reality: This is definitely a consideration that boards must confront. Boards have powerful rights to regulate the conduct of shareholders. However, boards have a less direct and effective legal path to eliminate nuisances that subtenants cause. A board must either give the shareholder a chance to act against his subtenant or act itself against the subtenant. Each has its pitfalls. Moreover, the subtenant usually can lose only the continuing right to live in an apartment for which he has a short-term lease. Those acting against a subtenant have little chance of successfully regulating his behavior or evicting him before the end of his lease term.

Myth: The number of sublet apartments affects a co-op's ability to refinance its underlying mortgage and the ability of purchasers of apartments to obtain "end loan" financing.

Reality: The trend is for lenders to consider apartments sublet by former residents to be "owner-occupied" for purposes of calculating the number of non-owner-occupied apartments in a co-op. However, many lenders will factor in the number of sublet apartments in their considerations. A waiting list keeping the number of sublet apartments under a certain level is an effective and legally enforceable way to deal with this issue.

Establishing a Reasonable Policy

Boards should establish clear sublet policies, distribute them to shareholders and prospective shareholders, and diverge from them only in special circumstances. This will send a message to shareholders that the board is serious about enforcing sublet policies and regulating the behavior of subtenants. However, if it is too broad or ambiguous, the policy will be a breeding ground for litigation by shareholders believing that they were not treated consistently with the policy.

Boards should insist on thorough review of sublet applications prior to allowing subtenants to occupy the co-op's premises. This review should include a credit check, discussion with several business and personal references (including prior landlords) and a personal interview. The fees for this should be paid by the applicant in advance and nonrefundable.

Boards should make sure that the consent of the shareholder's bank to the subletting is obtained, if required. Otherwise, if a problem arises after the board approves a sublet, the bank may challenge the co-op's ability to enforce its rights against the shareholder's apartment.

The sublease must contain adequate protections for the shareholder, and establish that subtenants must comply with the co-op's governing documents and that the board may elect to enforce the shareholder's rights against the subtenant. The board should be entitled to recover legal fees from the subtenant, as well as from the shareholder, if a subtenant violates a sublet agreement.

The shareholder or the subtenant should be required to obtain insurance at appropriate levels for the circumstances, naming the co-op and its board and managing agent as additional insureds. Proof of this insurance must be delivered before the subtenant is granted occupancy.

The shareholder applicant must agree to indemnify the co-op for the costs arising out of the subletting, including all legal fees and expenses incurred by the co-op in taking legal action against the shareholder or the subtenant. The co-op must be authorized to take legal action directly against the subtenant if the shareholder does not do so.

Boards should consider requiring shareholder applicants for sublet approval to deposit funds with the co-op to help defray the co-op's attorney fees in the event of a default. Boards should also consider adopting a penalty that shareholders must pay if their subtenants do not vacate at the end of the permitted term and the shareholder is not taking prompt and effective action to evict them.

Boards must have the willpower to insist on strict compliance with their rules in this (and every other) area absent special circumstances.

Appropriate Sublet Fees

Boards are deemed entitled to set sublet fees based on their authority to condition their consent to subletting. The amount of the fee can be based on a variety of factors—percentage of maintenance, percentage of profit, fixed dollar amount—and not necessarily done on a per-share basis. The fee may be related to the co-op's actual costs in allowing the sublet or be designed to generate revenues for the co-op.

However, there are a variety of pitfalls that boards must avoid.

Boards should carefully consider limitations on what a shareholder can charge his subtenant. In one case, a board attempted to limit the rent that a shareholder could charge a subtenant to no more than the shareholder's maintenance plus a 20 percent surcharge, together with a $1,000 deposit. An appellate court struck down that limitation, stating that "neither the proprietary lease nor offering plan limited the rental allowed to be charged to a subtenant by the holder of unsold shares."

Though this holding may not extend to subletting by ordinary shareholders as well as holders of unsold shares, especially in the current climate, boards should be wary of conditioning subletting on terms that have no necessary benefit to the co-op except to discourage subletting.

Sponsors and Holders of Unsold Shares

The rights of sponsors and holders of unsold shares to sublet is a complex and controversial topic currently evolving in the courts. The stakes are high, especially to investors who purchased large blocks of "unsold" apartments. Boards should not assume that such shareholders are free from all regulation (such as sublet fees and approval of the managing agent) just because board consent to the subletting may not be required. Also, whether a shareholder qualifies as a "holder of unsold shares" is open to interpretation. Variations in co-ops' underlying documents abound and clarifying legal decisions are imminent.

These fundamentals are not etched in stone. Their applicability will vary from co-op to co-op. Some are controversial now and all will require modification with evolving precedents, practices and realities. Boards should not be intimidated by the complex or protean nature of the problem. They should inform themselves as best they can and then act decisively to establish and implement fair and clear policies.

Mediation Alternative: "Wave of the Future" for Avoiding Lawsuits

By Chris Luongo

An unpleasant and often chaotic scene erupts each morning at the housing court on Centre Street in Lower Manhattan, where hundreds of people from all walks of life crowd into a dingy waiting room to search for their names and case numbers on long sheets of paper. When the doors to a large courtroom are opened, everyone scrambles in, to the constant slamming of the gavel by the judge, ordering silence, and the shouts of security guards, demanding that everyone take a seat on benches that are already full.

There's more confusion as cases are assigned to their individual courtrooms, as the complainants and defendants begin the hurried march out alongside their lawyers, who skim through their notes in preparation for the fight. While the outcome may be a legal victory for one, if it concerns an interpersonal matter involving residents of neighboring co-op or condo apartments, the two parties often return home with their bitterness still intact. And they may make it a point never to speak to each other again.

Many of these cases could be handled in a much more humane and less costly fashion, intended to leave both sides feeling like winners. With building boards, managing agents and shareholders constantly looking for ways to trim their buildings' legal bills and avoid the aggravation of senseless, time-consuming court battles, an alternative method of dispute resolution, known as mediation, is being introduced to the co-op and condo community. The directors of the program, along with volunteer mediators and co-op and condo attorneys and consultants, call mediation "a natural" for handling the kind of interpersonal building disputes stemming from such things as noise and animal complaints, broken contracts and harassment cases.

Mediation takes place in the neutral setting of a co-op meeting room or public meeting hall, where the two opposing parties are brought together and given control of their own destinies, with a neutral third party encouraging them to speak out their differences and steering the discussion toward an agreement that is meaningful to both. Often after just two or three hours, the problem is resolved, and everybody is shaking hands. But until the process is more widely accepted as an effective means for solving disputes, many of the disagreements that could have been steered along this much simpler path will continue to be fought out in court.

A Win-Win Situation

"As soon as problems and tempers flare up, the tendency of American society is to sue. We're trying to teach people about an alternative way of resolving problems, without getting to the point where the parties might end up shooting each other," says Thomas Christian, state director of the unified court system's community dispute resolution program. Various centers offering mediation as their primary service are now operating throughout New York under the guidance of his organization. "With mediation, we're working toward what we call a win-win solution. When it's over, while the two parties might still not end up having dinner together, at least they can say they got a fair shake."

Since Christian's program was established in 1981, more and more cases that used to be handled by the courts are being referred to dispute resolution centers, at which some two thousand volunteer mediators, with backgrounds that often include law and psychology, help people come to terms with their differences and work out ways of dealing with them in the future. Once an agreement has been reached, a contract is signed, and then, according to Christian, about 85 percent of parties are never heard from again.

"The two parties come in angry and hostile, saying 'I'm right and he's wrong,'" Christian says. "But once they state their positions, and look at the various issues, there's often some doubt in their minds, and they end up saying, 'I guess I misunderstood.'"

With mediation already a popular method in resolving disputes in both the corporate world and domestic situations, the process is expected to start catching on in co-ops and condos as well. One proponent of the process is real estate consultant Roberta Hendler, who says that with law schools now including mediation training, and building boards looking to cut costs and improve morale, mediation is "the wave of the future." Lately she has been busy making the rounds to various organizations to convince them that the method really works.

A Lesson in Conflict Resolution

One of Hendler's stops was *The New York Cooperator*'s Co-op & Condo Expo in January 1993 at which she suggested to a room full of managing agents that they introduce mediation to the buildings they manage. "If it works," she told them, "you look like heroes. And if not, at least it's barely costing you a thing."

Hendler is quick to point out the difference between mediation and arbitration, a more widely known method of dispute resolution, in which a judge sits down with the two parties in a private setting, and then is put in charge of deciding the outcome of the case. "With arbitration, it's over and done with and somebody is not going to be happy with the outcome," she says. "Mediation is an altogether different animal. It's a quicker, neutral platform for people to air their grievances, and its success rate is an attractive reason to give it a shot."

When a disagreement in Hendler's own Manhattan co-op, concerning noisy children bothering the tenant below, had escalated to the point of possibly becoming violent, the case was turned over to a mediator, who helped the two parties confront their hostility and work out a suitable arrangement. "The problem was never an issue again," says Hendler.

Mike Tarail, the city-wide director for the court dispute referral center, sees thousands of mediation cases go through his department each year, and has witnessed numerous situations in which even the most hostile people are taught how to communicate and resolve their problems. Tarail would like to see mediation someday be included as part of the terms of apartment leases or even as part of a building's by-laws "as something to try first." He says the process has proven ideal for solving problems involving people who have no choice but to continue living next to one another. Mediators are trained, he explains, to be good listeners and to help people work out agreements that will strengthen their future relationship as neighbors.

"If one has to lower his stereo, the other has to refrain from banging on the ceiling with a mop," Tarail says. "As a mediator, you try to balance it as best you can."

Co-op owner Wayde Harrison, who was trained as a mediator two years ago and works out of a dispute referral center in Brooklyn, says that part of what he does is to help people to talk out their problems, focus on their similarities and carve out an agreement in light of their future relationship.

"I'm seeing people who haven't spoken for twenty years suddenly shaking hands," Harrison says. "It's all quite extraordinary."

Now, as he works with Hendler to make building boards more aware of the mediation process, Harrison says he can't help but look back to past years in his own co-op and to all the neighbor disputes that could have been steered away from the courts and more effectively resolved. "Mediation certainly would have made life here a lot easier," he says.

Hendler says that many people have grown so accustomed to handing even their pettiest problems to their lawyers to squabble over that they are often hesitant to try a different path of recourse. "Mediation gets better results," she says. "But it's such a simplistic solution that people have a hard time believing it will really work."

Keeping Co-ops and Condos Healthy: A Legislative Agenda

By Chris Luongo

Ever since the co-op boom peaked in the mid-1980s and began its downward slide at the end of the decade, there has been pressure from apartment owners to reform the laws governing conversions and regulating the behavior of building sponsors. As the recession took hold, hundreds of buildings, most of which were converted with little tenant participation (current law allows a sponsor to convert with as few as 15 percent of the apartments sold), have experienced financial difficulties due to sponsor default or over-leveraging.

As the new legislative session begins in Albany, co-op and condo activists, lobbyists, owners and committed city officials are gearing up to fight for passage of a series of bills, many of which have been under consideration for years, designed to alleviate some of these problems.

"The wave of co-op and condo conversions that swept across our city in the 1980s brought many benefits, but also left in its wake a calamitous situation for tens of thousands of our city's families," says Queens borough president Claire Shulman. "One of the fundamental problems is the law that governs the conversion process—it is a prescription for disaster."

In 1991, Shulman formed the Co-op and Condo Task Force, made up of lobbyists, co-op and condo boards, real estate managers, bankers and attorneys, which has been pressing state lawmakers for reforms that would aid financially troubled co-ops and condos and prevent future problems.

Past lobbying efforts have resulted in three bills that are now helping buildings to extricate themselves from financial difficulties. The Direct Rental Payment Law, which Shulman and her delegates pushed for two years before it was finally passed in 1991, enables boards to collect rents directly from tenants if the sponsor defaults or the nonresident owners fail to pay their monthly common charges. Meanwhile, two tax exemption laws have helped Shulman and others save buildings such as the 617-unit Acropolis co-op, in Astoria, Queens, from foreclosure. One, passed in 1991, waives the Gains Tax paid to the state until an apartment gets sold, and another, passed in 1992, exempts co-ops from the real property transfer tax when they take back shares from defaulting sponsors.

But with seven additional bills now being pushed, and one more on its way, Shulman has been urging everyone not to give up the battle, and to join her on one of her regular bus trips to Albany to keep pressure on state legislators to push some of these proposals through.

Proposed Legislation

The following is a summary of the eight proposed bills being pushed for the 1993/1994 legislative session by the task force, six of which were passed by the State Assembly during the 1992/1993 session, before bogging down in the Senate:

1. Senate Bill 4397 would require that at least one resident owner be on the board of directors within sixty days of conversion, and that the sponsor relinquish control of the board within two years, instead of the current five.

2. Senate Bill 4979 would increase the minimum required number of apartments needed in order to declare an offering plan effective from the current 15 percent to 25 percent of the tenants in occupancy.

3. Senate Bill 6184 would require sponsors to correct serious code violations and dangerous or hazardous conditions prior to conversion.

4. Senate Bill 4399 would require sponsors to post a security to cover three years of financial obligations. This fund would have to be maintained until more than 90 percent of the shares or units are sold.

5. Senate Bill 2073 would allow shareholders to independently sue under the Martin Act if the sponsor promises something in the offering plan and then doesn't deliver it. Under current law, only the attorney general's office may bring an action against those who violate the Martin Act, which is the state securities law, requiring, among other things, that full and complete disclosure be made in the offering plan.

6. Senate Bill 1840 would establish a new Uniform Commercial Code filing system for co-op liens and provide co-ops with a "superior lien" for unpaid maintenance, meaning that the co-op gets paid before the bank can take over the shares of a defaulted unit.

7. Senate Bill 2887, the Condominium Lien Priority, would provide that an amount equal to six months' common charges be a superior lien due to the condominium association.

8. Assembly Bill 7148 would establish a financing program set up by the Mortgage Bankers Association. Legislation is needed to enable the State of New York Mortgage Agency (SONYMA) to issue securities that would be backed by subject share loans and underlying mortgages.

Pushing for Passage

Many of the proposals being pushed originated from bills first proposed by former attorney general Robert Abrams during the 1980s. Both the sales requirement bill (S4979) and the private right of action bill (S2073) were passed by the Assembly back in the 1982–83 session. Meanwhile, the code violation bill (S6184) was introduced to the Senate in 1988, and the board of directors' bill (S4397) in 1991. Some members of the task force blame the failure of these bills to become laws on partisan politics by the Republican-controlled Senate, while Shulman says counter-lobbying efforts by real estate developers and other professionals are also partly to blame.

"Most of the bills are caught up in the gridlock between the Senate and Assembly," says Gary Connor, chief of the Attorney General's Real Estate Financing Bureau. "Whether that's attributed to the Republican-Democrat split or other lobbying groups depends on how you look at it."

Republican senator Kemp Hannon, former chairman of the Senate Housing Committee, says that the bills' failure was partly due to lawmakers focusing their efforts on improving the rent regulatory system and to flaws in some of the bills. For instance, regarding the issue of board control, for which he has sponsored a bill, Senator Hannon says that the Senate body isn't convinced that increasing board control will actually help a co-op. In fact, he says, some believe that a professional might have a better sense of management than the resident shareholders themselves. "It's not that we're against it," he says, "but is it going to work?"

As to increasing the sale requirements to convert a building, Hannon says a case could be made that many co-op problems are the result of overpaying or too high an underlying mortgage. "I think we need to reexamine all the rules, but it strikes me on reading this bill that you may have a good argument but not necessarily the correct argument," he says.

Gary Connor disagrees, saying that it has always been the attorney general's belief that the more sales in a building, the better the cash flow and the stronger the co-op is to start with.

Benefits of Proposed Changes

"The way it is now is ridiculous," says task force member Charles Rappaport, president of the Federation of New York Housing Cooperatives, which endorses all of the bills in Shulman's reform package. Under current law a sponsor can make a promise and then say, "Sorry, I don't have any money," he points out. Regarding the security fund bill, he adds, "With this bill we're saying, 'Now if you make a promise, you have to put your money where your mouth is.'"

Rappaport says that while he considers all of the pieces of legislation important, they may be too late in coming, affecting just a small number of co-ops and condos. "It's like someone trying to close the barn door after a herd of horses got out, with only one crippled horse still in there," he says. "These bills are all great things that should have happened a decade ago, but now all the conversions under bad circumstances have already taken place."

But task force member Jimmy Lanza, founder of the Queens Co-op/Condo Coalition and president of the Woodside Co-op/Condo Coalition, points out that in the next couple of years many of the past problems affecting co-ops and condos will start to resurface, such as tax abatements running out and maintenance fees going up, putting a financial crunch on many co-ops that are right now just getting by. "If the market gets better, the same sponsors may come back under different names and do the same things all over again," he says.

As board president of Boulevard Gardens, a 963-unit co-op in Woodside, Queens,

Lanza has firsthand knowledge of how changes in the rules governing the conversion process can prevent future problems from happening. Lanza has witnessed numerous problems caused by shareholders being kept in the dark as to what the sponsor is doing. "And very often, unless residents have control of their boards from the outset," he says, "later on, it becomes much harder to work through a problem." Lanza has been lobbying for reforms in Albany ever since he and a few other members of his committee made the trip by car in 1989. That excursion grew into busloads of people once Shulman formed the task force two years later.

Widespread Support

Andrew Kelman, former director of housing in the Queens borough president's office, says that one key factor in making state lawmakers understand the urgency for housing reform has been the high level of support from individuals and organizations spread out across the five boroughs, such as Lanza, the Federation of New York Housing Cooperatives, the New York Association of Realty Managers and the Council of New York Cooperatives.

Kelman encourages co-op and condo owners wishing to be involved in the lobbying efforts and to be kept informed of the issues to take advantage of low-cost bus transportation to Albany that is provided for each hearing. "These Albany trips have become an annual pilgrimage," he says. "There's great camaraderie between the folks on the busses, who have included mothers with small children, retirees and apartment owners who have had to take off a day from work. And it's a great lesson in civics as well."

New York's New Lead Law: Defining and Treating the Hazards

By Sam Adler

In a bill passed in the summer of 1992, New York State empowered the state Health Department to establish a comprehensive lead program that will affect residential property owners. The new law, called the Lead Poisoning Prevention Act, was passed by the New York State Legislature in July, signed in September and went into effect on April 1, 1993.

The new lead law is directed at residential property, since its purpose is to limit the exposure of children to lead poisoning. The act establishes an advisory council on lead poisoning prevention to assist in the development of a statewide plan to eliminate lead poisoning, to recommend the adoption of lead policy and to coordinate activities of the council's member agencies.

The act goes on to authorize the state Department of Health to develop, implement and coordinate a four-point program to prevent lead poisoning. The department is authorized to:

1. Universally screen children and pregnant women for lead poisoning and to follow up where there are elevated blood lead levels, defined as ten micrograms of

lead per deciliter of blood or higher.

2. Enter into interagency agreements to coordinate lead poisoning prevention, exposure reduction, identification and treatment activities with other federal, state and local agencies and programs.

3. Establish a statewide registry of children with elevated lead levels, to be kept confidential except for medical treatment purposes and epidemiological data.

4. Develop and implement public education and community outreach programs on lead exposure, detection and risk reduction.

Hazards of Lead

The major sources of lead exposure in the home environment are lead-based paint, soil, dust and lead pipes that carry residential water. Infants and toddlers are far more susceptible to lead poisoning than are older children and adults.

Exposure to even low levels of lead increases a child's risk of developing permanent learning disabilities, reduced concentration and attentiveness, and behavior problems; higher levels of lead can cause mental retardation, kidney disease, liver damage and even death. If detected early, however, lead poisoning can be treated by introducing substances into the blood that bind to the lead and cause it to be excreted.

Currently, a child is considered to have lead poisoning if tests show twenty-five micrograms of lead per deciliter of blood. But the city is about to follow the state's lead and lower its definition of lead poisoning to ten micrograms per deciliter, although a home inspection by a New York City Health Department inspector would not be triggered until a child is found to have twenty micrograms per deciliter or greater.

Applying the old standard, in 1991 there were 648 cases of lead poisoning in New York City that triggered a home inspection. With the new standard in place, that number should jump to between six thousand and ten thousand cases per year, according to the New York City Department of Health.

Daniel J. Sitomer, a partner with the Environmental Law Group at Brown & Wood in Manhattan, notes that to the extent the state law addresses what constitutes a hazardous condition and how to respond to it, New York City's regulations must be at least as stringent. Sitomer notes, for example, that the new law provides for the removal of any paint containing more than .06 of 1 percent of lead, while the old law allowed up to .5 of 1 percent.

Sitomer also notes that the new law authorizes the state Health Department to require removal of contaminated soil or lead pipes supplying drinking water where they are deemed unsafe. Under previous law, this authority was limited to removal of lead-based paint.

"The law is vague on the issue of how to determine whether paint, a pipe or the soil is deemed a hazard," Sitomer says. "It doesn't stipulate how or when a material has to be tested and what the program for removal will be. We don't know whether the state Health Department will set up a comprehensive program for testing, require tests when renovations take place, as in the case of asbestos testing, or opt for some other method."

But at the very least the state's new screening requirement and new lead threshold will almost certainly increase investigations by New York City agencies looking for lead hazards, says Jim Raucci, program administrator for the New York State Department of Health's Childhood Lead Poisoning Prevention Program. He notes that the city lab is already gearing up to accept blood lead specimens (the test currently administered by the city can't detect lead below twenty-five micrograms per deciliter).

Raucci notes that with children being identified at lower levels, there will more than likely be increased follow-up activity and environmental investigations.

Taking Precautionary Measures

"The best advice we can give is to do a hazard assessment and address the problem," says Vincent Coluccio, vice-president of ATC Environmental, a lead consulting and management service. "The Williamsburgh Bridge and the lead-in-the-drinking-water issue are just the tip of the iceberg. I expect it to be a real issue in people's homes."

The lead problem is not limited to underprivileged areas, Daniel Sitomer points out. "In many older buildings, the first layer of paint was lead and it's been painted over a number of times. In poorer areas, the condition is allowed to deteriorate. While co-op and condo owners have been better able to maintain their apartments, exposure issues occur during renovation and that's what their concern should be. In addition, certain common areas bear watching, such as the boiler room where old paint is chipped and cracking."

According to federal estimates, 3.8 million children get lead poisoning by ingesting dust due to normal hand-to-mouth activity. According to Coluccio, who holds a doctorate in public health from Columbia University, "If lead paint is on a mouthable surface—even if it's intact—it can be a hazard. A child can bite a window sill and get enough to go to the hospital." On the other hand, he says, "Lead paint is especially hazardous if it's chipped, peeling or dusting" (exterior lead-based paint is designed to "dust" or shed the outer molecular layer to give it a fresh appearance). "Windows, doors, floor casings—anywhere there's friction, you'll find dust," he says.

Overreaction, more than inaction, may pose the greatest danger to public health. Decisions should be made with a cool head, says Sitomer, "beginning with the identification of consultants who are qualified to identify existing lead conditions in a building. From there, it's a question of developing a common-sense building-management program for lead similar to an asbestos operation and management process."

Unlicensed Abatement Contractors

Coluccio agrees that overreaction can worsen the problem: "My fear is that owners will improperly or unnecessarily strip lead paint, leading to a wave of lead-poisoning cases." He notes that there is no experienced lead-paint abatement industry in our region. Pointing to the whole asbestos-abatement experience, with its notorious "rip and skip" contractors, who kicked up more dust than they abated, Coluccio says that "strip and skip" operations are sure to appear in the lead-abatement industry.

Sitomer's firm prequalifies consultants and contractors. "The number who are qualified is very small—much smaller than existed at the beginning of the asbestos scare," he says.

One of the things the new state advisory council has been mandated to do is to make recommendations to ensure the qualifications of persons performing inspection and abatement of lead through a system of licensure and certification or otherwise.

Coluccio is a strong advocate of certification requirements. "I've seen improper abatements that have exacerbated existing lead poisoning," he says. "The basic problem is that contractors fail to grasp the fact that dust is a hazard. It's difficult to get contractors, who are used to working with dust, to contain it."

To suppress dust, Coluccio recommends frequent wiping down of surfaces. If a child rides a bike into a wall, kicking up lead dust, address the problem immediately. And when doing any kind of apartment renovation, insist that the contractor work in a contained area to keep dust from spreading. At the end of the job, have a lab come in and take a wipe test to see how much dust remains.

Joseph Giamboi, an attorney at Stroock & Stroock & Lavan, says buildings can try to protect themselves against a consultant or contractor botching the job by insisting on having an indemnification or hold-harmless clause in the service contract. "But you must make sure that the contractor is properly insured or has sufficient assets to make good on a hold-harmless or indemnification clause."

"You want to look at the consultant's insurance policy to see that they have liability and errors and omissions coverage for working with lead," advises Sitomer. Buildings should also review their own insurance policies to determine if they exclude lead coverage within the pollution exclusion.

Property Owners Bear the Burden

The new state law also authorizes the advisory council to recommend strategies for financially assisting property owners in abating environmental lead, such as tax credits and loan funds. "We can't expect individual citizens like property owners to underwrite the solution to this serious public health problem," says John Gilbert, past president of the Rent Stabilization Association, which represents landlords. "If that decision is made, then there will never be a solution to the problem, there'll just be less housing." Gilbert urges property owners to look closely at efforts to modify local laws so they don't place the entire burden on the property owner.

Coluccio is enmeshed in that process. As he explains it, in 1985, a coalition of groups successfully sued New York City, maintaining that its lead laws were antiquated. The state Supreme Court in the case held that all lead paint—not just that which is chipped or peeling—is a hazard. The court decision was "staggering in its implications for property owners," says Coluccio.

Because of it, he says, the City Council is currently considering legislation requiring lead abatement in all dwellings inhabited by children under age seven or pregnant women, as well as in common areas where these two groups could be expected to frequent. The City Council's approach—full removal or enclosure of all lead paint at a cost of $15,000 and up per apartment—would be too much of a financial burden on property owners, says Coluccio, who is a member of the mayor's Advisory Committee on Lead Poisoning. The committee is pushing for a less costly approach: finding where the lead paint is and managing it. Only where it is very bad would a major abatement be required. The two-pronged approach—risk assessment and in-place management—mirrors the "operations and maintenance" approach taken with regard to asbestos several years ago.

Under the mayor's plan, risks would be classified according to three dust levels: Level One, a low dust level, would involve wet-scraping on a spot basis at an average cost per apartment of about $1,200. Level Two, an intermediate dust level, would require more abatement, including use of a high-efficiency vacuum and trisodiumphosphate detergent. Cost per apartment would be about $3,000. Level Three, a high dust level, would require replacement of windows and carpets, sealing of floors and encapsulation or replacement of surfaces. The cost would be about $8,000 per apartment.

While the new state law will soon require screening of young children and pregnant women, how can everyone else find out how much lead they are living with? Under current regulations, New York City health inspectors will pay your building a visit under only two circumstances: if a child in your building develops lead poisoning, or if you live in a pre-1960 building and an inspector happens to see chipped paint. In that case, there's a presumption that it's lead paint and the owner will be cited for a violation and ordered to perform an immediate abatement.

"If people want to know if their building is safe, they're on their own," Coluccio says. "They have to find a company to do testing. But there are no certification requirements, so it's buyer beware."

CHAPTER ELEVEN

Taxation Issues

- *Tax reform efforts*
- *Real estate taxes*
- *Inheriting co-ops*

A Deluge of Taxes for Owners: Take Action to Reduce Burden
By Laura Rowley

"Taxes are what we pay for civilized society," Oliver Wendell Holmes, Jr. said in 1904, a statement he might be inclined to revise if he saw New York City in the 1990s. New York apartment owners are being deluged with taxes from every side—federal, state and city—and they don't show signs of abating. Below is a review of the state of co-op and condo taxation in a less civilized time than Holmes envisioned.

Your Building's Tax Assessment

Real estate tax assessments have continued to climb over the last three years in spite of the fact that the market nose-dived deeper and faster than a stunt man leaping off the Empire State Building. From 1987/'88 to 1988/'89, the average increase was 26 percent; from 1989/'90 to 1990/'91 the hike averaged 9.5 percent, although some individual buildings were hit with increases as high as 20 percent, according to the law firm of Tuchman, Katz, Schwartz, Gelles & Korngold, which studied the assessment valuations issued by the New York City Department of Finance for those periods. Finance records released in January show that the assessments on Class II properties were up an average of 6 percent in 1990/'91 to 1991/'92.

Paul Korngold, whose firm represents eight hundred co-ops and condos, suggests that most buildings should have their certiorari attorney file protests with the city every year. As real estate values continue to fall, the number of owners protesting their new assessments is rising sharply.

"Unless you protest you don't really know how you stand vis-à-vis the other buildings," says Korngold. "People should try to understand as much as possible about their buildings' taxes and how it affects their bottom line." Class II properties—co-ops and condos—have until March 1 to file their protests. Protests are filed with the New York City Tax Commission, usually on the grounds that the assessment is unequal or excessive.

The hottest political potato in this arena is the way co-op and condo owners continue to get hit with disproportionately higher taxes than single-family home owners, since tax policy in the early 1980s capped the increase in assessments for Class I properties (one-, two- and three-family homes) but not Class II. Finance commissioner Carol O'Cleireacain has indicated that she favors phasing in a merger of Classes I and II, which would provide more equity between the two kinds of housing and most certainly result in tax increases for small home owners. However, such a change would have to be approved by both the City Council and the state Legislature.

J-51 Tax Abatements

The expiration of J-51 tax abatements is creating budget havoc for some city buildings faced with tax bills that are doubling or even tripling. For those who haven't yet heard, the J-51 Program was enacted in 1955 to help building owners upgrade their properties rather than abandon them. In the 1980s, hundreds of co-ops and condos used the tax abatements provided by J-51 to rehabilitate their buildings. J-51 exemptions forgive, generally over a period of twelve years, the increased property taxes based on the increase in assessed value that results from the physical improvements made to the building.

As owners who rehabilitated their buildings under the J-51 Program clearly know, the abatement period is expiring in many city buildings. "It's a terrible problem, due to ignorance, bad offering plans and overestimates," says Korngold. "People who bought who figured they could afford $500 in maintenance are now faced with paying $1,000."

Some boards have dealt with the problem by phasing in maintenance increases, selling retail space, refinancing underlying mortgages or even paying them off entirely so they could absorb the tax blow when it came. Others were asleep at the wheel, and are faced with a skyrocketing increase in maintenance when shareholders and unit owners can least afford it.

IRC 277 and 421a

Internal Revenue Code Section 277, or the "country club" tax, as it might be called, taxes member organizations on income from nonmembers—greens fees in a country club, for example. For some time the IRS has been trying to apply this section to the interest on reserve funds and rents from commercial and professional leases, reasoning that these funds constitute nonmember income to cooperative corporations. Co-op lawyers and lobbyists argue that Section 277 applies only to organizations that provide goods and services, not housing and facilities, and point out that housing cooperatives are addressed in a completely different section of the Tax Code.

Every year, bills exempting housing cooperatives from IRC 277 are submitted to Congress. Several cases are still pending in federal tax court that may resolve the issue.

Another taxing problem is occurring for some twenty thousand co-op and condo owners in buildings affected by the city's 421a tax-abatement program, who may be overpaying their real estate taxes by as much as 10 percent. The state Supreme Court recently ruled that the city is using a calculation method that illegally double-taxes the owners of units receiving 421a benefits after a real estate law firm filed suit against the city. The double-taxing is all but undetectable on the annual tax bill because the tax-setting formula is so complex. During a routine audit of a condominium's tax records, the firm of Seiden, Stempel, Bennett & D'Agostino discovered the double taxation. The owner of a typical one-bedroom 421a Manhattan apartment faces a tax overcharge averaging $320 a year—about 10 percent. Owners in 421a buildings should ask their attorneys to audit their tax bills since the overcharge is not readily apparent.

The City Franchise Tax

Through a special provision of the Corporate Tax Code, the city taxes all co-op corporations on their real estate assets (rather than their income, the way a normal corporation operating in the city would be taxed, since co-ops do not exist to make a profit or generate any income in most cases). However, some co-op attorneys are complaining about the way the city is playing hardball with this tax, using different methods of valuation on different buildings to determine the tax in an effort to rake in the most income for the city.

The city uses several methods to determine a co-op's franchise tax, each with its own difficulties, according to Richard Siegler, a partner with Stroock & Stroock & Lavan. First, the city can base the tax on a current appraisal, which is onerous and expensive, requiring the co-op to have an appraisal done every year. Or it can base the tax on the co-op's historic book costs, the real property transfer tax at the time the property was purchased (the total value of the share acquisitions). The problem here is that a co-op that converted in 1950 would have a much lower historic book cost than one converted in 1987. Third, the city can use a formula that takes the current real estate tax assessment and doubles it. The city generally uses the second and third methods.

"What the city has done is pick and choose its valuation methods in the most artful way to yield the most revenue for the city," says Siegler. For example, he represents a co-op on Fifth Avenue that converted in 1950 and has a historic book cost of about $6 million. Instead of this figure, the city uses the third method, doubling the co-op's assessment of $16 million to come up with a figure of $32 million to base the tax on. On the other hand, Siegler represents a building on East 54th Street that has an historic book value of about $57 million because it converted under an eviction plan in 1983. In this case, the city chooses to use the historic book value to determine the building's taxes because the method of doubling the co-op's tax assessment would result in a lower figure to base the franchise tax on.

"We would like to see the administration adopt a uniform method," Siegler notes. "This would put all co-ops on a level playing field." He adds that a corporation's accountant should challenge the city's method if it seems unfair. In most cases, he says, he has seen the city back down rather than take a challenge to court, where the city might be ordered to stick to one method.

At a time when co-ops and condos are also struggling to cut costs, it is important to take the closest look possible at your building's taxes and be vigilant in challenging them. It could save the building many thousands of dollars in taxes, help keep maintenance down and, consequently, keep overall apartment values up.

Stop Your Taxes From Going Up: Class II Owners Must Act Now

By Greg Carlson

As you may or may not know, the mere fact that you either own shares of stock attributable to a unit in a housing cooperative or own the unit outright in a condominium makes your share of real estate taxes two, three or more times greater than that of a private home owner in New York City. Although a single-family home owner can demand a sales price two to three times greater than a comparable co-op or condo unit, he or she pays about one-third the real estate tax of a unit owner. A building's tax liability is determined by two factors: its assessment and the real estate tax rate.

When the Action Committee for Reasonable Real Estate Taxes was formed in 1990, real estate taxes for Class II buildings (which includes most co-ops and condos) were rising at an alarming rate, quickly surpassing increases on Class I buildings (one-, two- and three-family houses). Within a very short time, the committee was able to convince the City Council of the problem facing Class II buildings, and the result was a rollback in the real estate tax rate to what it was in 1987. This was a major accomplishment.

In 1991, the action committee joined with other real estate organizations from all classes of real estate to form Taxpayers for an Affordable New York. This joint effort applied the pressure necessary to force the Dinkins administration and the City Council to change the annual practice of raising the real estate tax rate in an attempt to balance the city's budget, or at the very least, "make ends meet." (Regulation of the tax rate is one of the very few taxing areas that the city controls without the need for state approval.)

Another part of the taxpayers' strategy was to bring to the forefront the inequity among building classifications in treatment of real estate taxes. Despite pledges from both Mayor Dinkins and the City Council to freeze the real estate tax rate, New York State stepped in. Under the guise of the State Board of Equalization and Assessment (SBEA), using data that was over three years old, the board determined that Class II buildings were not paying enough in real estate taxes. So, in 1992 the board issued its findings calling for an increase of almost 8 percent. Fortunately, thanks to the action committee drumming up support among members of the

City Council and various state legislators, what would have proved to be a disaster was averted. Although the outcome was not the ideal (no increases), the hardship was minimized.

Unfortunately, despite pledges from both the mayor and the City Council to freeze the rate, Class II buildings received a 4.5 percent increase. Again, SBEA, using three-year-old data, determined that Class II buildings should have their share of the tax load increased while Class I buildings should receive an increase of less than 1 percent. While battling their own budget crisis, the city legislators forgot to lobby Albany, and the increase was allowed to pass through without a fight.

The Action Committee for Reasonable Real Estate Taxes under the leadership of Martin Karp has accomplished much in a short time. Although progress has been made, there is still a long way to go in order to achieve equity in real estate taxes. The committee needs the help of every co-op and condo owner.

When the action committee held its meeting in October 1992, the guest speaker was New York City finance commissioner Carol O'Cleireacain, who told the audience that if unit owners want real estate tax reform, they had better "squeal like stuck pigs." When we speak to various state and city legislators, the consensus is that they hear nothing from co-op and condo owners (except for some parts of Manhattan). The legislators also tell us that no matter what type of legislative proposal is contemplated concerning Class I, the phones ring off the hook.

What can you do to get involved? Pressure the candidates running for city office and your City Council district representative for their position on this issue. Invite the candidates or representative to your next annual shareholders' meeting. Form a committee to address either just the real estate tax issue or several issues that may concern your buildings. This committee can put together a letter-writing campaign. The voice of the individual unit owner is the most effective tool to reach elected officials, and with enough voices we can create a voice loud enough to force a change.

In December 1992, the action committee brought its meeting to Queens. This meeting was standing room only, and guest speaker Martha Stark, former special counsel for property tax reform at the New York City Department of Finance, reinforced what her boss had told the audience the October before. (Ms. Stark recently left the commission to assume a position in Washington.) As a result, people from buildings represented at the meeting wrote to their legislative representatives and the legislators took notice—they told us something must be going on because Class II people never write them.

Real Estate Tax Reform: Moving in the Right Direction

By Andrea Conrad and Chris Luongo

With the owners of co-ops and condos being hit with taxes three to five times higher than those paid by owners of one- to three-family homes, a growing chorus of voices, including real estate advocates, neighborhood associations, local politicians and co-op and condo owners, are calling for a full-scale reform of the current property tax system. Recognizing this inequity, former mayor David Dinkins and the City Council appointed a special commission last September to study reform options. And while the seven-member New York City Real Property Tax Reform Commission postponed making any formal recommendations until it receives some guidance from the new administration, it did recently issue a report that shows how the current system is imbalanced, causing co-op and condo owners to be saddled with a disproportionate share of the property tax load.

Apartment Owners Speak Out

Late last year the reform commission held a series of public hearings throughout the five boroughs. Apartment owners showed up at all of these events to share tales of how the present tax system has negatively affected their lives. At an October hearing at City Hall in Manhattan, the board president of an Irving Place co-op "operating on a shoestring," as she said, told how her building's plumbing and wiring were about to give out while half of its budget went into paying real estate taxes. "This state of affairs is intolerable!" she shouted.

Board president Suzanne Fass offered a grim account of her Nassau Street co-op, in which the maintenance has jumped 60 percent in a year to keep up with rising real estate taxes. "Contrary to popular belief, not everyone who lives down here is a Wall Street lawyer," she said. "Is it hard for us? Of course it is."

The owner of a Bank Street co-op, who also claimed to be barely able to keep up with her tax payments, pleaded to the commission for some major reforms and then described an occasion in which she found herself looking into the eyes of a homeless person on the street, while thinking to herself, "This could be me someday."

City councilman Charles Millard blames the current tax system partly on a misperception among many city officials that co-op and condo owners are wealthy enough to shoulder the burden of higher taxes. "The truth is that co-op and condo owners look, work and earn just the same as anyone else in this town," Millard says. "People balance their checkbooks the same way in Turtle Bay as they do in Sheepshead Bay. We are subsidizing other New Yorkers simply because our homes happen to stand vertically rather than horizontally. This has to stop. We need action from this commission and we need it quickly."

Unfortunately, that action never materialized, as the December 31 deadline, by which the commission was supposed to come up with its list of recommendations for reforming the real property tax system, came and went. But in its thirty-five–page report, handed over to Mayor Rudolph Giuliani for his input, the commission, which was charged with developing a local consensus on a real property tax reform proposal that could be taken to Albany for state legislative approval, states that "the property tax in New York City not only appears unfair, it is unfair." The report goes on to point out areas that need special attention and review the testimony received at the hearings.

"The commission decided, given the new mayor, not to recommend any specifics until he (Giuliani) comes to his own conclusion," says Kurt Richwerger, a member of the City Council Finance Division. According to Andrew Kelman, former director of housing in the Queens borough president's office, the commission's task of having to review housing data, hold a series of public hearings and draw up a list of recommendations, all within a three-month period, was nearly impossible to carry out. "Given those time constraints, it was quite remarkable to see how feverishly the committee members worked," he says.

In the meantime, other advocates of tax reform, also thankful that some sort of reform movement has at least finally begun, plan to continue to lobby for a more equitable system, especially in the wake of Mayor Giuliani's January 10th decision not to include in his budget City Council speaker Peter Vallone's proposal for a 40 percent tax cut for co-ops and condos, although the mayor said he agrees that the current property tax system needs to be reformed.

The Commission's Report

The report issued by the commission recognizes that owners of rental buildings, co-ops and condos often pay far higher taxes than owners of one-, two- or three-family homes with identical market value; that homes of similar market value in different neighborhoods or even on the same street can bear very different tax burdens; that the property tax consumes a far greater percentage of the income of the less well off than that of the more affluent and that current relief programs are inadequate.

"Testimony received at the public hearings...pointed time and again to the inequities and burdens and the need for serious reform of the existing property tax system," the report reads. "With the growth in co-op and condo residency, this discrepancy has become more apparent and more burdensome for many New Yorkers."

The commission recommends that the following areas, among others, be addressed: revision of the class system to eliminate the artificial distinctions among residential properties; replacement of the system of class shares with a system whose primary objective is to achieve the city's policies through simple and equitable tax rates and creation of a property tax structure that enhances the city's ability to compete in the commercial and industrial sectors.

Martin Karp, chairman of the Council of New York Cooperatives' Action Committee for Reasonable Real Estate Taxes and a vocal participant at nearly all of the commission's hearings and meetings, says he felt that the members of the commission were successful at identifying the critical issues, "confirming that there is, indeed, tax inequity." He goes on to say that had the committee members been appointed back in April, when the commission was created by local law of the City Council, "there might have been enough exchange of data for it to say 'OK, everybody's been heard.'"

Reasons for Tax Reform

The underlying issue raised by Karp and other tax-reform advocates is the discrepancy between the taxation of Class I and Class II housing, leaving co-op and condo buildings bearing an unfair burden. "Class I property (made up of one-, two- and three-family homes) is assessed at 8 percent of full value, which for Class I is essentially market price," Karp says. "Whereas in Class II properties (all multifamily buildings over three units, including most co-ops and condos), the target assessment is 45 percent of value. And the standard for setting value in Class II is a little more complicated: the capitalized income method, which is a classic method of valuing property that has some income potential."

Karp goes on to explain that if one starts with a situation in which—by law—the maximum assessment in Class I is 8 percent of value and for Class II is 45 percent of value, you get a five to one differential. He also notes that New York City has the highest effective tax rate on multifamily residential property in the country. "Whatever the economic and political reasons," he says, "that's a fact.

"The question of what is the full value of a co-op and condo is still subject to debate, and that has to be resolved," he continues, adding that the action committee will continue to pursue its efforts to achieve tax reform for all classes of real property. "Until the total issue is addressed," he says, "New York City won't have an equitable real estate property tax system." He points to the problems with Class IV properties (commercial real estate) that still need to be addressed. "And there is, as the commission and many of us have noted, the fact that, due to the regressive nature of the real estate tax, low-income people still have problems."

Part of the reason for inequity stems from the fact that the major pieces of legislation defining classes of real estate were passed in 1981, when there were very few co-ops and condos in the city. "The current tax system was designed for an environment that no longer exists and I doubt will ever return," Karp says.

Assemblywoman Catherine Nolan agrees, pointing out that there were just five thousand co-ops when the New York real property tax was adopted in 1981, while today the number has grown to nearly half a million. "Clearly you can see emerging a strong sentiment, citywide, to protect the owner-occupied co-op because of those numbers," Nolan says. "But nobody wants to put this on the backs of the one-, two-, three-family home owners or the commercial property owners. If you think the solution is to say that Class I people are paying too little, that's not the way to achieve anything. Everybody thinks they pay too much."

Solutions to the Problem

In Councilman Millard's testimony, he told the commission that any solution to the existing problem would have to be implemented over time, with appropriate "circuit-breaker" protections for seniors, owners with low income and so on. "And, of course, just as it took years to create this unfairness, no one is asking you to quadruple home owners' taxes immediately," he adds. "People must be protected against disaster, but the unfairness must stop."

Many of those who spoke at the hearings in regard to the unfair tax treatment of co-op and condo properties, endorsed a two-class system, one for residential and one for commercial, to be taxed at full value as presently defined by law, with caps and phase-ins to protect individuals against anticipated jumps in the property tax, and safety-valve provisions for people with limited incomes and senior citizens. It was argued that choices regarding tax burdens on different types of property should be expressed through the tax rate, rather than on the more complex system currently in use.

Karp stresses the need for any reform to be "revenue neutral," meaning that "We do not want the inequities to be resolved by simply reducing the excess tax burden on one class and leaving the city short of money," he says. "Mr. Valone addressed this by pointing out that his tax-cut proposal would cost $44 million a year and that money would have to be found someplace else."

Now with the thirty-five–page tax reform report left in the hands of Mayor Giuliani, Karp says he hopes that soon the commission, or some similar group, will be able to pick up where it left off, "so that we can get some actual proposals out on the table."

Reduce Your Tax Bite: Challenge Assessments Annually

By Christina Johnson

Every year on January 15, the New York City Department of Finance unveils its new tax assessment roll and puts it on display in borough offices. Every co-op and condo board is urged to go and take a look. There will be a stack of books. Go to your borough office, locate your block and read down to your lot number. There you'll discover not only what the market value of your building is this year, but its taxable value, which determines its tax liability as well.

If your assessment looks too high, you have until March 1 to challenge it before the New York City Tax Commission. If you receive a reduction, it could mean big tax savings for every shareholder or unit owner in the building. Thousands of co-op and condo boards appeal their tax assessment each year; of those, about a third succeed in paring down the bill.

How Your Property Is Assessed

Each year, every parcel of real estate in New York City is reassessed. The Property Division of the Department of Finance calculates the market value of each building by one of three methods: comparable sales, "reproduction cost" minus depreciation or capitalization of income. For many years, comparable method was most commonly used for co-ops and condos. Within the past few years, however, the city has favored the income-capitalization method, which is based on how much income the building would generate were it a rental property. The city then computes market value by capitalizing the net income before interest, amortization of mortgage and depreciation. The capitalization rate depends on the type of building, its age and neighborhood. The "reproduction cost" method is used only for certain unusual buildings that could be described as "specialties."

Once the market value has been determined, and any abatements or exemptions subtracted, a formula is used to determine the building's tax liability. Class II properties, which include all residential buildings of four units or more, are assessed on the basis of 45 percent of market value. The current tax rate for Class II properties is 9.91 percent, up significantly from 8.85 percent in 1981. Thus, a building whose full market value is $10 million would pay a real estate tax of 9.91 percent multiplied by $4.5 million or $455,950.

Increases or decreases in assessment are phased in over a five-year period, to soften the blow of the increased tax bite. For example, if a building's assessment goes up from $100,000 to $150,000, the $50,000 increase will be phased in at the rate of $10,000 per year. The "transitional" assessment value for the first year would be $110,000 with an "actual" assessment value of $150,000. The building pays taxes based on the transitional assessment, which is increased by $10,000 per year until it reaches the actual value of $150,000.

If the assessment goes up again in the following year by another $25,000, that creates an additional $5,000 per year phase-in for the next five years, which is added to the existing $10,000 until the full new assessed value of $175,000 is reached.

Only three years ago, most buildings were paying on transitional assessments. Today, approximately 60 percent are still paying on transitional assessments, says certiorari attorney Eric Weiss, who handles over six hundred assessment challenges a year from his midtown office. This is due to the fact that in recent years, with real estate values dropping, many buildings have actually experienced assessment reductions.

"In a rising market," says Weiss, "you're not paying based on the actual assessed value, you're paying on something less than that [that is, the transitional assessment]. In a falling market, your taxes may still be going up over previous years, but you'll still pay no more than taxes based on the actual assessed value of the property."

Weiss stresses that although assessments are coming down, buildings should still challenge them annually. "Many co-ops, especially on the East Side, were hit hard with assessment increases in the eighties," he points out. Thus, many deserve reductions now that property values have dropped. Even if your building's new assessment is lower than last year's, it is still possible to get a further reduction by challenging it.

The numbers speak for themselves. In the building cited above, valued at $10 million, a $1 million reduction in market value would not be out of the question in today's market. That would produce a tax savings of 9.91 percent multiplied by $450,000, or $44,595. This savings would be divided among all unit owners or shareholders, less the lawyer's fee of perhaps 25 percent, or $11,148.75. If there are one hundred units in the building, that represents a net savings of approximately $335 per unit. Done consistently, challenging the building's tax assessment can save owners thousands of dollars over the course of their ownership.

Who Challenges Your Assessment?

If your building decides to challenge its assessment, members of the board may opt to hire an attorney who specializes in reducing assessments. They are called "certiorari" attorneys, from the Latin word that refers to case review. They generally work on a contingency basis, for a predetermined percentage of the reduction, or sometimes on a straight fee basis. It is not mandatory, however, to hire a certiorari attorney; some cases are presented by tax consultants, building managers, board members or a shareholder representing the building.

"Boards may not be aware they can bring their own case," says Glen Borin, the counsel to the City Tax Commission, the quasi-judicial body that holds reassessment hearings, and that is staffed mostly by appraisers, not attorneys. "It's not out of the question for a two hundred–unit high-rise to do it themselves," he adds.

Not everyone agrees—particularly lawyers. "You can't afford to do it yourself," scoffs attorney Stanley Dreyer, a partner with Gallet Dreyer & Berkey and co-chair of the Committee on Condos and Co-ops of the New York State Bar Association. He doubts that an amateur would be able to successfully maneuver through the application procedure, the rounding-up of financial statements and the haggling with city agencies. "They'll run you ragged," he says.

Telling It to the Judge

According to professionals, the process of challenging a high assessment can be very simple—or very complicated. Daily hearings, which are held in Room 910 of the City Tax Commission headquarters at One Centre Street, begin in late January, and may run all the way through August. A single hearing officer considers the case, and a decision is typically made on the spot. Winners have fifteen days to accept the offer of reduction—which can slice anywhere from 3 percent to 40 percent off the tentative tax assessment. Those who are dissatisfied with the offer, or unsuccessful in their appeal, may take their case to the New York State Supreme Court.

"In some cases, we don't find a receptive audience at the Tax Commission," says Isaac Sherman of the law office of Moroze, Sherman, Gordon and Gordon, an office that handles assessment challenges. At the Supreme Court level, litigants must first talk it out at a pretrial settlement conference with the Corporation Council of the City of New York.

The appeal must be made by October 24, and disbursement costs for the client must be considered. The state requires challengers to purchase an index number, which costs $170, and a calendar date for $75. An appraisal report can run anywhere from $3,500 to more than $10,000. However, an appraisal is not a prerequisite at this hearing.

"Some cases are successful immediately," Sherman says, "and for others, several years have to go by until there is a fair adjustment."

Other Sources of Information

The Tax Information Line, provided by the Finance Department, is a catalogue of recorded information concerning real estate taxes. There you can obtain information such as this year's rates and how real estate taxes are evaluated. Message 126 explains how to appeal your tentative assessed valuation through the New York City Tax Commission. The phone number is (718) 935-6736.

The New York City Tax Commission counsels callers on how to appeal assessments. The number is (212) 669-4410. If you are looking for a certiorari lawyer, the New York City Bar Association and the New York County Lawyers Association operate a legal referral service, at (212) 626-7373.

Save on Estate Taxes: Set Up a Personal Residence Trust

By Aaron L. Danzig, Esq. and Christopher J. Lagno, Esq.

A new idea has come upon the co-op horizon, especially in view of a recent ruling by the IRS: Create a trust that will own your apartment, permitting you to live in it for a period of years, after which the ownership passes to your children (or any other family members who you want to select). The result is a dramatic reduction in gift and estate taxes. The idea behind this legal maneuver is that when you give away a future interest in something, the gift is worth a lot less than if you give the asset away now.

Let us explain. Say you own a cooperative apartment worth a million dollars. You hold onto it until you die. In comes Uncle Sam and says to your kids, "OK, you owe us estate taxes on a million dollars." That can be a stunning sum: as high as $550,000, depending on the tax bracket of your estate.

Now, instead of doing that, you turn to your children today and say, "I give you my entire interest in my apartment fifteen years from now. Meanwhile, I reserve all rights to it, including, of course, the right to live in it."

Reduced Tax on Future Interest

We must stop here and explain that there is a tax on everything you give away while you are alive. The rates are exactly the same as the estate tax rates that your estate would have to pay on the property if you didn't give it away. The simple logic of the government is that if they don't tax gifts during your life, you'll give it all away and there'll be nothing to tax when you die.

So the question now is, what is the amount of the gift that you have made? You must pay a gift tax on that amount (there are certain annual gift tax exemptions, $10,000 per person, but they have only a minor effect when you're making a major gift). The answer: only a fraction of the million-dollar value of your apartment.

Here, too, a simple logic applies: If I give you a million dollars today, it's worth just that, but if I say to you that I'll give you a million dollars fifteen years from now, that's like saying, I'm really only giving you $250,000, or some other sum, that if safely invested, will bring you a million dollars fifteen years from now. This is called a "future interest" and the IRS provides tables that show you the value of future interest in this sort of situation. If, for instance, you consult the table and want to find the present value of a gift by a person age sixty of a million dollars, effective fifteen years from now, you will find it to be in the area of $250,000.

So now, in the example given, Uncle Sam comes in and says, "Pay the tax on that gift," and your answer is "OK. The gift has a value of only $250,000." It doesn't take long to figure out that you have saved the estate tax on the difference between $250,000 and $1,000,000—a tax savings of roughly $412,000, if your estate is in the maximum bracket.

To pursue this strategy, you need a lawyer. That's because the way to create a future interest in this situation is by creating a trust, or more particularly, what is known as a qualified personal residence trust. The manner of setting up such a trust is explained in the Internal Revenue Code and regulations, and you would be foolhardy if you attempted it without legal assistance.

What's the Catch?

You can create such a trust in a cooperative apartment and, in fact, in almost any type of single-family residence, and we think you can see that in the type of arrangement we have described, you have a triple benefit. You have done what you would have done anyway: given your apartment to your children at a future time. But by doing it through a trust, you are saving a whopping amount of taxes, while retaining all the benefits of being a co-op owner, such as the right to deduct your pro rata share of the mortgage interest and real estate taxes paid by the co-op cooperation and the interest on any mortgage that you have on your individual co-op.

There is one catch. To get the benefit of the reduced amount of the gift, you must outlive the period for which you reserve all rights to yourself. If you don't, the full value of your apartment becomes a part of your estate and is taxed accordingly (with credit given for any gift taxes that you have previously paid). However, you are no worse off than if you had done nothing.

So the trick is to pick a period that you feel you will safely outlive. Of course, the shorter the period you reserve for yourself, the greater will be the value of the gift, because you are not putting it too far off in the future. While the failure to outlive the period is a risk, the possible benefit to be derived if you do outlive the period seems to be well worth the gamble.

Co-op Board Reaction

How do co-op boards react to this type of trust? First of all, we should make clear that the Internal Revenue Code, as amended a few years ago, specifically permits a trust to hold co-op shares, with no loss of benefits. Of course, you would want board approval to make the transfer to the trust, and the board may be hesitant to approve someone who will take over ten or fifteen years from now, but the answer to that is that they only have to approve the present tenant in occupancy, which is you. They can reserve their approval of the future tenant until such time as he or she takes over. Even this does not present a problem because the future tenant will probably be your offspring and most leases permit occupancy by members of your immediate family.

The fact is that co-op boards are getting increasingly accustomed to trusts as tenant shareholders, as revealed in an article in *The New York Times* on May 16, 1993 ("New Legal Wrinkles for Co-ops," by Andree Brooks).

Suppose the board doesn't approve the transfer to the trust? According to a letter ruling issued by the IRS, even this does not present a problem. In the case dealt with in the letter ruling (which is not binding on the IRS but shows the way it views particular problems), the co-op board refused to approve the transfer. The tenant shareholder nevertheless assigned his interest in the apartment to the trust and held title as nominee for the trust. This was good enough for the IRS, who treated the transaction as an effective transfer to the trust, with all of the benefits described above.

If the period that you reserve for yourself runs out and you have survived it, the apartment belongs to your children, assuming they are the ones to whom you have made the gift. What you have to do at that time is to enter into a lease with your children to rent the apartment at fair market rent. If you don't, there is the danger of the entire value of the apartment falling back into your estate when you die. Does this present a problem? To the contrary, it is a way of channelling funds to your offspring and correspondingly reducing your estate. It is true that subleases ordinarily require board approval, but once again, you are the occupant of the apartment and the proprietary lease permits it.

Building-Wide Insurance

- *How much insurance*
- *Reducing premiums*
- *Protecting board members*

Buying Insurance: How Much Is Right for Your Building

By Anne Gaddis-Marcus

If you live in a typical co-op or condo, one of the major items in your building's budget is insurance. Like other insurance policies in your life, it probably makes you feel secure to have it—and have as much of it as possible. But how do you know if your building has enough—or too much—insurance?

Managing agents, insurance brokers and accountants say that co-op and condo owners often don't take the proper steps in making sure that their buildings' insurance policies are accurate. They recommend that owners have their insurance policies reevaluated periodically, and their buildings thoroughly inspected, which can often result in considerable premium reductions.

Overinsuring Property

According to Oskar Brecher of American Landmark Management Corp., many owners are wasting money by overinsuring their buildings, a mistake he says stems from arbitrary methods used to determine insurance coverage. He cites as an example a building from his company's portfolio, 117 Beekman Street.

Shortly after Brecher's firm took over the management of the building, it became apparent that the property might be insured for far more than it was worth. An audit was ordered, and sure enough, the appraiser determined that the building was overinsured by about one-third, or around $15,000 per year. Brecher says that the audit ended up saving each of the twenty-six–unit owners nearly $600 annually.

"Whether a building is adequately insured or overinsured is very rarely tested," Brecher says. "Insurance is one of those things that boards just pay every year without thinking about it. And the problem with the system for insuring buildings is that often there's no system at all."

Ken Chodkiewicz, the appraiser for the Beekman Street building, agrees, and points out that he has also come across many buildings that are underinsured. "I would say between 25 and 50 percent of the buildings I look at have too much or not enough insurance," he says. "And both are mistakes."

Chodkiewicz says that the inaccuracies stem from owners' having little idea of how the numbers that make up their insurance policies were determined. "People will pick any number—the amount they paid for the building in 1926, or just some number that has been used for the last forty years," he says. "And they don't even know where it came from."

Mark Shernicoff, a CPA with Zucker & Shernicoff, and treasurer of the Council of New York Cooperatives, says buildings overspend on insurance for two reasons: first, because they don't shop around enough for the best price, and second, because they buy more than they need. "People like security, and so five million dollars' worth of insurance sounds better than one million dollars' worth," he says. "And ten million sounds even better."

How Much Is Enough?

To figure out whether one has enough, too little or too much insurance, experts suggest that owners consult appraisers to determine the accuracy of their policies and examine the structure of the building itself. Insurance policies consist of liability insurance, which protects the building owner from being sued for accidents that might occur on the premises, and property insurance, which reflects what it would cost to repair or replace the structure in case of fire, flood or other destruction. According to industry professionals, it is in the area of property insurance that most miscalculations occur.

Alex Seaman, president of Seaman, Ross & Weiner, an insurance brokerage firm, says that in the case of fire-resistant buildings, he typically recommends a minimum of $120 per square foot for insurance, subject to the inspection of insurance companies. If the building is a designated landmark, he adds, that cost can often run much higher, maybe as much as $200 a square foot.

Meanwhile, Stephen Beer, an accountant with Czarnowski & Beer, says he comes up with an insurance figure by comparing what the building is currently spending on insurance and the city's assessed market value for the building. "Of course, you first have to have some idea of what buildings in this city are worth," he says.

But Brecher points out that by using formulas alone, without having a formal appraisal and an on-site study done, owners will end up with miscalculated insurance plans. He says that if a board determines its replacement costs simply by picking a construction cost estimate and multiplying it by the number of square feet, "it doesn't work, because every building is different."

Appraisers should "come out and take a look at the building, see the quality of construction and the type of detailing the building has," Brecher says. "And then they can give you a fairly accurate estimate of the replacement costs of the building."

Chodkiewicz says that his company, GAB Business Services, recommends that every building be looked at by a professional. He agrees with Brecher that the structural elements of the building, including construction materials, air-conditioning and the amount of plumbing and finishing work, should be considered before an insurance plan is agreed upon. The amount can then be adjusted over a five-year period to keep up with inflation, he says.

According to the director of management for Walter & Samuels, his firm goes so far as measuring buildings with a tape measure to determine the proper level of insurance for the co-ops and condos they manage. "Often we find a building is insured 'full to lot' when actually many sections are set back," he says.

In the case of the Delegate, a condo on East 45th Street, he continues, "the insurance company had counted the setback, and when we subtracted those twenty-five feet, we were able to reduce their insurance premium by $8,000 a year." Other mistakes that Moran notices people making when drawing up their insurance policies are counting lobby floors as regular floors and forgetting that, in many cases, there is no thirteenth floor. Also, basements don't have true value, he says.

Walter & Samuels estimates that insurance rates for buildings are wrong about half the time. "It's because certain insurance companies, given the open market, will accept the figures, and not inspect," says their director of management.

What About Liability?

Liability insurance has its own set of difficulties when trying to determine the right amount, says Shernicoff. "It depends on how much risk you're willing to bear, and the likelihood of a settlement in a negligence litigation case," he says. "If you're negligent and it results in a death, there can be a big reward. Is $5 million enough? Is $10 million enough? A good person for the board to talk to about liability insurance is its counsel."

These experts all agree that insurance can be a tricky area that's not going to get any easier in the near future. Whereas insurance rates have been dropping for years due to increased competitiveness in the industry and some well-placed investments made during the last decade, now, due to a number of recent hurricanes and other catastrophes, many insurance companies' coffers are seriously depleted. With premiums expected to go up, professionals in the field predict that overspending on insurance will become an even more important issue.

"People have gotten lulled into thinking that insurance is under control, but the insurance companies have been devastated by three or four disasters that have happened in the last few years, and I think that's going to be reflected in the premiums fairly soon," says Brecher. "I think insurance is going to be a very hot topic again."

Comparative Shopping: Reduce Premiums and Increase Coverage

By Hilory Wagner

Cutting building insurance premiums isn't as simple as changing a deductible or lopping off certain types of coverage. But insurance is an area in which your building can save substantially if the coverage is reviewed regularly and if the board seeks out a reputable, experienced broker, preferably one who specializes in habitational insurance. In addition, the experts say, premiums can be kept to a minimum by limiting the number of claims, installing safety devices to prevent claims from arising and taking advantage of the most up-to-date comprehensive programs designed specifically for co-ops and condos.

Like any other business, insurance is a competitive industry. To see where your building stands in terms of spending, talk to other co-op and condo boards in your area, and get an idea of where your building's insurance costs rank in comparison.

Comparison Shopping

Dinnene Hallahan, a board member of her Brooklyn co-op, says such a comparison process launched her search for a new broker and policy. "While talking to other board members in our area, we found that our premium seemed quite high," she recalls. "We had a new broker give us quotes from three companies, and consequently our next plan saved us 50 percent with double the coverage." However, this package did not include directors' and officers' liability (D & O), an essential part of any co-op's policy, so the board purchased that coverage from a second carrier. Eventually, members of their neighborhood co-op league recommended another brokerage firm, which was able to provide Hallahan's co-op with equal coverage, plus D & O, for less money.

Purchasing comprehensive insurance through a specialized company can be more economical than buying standard forms. For the same cost, or even less, these packages include traditional property and liability, plus extras not seen in basic building coverage, including substantial umbrella liability protection, extended boiler and machinery insurance (which also covers air-conditioning equipment, electrical apparatus and more) and crime coverage. Harry Hicks, resident manager of Seacliff Towers on Staten Island, says he was able to increase his building's coverage by more than $2 million at a much lower premium by switching to a carrier that specializes in mid-sized cooperative buildings.

Edward Finkelstein, formerly of Versatile Insurance Programs Corp. (VIP), says the firm introduced its Cooperative and Condominium Insurance Program in June 1991. According to Finkelstein, this comprehensive program offers "the most competitive price available and the broadest coverage we've seen." The new package, offered exclusively by VIP, includes higher and more comprehensive coverage than most packages, with a broader definition of the building itself.

Jane Groveman was on the board of her Greenwich Village co-op when they decided to switch insurance companies. "We shopped around and evaluated different policies," she says. The board chose the VIP program because it gave them "much better D & O and umbrella coverage" and they were able to cut their premium costs by "about 10 to 15 percent," says Groveman.

Lower Risk Means Lower Cost

According to Robert E. Mackoul, president of Mackoul & Associates, these lower-priced comprehensive plans are available "because co-op and condo owners take more pride in their property than the landlords of apartment buildings might, and the boards make the effort to install security features and provide better maintenance." As a result, he explains, "There are usually fewer claims."

These types of buildings are a better risk for insurance carriers, and that results in lower premiums. "And if a co-op or condo fits the requirement for certain programs, they can usually save 25 to 75 percent," Mackoul notes. These requirements are basically structural and safety improvements, such as updates on electrical and plumbing systems, roof repairs and installation of sprinklers. Understandably, a fire-resistant structure is going to command a much lower fee than a joisted-masonry (or wood or brick) building.

"The key to long-term insurance savings is the prevention of claims," explains Thomas R. Kozera, C.P.C.U., president of the Co-op/Condo Insurance Agency. By upgrading what are called "life safety" factors in the building—for example, installing emergency lights in stairwells, placing smoke detectors in common areas and providing manual pull-box alarms—boards not only increase the safety of residents and protect against potential legal expenses, but might also qualify for more competitive insurance programs or credits on existing ones.

More Claims Mean Higher Premiums

In addition, a board might consider covering small claims out of its own pocket. With automobile insurance, drivers who submit numerous claims will face rising fees; the same rule applies to building coverage. "The loss history of a building greatly affects the premium. It might make more sense not to submit every small claim to insurance companies," Kozera explains. For example, if the building has a $1,500 claim with a $1,000 deductible, it might be worth it to just absorb the $500.

"Building owners should learn to view insurance as coverage for large, catastrophic claims, not every small incident," Kozera suggests. "It's easier to explain one bad loss than many small ones."

Although some types of coverage might seem expensive and unnecessary, such as earthquake or flood protection, cutting them out seems to be an unpopular idea. "Boards almost never give up coverage," notes Mackoul. "Earthquake and flood protection are profit centers for insurance companies. They sound good, but the deductibles are usually so high that the chances of clearing them are slim. But no one on the board wants to be the one to make the decision to cut out the coverage. Directors and officers can be held personally liable in a lawsuit."

In this soft market, insurance rates have been dropping, in some cases so low, according to one broker, that the carriers can't make a profit. This means a buyer's market for boards. But don't be lured primarily by a low price that could skyrocket twelve months later. Premiums can vary drastically from year to year, but boards can try asking for contracts or long-term price guarantees.

"Saving money is a long-term issue," Kozera says. "Choosing an insurance package just because it's cheap is like doing a roof repair that will only last a year. The bottom-line price should not be the main concern. Look at how the program will save money in the long run."

Avoid Insurance Lawsuits: Hold Adequate Personal Coverage

By Robert E. Mackoul

"See you in court!" A truly American phrase. Increasingly, co-op and condo boards and individual apartment owners are uttering this threat due to losses of personal property that was uninsured. Most co-ops and condos have adequate coverage to protect the building against almost any contingency, but that coverage doesn't extend into the apartment units to cover the resident's improvements, alterations or personal property. Many boards are insisting that residents provide certificates of insurance to prove that insurance is maintained.

"It's a problem that we can't sweep under the rug any longer," says Andrea Bunis, president of ABR Management. "We strongly recommend to our boards that they amend their by-laws to require unit owners to purchase adequate personal coverage." Failure to do so will ultimately lead to problems in the future, says Bunis. "When a fire destroys a $75,000 designer kitchen, the unit owner had better have insurance because the building's coverage is not going to pay for the restoration."

Very few co-op and condo owners are going to be complacent when they feel that the building should be responsible for their damages due to burst pipes, leaky air-conditioning systems and the like. Joni Stern, an underwriting specialist for The Hanover Insurance Company, a major insurer of co-ops in the New York area, states, "Yes, pipes burst and cause damages, and our obligation is to our insured: the co-op board. Our coverage conforms with the proprietary lease." This can cause big problems for the shareholders who mistakenly believe that permanent expensive alterations in their units are covered under the building's insurance. The fact is, the co-op's insurance is not going to pay for replacement of improvements, alterations, built-in units, custom cabinets, flooring or fixtures. "Even the cost of the wallpaper and paint to complete the restoration falls on the shoulders of the unit owner," Stern advises.

Because there's much that can go wrong even when there are two different insurance companies representing both the shareholder and the co-op, owners are advised to save themselves frustration, anger and the possibility of an enormous financial loss by insuring themselves properly.

"I was totally disgusted," claims Dr. Alan Langsner, a physician who spent over $150,000 improving his Park Avenue unit only to have a pipe burst and flood the apartment while he was in Europe. "I was caught between two insurance companies and nothing was getting done because of different interpretations of who was responsible for what." Ultimately, he concedes, "I should have spent ten minutes on the phone with my insurance agent somewhere along the line to make sure I was adequately covered before the claim."

So what can apartment owners do to protect their interests? First, understand that apartment owners' policies written by most insurance companies are relatively inexpensive. The following is a brief look at coverages in such a contract:

Personal Property: This is the unit owner's contents, and while this includes most types of personal property, it probably will not cover most jewelry, furs, fine arts, antiques and collectibles (these can be itemized and covered under a rider). The minimum amount companies will usually insure is $20,000. You're covered for a host of "perils" including fire, water damage and theft.

Improvements and Alterations: This is the coverage for permanent apartment additions such as kitchen cabinets, built-in wall units, carpeting, lighting, wallpaper, paint, bathroom fixtures and tile/wood flooring. The basic unit owner's policy only provides $1,000 coverage so you need to assess what improvements have been made to the unit and increase this coverage to an amount that will enable you to restore the unit.

Loss of Use/Additional Living Expense: If your apartment becomes uninhabitable because of fire, severe water damage or any other covered claim, this coverage will provide for the extra cost of living elsewhere (hotels, rentals) and any other extra expenses you incur.

Comprehensive Personal Liability: This protects you and your household family members against lawsuits due to injuries to other people or damage to their property. You are protected away from your premises as well (for example, you injure someone while participating in sports, or your dog bites someone on the street). The standard unit-owner policy provides for $100,000 of liability insurance, which may be increased for a minimal premium.

Loss Assessment: If the building doesn't have adequate insurance to pay for property damage or a liability lawsuit, and apartment owners are assessed, this will cover your assessment amount.

The co-op/condo unit owner's policy is a package policy, and premiums can vary depending on the amount of personal property, improvements and alterations, and any additional coverages taken. A basic policy insuring $25,000 of personal property and $25,000 of improvements and alterations, with a $250 deductible, should be about $250 a year. Options can add to the price. Expect to pay about 20 percent extra for "guaranteed replacement cost," a rider that pays the cost to replace older items at today's prices. Add another 25 percent for "off-premises theft," which covers property stolen away from your unit (for example, your luggage while traveling or your bicycle while you buy a loaf of bread).

Because of sheer neglect, many co-op and condo owners have not updated their older policies or purchased the right coverage. All it takes is one bad experience leading to a lawsuit to make boards insist that owners insure themselves properly. In the words of Michael Abeloff, managing director of PRC Management, "If both boards and unit owners would exercise an ounce of prevention, it would be worth a pound of cure."

Directors' and Officers' Insurance: Be Sure Your Co-op Carries It

By Samuel Schiff

Congratulations! You've been nominated as a member of your building's board of directors. You know that the rewards are few and the headaches many. Still, you have a vested interest in the building and you want to be a good neighbor, so you accept. But suppose something happens and there's a lawsuit against the board. Will you be held personally liable?

While there are many people ready, willing and able to serve on building boards, there exists a real fear among some that in the event of a serious problem or dispute, they could be faced with a lawsuit. That problem, according to a number of insurance agents and brokers, can be significantly reduced or eliminated if the building has directors' and officers' (D & O) liability insurance.

What Does D & O Cover?

The D & O policy is designed to protect the co-op board or condo association against financial loss due to indemnification of a board member. It also protects board members against personal liability lawsuits. The policy does not insure against negligence claims that may arise from slips and falls, water damage to the property of others or suits that may be brought against a board. Those situations are covered by the building's general liability policy.

"The importance of D & O liability insurance for those serving on the board of a co-op or condo can't be stressed enough," says Barbara Strauss, vice-president of the Owens Group, a New York–area insurance agency. "Knowing that such a policy is in place enables the board members to do their job properly without fear of a costly lawsuit."

Strauss notes that there are many different types of complaints that may be lodged against those running a co-op or condo. Her list includes complaints about poor judgment in the conduct of the association's affairs, misleading representations to unit owners, acts of bad faith, mismanagement of funds, failure to collect assessments, breach of loyalty, failure to obtain competitive bids and lawsuits involving board members and the sponsor.

"The nation's litigious society presents a major problem to all kinds of organizations, and co-op and condo boards are no exception," says Nancy Gelardi, vice-president of Gallagher Newman, insurance brokers. "Thus D & O liability insurance is a must. While most of the suits are settled out of court or prior to trial, it's the defense expense that is the costliest part of any settlement process. It's not unusual or out of the ordinary to see defense costs running into the six-figure range," she says. She agrees with Strauss that potential board members should make sure that a D & O policy is in place before agreeing to serve.

All Policies Are Not Alike

While it is possible to obtain D & O liability coverage as part of a package policy for co-ops and condos, very often a board may be better served by going with a more specialized policy. "Many boards do not realize that all D & O liability insurance policies are not the same," says Allyson Martin, senior account executive with Distinguished Properties Associates, a division of Douglas Elliman. "For example, the D & O liability coverage contained in a special multiperil policy is more limited than the coverage provided in a stand-alone D & O liability policy. A stand-alone policy will typically provide coverage for claims arising from wrongful termination and discrimination, whereas the coverage is typically excluded when the D & O liability is included in a special multiperil policy," she points out.

"When purchasing D & O liability protection, boards should be aware that each policy differs significantly from one company to the next," says Strauss. "Each company has its own terms and conditions and each policy should be reviewed carefully before a decision is made. By going with a more specialized policy, the board can get protection over and above what is available from the standard policy, and if there is something unique about the building, its tenants and the board, these concerns can be addressed in a special policy," she explains.

When choosing a policy, boards should question the insurance agent or broker to make sure that adequate and proper coverage is available for the board of directors. "Although D & O policies contain exclusions, certain companies have the ability to delete them and give the board the coverage it wants," says Strauss.

How Much Coverage?

Unlike an automobile policy, where a good driving record can reduce premiums, such is not the case with D & O policies. "The amount of the premium is determined by the breadth of the coverage," says Gelardi. "The more that's covered, the higher the premium." Normally, she notes, D & O policies start with one million dollars' worth of coverage. However, depending on the size of the building and other factors, a figure of $5 million coupled with an umbrella liability policy that provides still higher coverage may be advisable. "If the building is especially unique or highly visible, insurance programs are available with up to $20 million in D & O liability coverage," she says.

According to Martin, "Directors and officers should focus on more than price when they consider their building's insurance program." The decision should also include the financial strength and reputation of the insurance company, the policy limits, the deductibles that may be available, the broadness of the coverage that is offered and the quality of service offered by the broker.

While there has been a decline in the number of companies writing D & O liability coverage for co-ops and condos in recent years, "there should be no problem in purchasing the coverage your building needs," says Gelardi. Strauss agrees, adding, "Litigation costs as well as indemnification, especially in the New York area, have caused several insurance carriers to withdraw from the marketplace, while others are requesting rate increases when the policies come due for renewal. Nevertheless, D & O coverage is available."

Professionals agree that co-ops and condos, regardless of their size, need adequate insurance coverage, including general liability coverage and D & O liability for their board members. This coverage will not only protect board members, but ensure that the building has the most capable people serving on its board, knowing that they can make their decisions without fear of facing personal liability.

Insure Against Pollutants: Toxic Contamination Is a Building Risk
By Tod C. Powers

The unmistakable odor of fuel oil is strongly present in your building's basement. An investigation of the boiler seems to show no sign of a problem. Baffled, you call in your heating contractor. The smell is discovered to be fuel oil seeping in through your foundation wall. How many gallons are in the ground? Is it your oil? How far has it traveled? Your heating contractor calls an environmental clean-up company and you call your insurance broker.

Many pollution exposures exist in the real estate business: stored fuels and chemicals, asbestos and new energy construction that creates air-quality problems. Moreover, who knows what dangers exist from past tenants and owners, or the land itself, which may have had pollutants before the facility was even built?

Over the last five to ten years, your insurance broker would have commonly answered your call by telling you that "pollution is excluded from your policy." This unfortunate fact is the result of legal attacks on past pollution coverage language. The old language included pollution liability arising out of "sudden and accidental" occurrences. Courts liberally ruled that years of contamination were nonetheless "sudden and accidental," and the insurance industry moved to protect itself by excluding pollution in a more absolute fashion. The current modified and "improved" pollution exclusions are thought to be ironclad.

However, pollution liability coverage is beginning to reemerge. Recent U.S. government mandatory requirements of insurance coverage for marketers using underground storage tanks (soon to be expanded to nonmarketers) has brought some major carriers back into underwriting pollution coverage.

This limited availability is still complicated by restrictive language and a difficult application process. You may be required to spend thousands of dollars per location for environmental assessments before coverage is offered. Plus, any location found to have existing contamination will be excluded. Many recent applicants who have pursued a pollution liability premium quotation subsequently decided the policy was too costly, the application process too difficult and the coverage too limited to warrant the purchase.

Still, the pollution liability market is changing rapidly in both the types of coverage available and the cost of premiums. A call to your insurance broker should determine whether your specific need can be addressed and what will be required before a policy can be purchased.

Whether coverage is available or not, basic risk management techniques are still recommended to the prudent property owner or manager. Analyze your exposure, then eliminate or control that exposure.

Areas of Concern

Fuel Storage: How old is your tank and should it be replaced? Can an underground facility be converted to above ground? Fuel use versus delivered volume should be monitored as often as possible (a twenty-gallon leak is less expensive than a thousand-gallon leak).

Asbestos: Identify and monitor all asbestos and find out whether it should be removed or encapsulated.

Air Quality: Is there enough air exchange in the building to avoid health problems? Are you aware of what your maintenance people may be releasing into the air of this closed environment?

Contamination: You should complete an environmental assessment of property you intend to purchase—will the use of your property create a pollution exposure?

The expertise to help you with the risk management effort can be found in a number of areas: your insurance broker's loss control division, environmental consultants, fuel and chemical suppliers, material safety data sheets and your own maintenance and engineering staffs. Thoughtful precaution and professional guidance may make a property more eligible for insurance protection.

About the Authors

Sam Adler
Mr. Adler is a freelance writer living in New York City.

Steven M. Alevy
Mr. Alevy is a vice president with Bankers Capital, a firm that specializes in obtaining underlying cooperative mortgages through the secondary lending markets.

Robert B. Anesi, Esq.
Mr. Anesi, a former Manhattan assistant district attorney, is a partner with the law firm of Aborn & Anesi in New York City.

Alvin I. Apfelberg, Esq.
Mr. Apfelberg is an attorney based in New York City who has represented over two hundred co-ops and condos and written and taught extensively on co-op and condo law.

Stephen William Beer, CPA
Mr. Beer is a partner with the accounting firm of Czarnowski & Beer and a member of the Queens Borough President's Co-op/Condo Task Force and the New York State Society of Certified Public Accountants' Real Estate Committee.

Roberta Faulstick Benzilio
Ms. Benzilio is executive vice-president of the William B. May Co., a New York real estate brokerage firm.

C. Jaye Berger, Esq.
Ms. Berger, of Law Offices of C. Jaye Berger, is an attorney in New York City specializing in building construction, real estate, co-op and environmental law, bankruptcy and litigation. She has written books on both hazardous substances in buildings and interior design law.

William Brangham
Mr. Brangham is a freelance writer living in New York City.

Oskar Brecher
Mr. Brecher is managing director of American Landmark Management Corp., a residential management firm located in Manhattan.

Louise Brodnitz
Ms. Brodnitz is a freelance writer and president of Louise Dunford Brodnitz Architecture/Preservation.

Marc Broxmeyer
Mr. Broxmeyer is a principal with Bellmarc Management and a communication consultant to corporations.

Greg Carlson
Mr. Carlson is director of management services and will be an equity partner of Castle Management. He is on the board of governors of the Registered Apartment Manager (RAM) certification program of the Associated Builders and Owners (ABO) of Greater New York and the National Association of Home Builders (NAHB). He is on the board of directors of the Federation of New York Housing Cooperatives (FNYHC), a member of the Queens Borough President's Co-op/Condo Task Force and an adjunct instructor at New York University.

Victoria A. (Vicki) Chesler
Ms. Chesler is executive editor, co-owner and co-founder of *The New York Cooperator.*

Bruce A. Cholst, Esq.
Mr. Cholst is a senior attorney with Rosen & Livingston, a Manhattan law firm specializing in representation of cooperative and condominium boards.

Joseph V. Clabby
Mr. Clabby, a former New York City police detective, is president of Corporate Loss Prevention Associates, which provides investigative services for large corporations and financial institutions.

Andrea Conrad
Ms. Conrad has been a business/real estate reporter for more than twenty years. She is currently publishing a regional newspaper on relocation and tourism in the Hudson Valley.

Andrew Cursio
Mr. Cursio is a financial consultant and treasurer of his co-op board in New York City.

Aaron L. Danzig, Esq.
Mr. Danzig is a member of the law firm of Baer Marks & Upham in New York City.

Barbara Dershowitz
Ms. Dershowitz is a professional writer and president of Business Communications Workshop and B. Dershowitz Communications.

Angelina Esposito
Ms. Esposito is assistant publisher of *The New York Cooperator.*

Andrew Essex
Mr. Essex is on staff at the *New Yorker.*

Barbara S. Fox

Ms. Fox is president of Fox Residential Group, a Manhattan real estate brokerage firm that caters to buyers and sellers of cooperatives, condominiums and townhouses. She has been a Manhattan broker for twenty-two years.

Anne Gaddis-Marcus

Ms. Gaddis-Marcus is a freelance writer living in New York City.

David A. Goldstein, Esq.

Mr. Goldstein is an attorney with thirty-four years' experience as a litigator and is a former New York County prosecutor specializing in commercial and real estate litigation.

Marilyn L. Herskovitz

Ms. Herskovitz is executive vice-president of Ambrose-Mar Elia Co. She has twenty years' experience as a real estate broker and has served as executive vice-president of three residential real estate firms in New York City.

Christina Johnson

Ms. Johnson is a reporter for the *News Tribune* in Woodbridge, New Jersey.

Leslie Kaminoff

Mr. Kaminoff is president and chief executive officer of AKAM Associates, a residential management firm located in Manhattan.

Mark Klein

Mr. Klein is a project engineer with Haven Technical Associates, specialists in commercial and residential heating systems, energy conservation and co-generation.

Gary Q. Kokalari

Mr. Kokalari is a financial consultant with Merrill Lynch in New York City and a specialist in financial management for cooperatives, condominiums and commercial properties. He is also president of his co-op board.

Richard L. (Dick) Koral

Mr. Koral is director of the Apartment House Institute of New York City Technical College.

David Kuperberg

Mr. Kuperberg is president of Cooper Square Realty, a Manhattan-based property management firm.

Alex Ladd

Mr. Ladd is a freelance writer living in New Jersey.

Christopher J. Lagno, Esq.

Mr. Lagno is a member of the law firm Baer Marks & Upham in New York City.

Peter I. Livingston, Esq.

Mr. Livingston is a senior partner in the law firm of Rosen & Livingston in New York City, which specializes in representing cooperatives and condominiums.

Chris Luongo

Mr. Luongo is a columnist for *The Hour*, a daily newspaper in Norwalk, Connecticut.

Robert E. Mackoul

Mr. Mackoul is president of Mackoul & Associates, an insurance agency specializing in co-op and condo coverage.

Peter R. Marra

Mr. Marra is president and owner of William B. May Company, a New York City real estate brokerage firm.

Paul Millman, PE, RA

Mr. Millman is a principal with SUPERSTRUCTURES, a New York City engineering and architectural firm that emphasizes building rehabilitation and repair. He is both a professional engineer and a registered architect.

Patrick Niland

Mr. Niland is managing partner of First Funding, a brokerage firm that has specialized in underlying mortgages since 1987. Hew has written two books about refinancing underlying mortgages as well as numerous magazine articles on the subject.

James J. O'Brien

Mr. O'Brien is president of Rockmills Steel Products, a forty-year-old manufacturer of commercial boilers and tanks located in Queens.

Tod C. Powers

Mr. Powers is a senior vice-president of Kaye Insurance Associates in New York City.

Duke Ratliff

Mr. Ratliff is a writer living in Manhattan.

Laura Rowley

Ms. Rowley is editor-in-chief of *Multi-Housing News*, a national magazine for builders, developers and property managers.

Stuart M. Saft, Esq.

Mr. Saft is a partner with the law firm Wolf Haldenstein Adler Freeman & Herz, has written eight books and over two dozen articles on real estate and is chairman of the Council of New York Cooperatives.

Samuel Schiff

Mr. Schiff is a freelance writer living in New York City who specializes in insurance and finance. He is also on the board of his co-op building.

Craig Schiller, Esq.

Mr. Schiller is an attorney with Schiller & Associates, PC, a Madison Avenue law firm that provides problem-avoidance and problem-solving advice to condominium and cooperative boards.

Paul Schreyer
Mr. Schreyer is a partner with the law firm of Postner and Rubin, specialists in construction law.

Ed Serken
Mr. Serken is the former associate editor of *The New York Cooperator.*

Robin Shamburg
Ms. Shamburg is a freelance writer living in New Jersey.

Mark B. Shernicoff, CPA
Mr. Shernicoff has held every corporate office on the board of directors of his 170-unit cooperative during his years of service. He is treasurer of the Council of New York Cooperatives and regional vice-president of the National Association of Housing Cooperatives (NAHC). Mr. Shernicoff is a CPA and a partner in the accounting firm of Zucker & Shernicoff, which represents over one hundred co-op and condo buildings. He is a frequent speaker on issues relating to cooperatives and condominiums.

Kate Shogi
Ms. Shogi is an associate director of research at Thirteen/WNET, the public television station in Manhattan.

Jill Smith
Ms. Smith is vice-president of finance at AKAM Associates, a residential management firm located in Manhattan.

Robert D. Tierman, Esq.
Mr. Tierman is a partner in the New York City law firm of Salon, Marrow & Dyckman, and represents the boards of approximately fifty cooperatives and condominiums in and around New York City.

Allen M. Turek, Esq.
Mr. Turek is a partner in the Manhattan law firm Schiff, Turek, Kirshenbaum, O'Connell, LLP, specializing in real estate law, particularly cooperative and condominium issues.

Hilory Wagner
Ms. Wagner is a freelance writer.

Gregg Winter
Mr. Winter is president of Winter & Company mortgage services, a firm specializing in the placement of cooperative underlying mortgages.

Glossary of Terms

Following is a list of words found in the text of this book, with brief definitions. Please note that these are layman's definitions and are not intended to be used for technical or legal purposes. As always, if you need specific legal or technical definitions, consult an experienced professional.

Adjustable rate – A mortgage interest rate that fluctuates on a periodic schedule—every one, three or five years, for example—and is tied to the prime lending rate or some other index at several percentage points above.

Amenities – Those attributes that a building or apartment has to offer above and beyond the usual, such as a doorman, swimming pool, rooftop deck, health club, valet or other luxury services.

Arbitration – An alternative form of conflict resolution designed to keep feuding parties out of court. Binding arbitration is an exchange between two parties in conflict before a licensed arbitrator who will then make a decision based on the facts presented. The parties, once they agree to enter into arbitration, are bound to abide by the arbitrator's decision.

Arrearages – Any overdue financial obligations, generally referring in co-ops and condos to overdue maintenance fees or common charges.

Assessed value – The value attributed to a piece of real estate by the city of New York for the purposes of assessing real estate taxes. There are several different methods of assessing buildings and the assessment can be challenged in court.

Assessment – A one-time charge (which may be billed all at once or over a period of several months) by a co-op or condo to its shareholders or unit owners to cover the cost of any over-budget item that the maintenance fees or common charges do not already cover. Usually used to pay for capital improvement projects.

Balloon mortgage – A nonamortizing mortgage that requires the mortgagee to pay only the interest portion (not the principal) to the bank on a monthly basis. At the end of the mortgage term, the principal, which remains the same throughout the term of the loan, is due in full.

Balustrade – A row of upright supports topped by a rail.

Bid – A proposal from a contractor or any vendor or service company to perform a

219

specified task for a specified price.

Board approval – When purchasing a cooperative apartment, the potential buyer must go through the board approval process, submitting an application and financial statement and participating in a personal interview. The board must approve the buyer in order for the sale to take place.

Board of directors – Like any corporation, a cooperative corporation is run by an elected board of directors that has the right and duty to make financially responsible decisions about the operation of the co-op.

Board of managers – The condo equivalent of a board of directors.

Budget – The total amount of money an entity spends in a given time period. In co-ops and condos, the annual budget includes all the expenditures the building will have to make in the course of the year.

By-laws – One of the governing documents of a cooperative or condominium.

Capital expenditures – Money spent on long-term projects to upgrade the building, including boiler replacement, window replacement, lobby renovation, and so on.

Capital improvements – Long-term upgrades made to the building's physical plant.

Certificate of occupancy – A certificate issued by the New York City Department of Buildings giving an owner the legal right to use a specific space for a specific purpose, as stated in the certificate.

Certiorari – An area of tax law specializing in the assessed valuation of real property. Certiorari attorneys are often hired by co-ops and condos to challenge their

real estate tax assessment in an effort to reduce real estate taxes.

CIRA – Common Interest Realty Associations, another name for the type of group ownership that includes co-ops and condos. CIRA guidelines, affecting co-ops and condos, were issued by the American Institute of Certified Public Accountants (AICPA) in 1992, calling for an assessment of the useful life remaining in a building's major components and a cost proposal and projection for any anticipated repairs or upgrades.

Code violations – Any building conditions that do not meet the requirements of the New York City Department of Buildings' Building Code or other applicable municipal and national codes, such as the New York City Housing Maintenance Code or Fire Prevention Code.

Common charge – The monthly fee charged by a condo to its unit owners to cover the costs of operating the common elements of the building.

Condominium (condo) – A building or complex divided up into residential units owned separately as real property by the individual residents. The common areas, including the costs of operation, are shared by the owners.

Conversion – The process by which a rental building is transformed into a cooperative or condominium.

Cooperative (co-op) – A corporate form of building ownership, governed by a board of directors, under which the shareholders jointly own the property and lease themselves residential units within it.

Debt service – The cost of paying for your debt (that is, interest payments).

Default – Failure to meet the financial obligations of owning property (that is, failure to pay off a co-op loan, condo mortgage, maintenance fees or underlying mortgage on time).

Directors' and officers' (D & O) insurance – An insurance policy that protects corporate directors and officers, while they are in office, against monetary damages incurred through lawsuits resulting from their actions as board members.

80/20 rule of the Internal Revenue Code – IRS Code Section 216, which states that in order to retain homeowners' interest rate tax deductions on mortgage payments, no more than 20 percent of a co-op's annual income can come from sources other than shareholders.

Errors and omissions insurance – An insurance policy that insures professionals, such as residential building managers, against monetary losses resulting from mistakes made that cost their clients money. The policy will reimburse a building if it is found that the insured manager made an error costing the building money.

Escrow account – A bank account set up to put aside money that is legally intended for a specific purpose.

Facade – An exterior wall of a building, facing a street, court, garden or other public space.

Fannie Mae – The Federal National Mortgage Association, a government lending organization.

FDIC – The Federal Deposit Insurance Corporation, the government-established insurance fund that protects bank deposits.

Fiduciary duty – The responsibility of being entrusted with other people's property, as in the duty of co-op or condo board members to act responsibly and in good faith in their decision-making on behalf of their fellow shareholders and unit owners.

Fixed rate – An interest rate that does not fluctuate, but is locked in throughout the term of the loan.

Flashing – An impermeable membrane, often sheet metal, used to waterproof the junctures between adjacent building components.

Flip tax – A fee charged by a co-op or condo when a unit changes hands.

Floating rate – See adjustable rate.

Foreclosure – The act of terminating a mortgage and repossessing a piece of property when a mortgagee has failed to make his payments on time.

421a tax abatement – A New York City tax incentive program that provided reduced taxes to building developers who met certain requirements.

Freddie Mac – The Federal Home Loan Mortgage Corporation, a government lending organization.

House rules – Rules set by the board of a co-op or condo to govern the behavior of building residents.

Insider price – The price offered by a conversion sponsor to those rental tenants living in a building at the time of conversion. The insider price is generally substantially lower than the market price offered to nonresidents.

Internal Revenue Code Section 277 – Also known as the "country club" tax, because it applies to greens fees and other nonmember income at country clubs, this taxes member organizations on income from nonmembers. The IRS has been trying to apply this section to interest from reserve funds and rents from commercial and professional tenants in co-ops and condos.

J-51 tax abatement – A New York City building upgrade incentive program that grants tax abatements and tax exemptions to residential buildings that undergo renovation or major capital improvements.

Laddering – An investment term referring to the purchase of securities on a staggered maturity schedule to minimize interest rate risk.

Lintel – A horizontal piece spanning the top of an opening that supports the weight of the structure above it.

Maintenance fee – The monthly fee charged by a co-op to its shareholders. The fee covers the costs of operating the common elements and staff of the building and pays the real estate taxes and underlying mortgage on the building.

Managing agent – A professional hired by the owners of a building to oversee the day-to-day requirements of operating the building, including collecting rents or monthly charges, paying taxes, maintaining the physical plant and so on.

Mechanic's lien – A lien placed on a building by a contractor who has not received full payment for a job. A lien can prevent future sales.

Mediation – An alternative form of conflict resolution whereby a trained mediator sits down with two parties in an effort to work out a mutually agreeable solution to a problem.

Negative cash flow – A situation in which expenses are higher than income.

Offering plan – Also called the prospectus, this is a legal document offering securities for sale, including co-op stock and condo common interest allocations, which outlines the specifications of the property and the terms of sale.

Owner-occupied – Occupied by the owner, as in a co-op or condo unit in which the actual owner, not a subtenant, resides or which he keeps vacant for his own use.

Parapet – A low wall or railing, as at the edge of a roof.

Pointing – Raking out and replacement of the mortar between the bricks on the outside wall of a building to maintain soundness and water-resistance.

Prepayment penalty – A fee charged by a lending institution for paying off a loan or mortgage earlier than the original term states.

Proprietary lease – The document that spells out and governs the rights of a tenant/shareholder to use and occupy his unit.

Prospectus – See offering plan.

Proxy – The authority or right to act for another, or the document granting such a right. Proxies are used during co-op and condo board elections when a voter is unable to be present and gives his voting rights to another shareholder to vote for him.

Purchase money mortgage – Also known as owner financing, this is a loan note held by the seller of real property and payable by the buyer.

Quorum – The minimum number of

voters required to be present—in person or through proxy—at a meeting in order to make decisions, vote on them and have them enacted.

Real Property Law – The body of law governing the ownership and exchange of real estate.

Receivership – Being in the hands of a receiver, or one who has been legally appointed to have charge of and collect money involved in a lawsuit. When a property is in receivership, it means that the owner has defaulted on a loan, and the lender has begun foreclosure proceedings. Throughout the proceedings, which could take years, the monthly maintenance fees or common charges are collected by a court-appointed receiver.

Refinancing – The act of paying off one loan and replacing it with another. Co-ops refinance their mortgages either when they come due, and principal is still unpaid, or when interest rates have fallen and they can get a better rate, or when they need cash and can refinance the loan for a higher amount.

Resale – The sale of a piece of real estate that has been owned at least once already (that is, it is not newly built).

Reserve fund – A savings fund held by a co-op or condo to be used for capital improvements or other one-time expenses. Not intended for paying regular budget items.

Resolution Trust Corporation (RTC) – A corporation set up by the federal government to dispense with the holdings of bankrupt savings and loan institutions.

Right of first refusal – A condominium's right to refuse the sale of a unit to a buyer if the building intends to buy the unit itself.

Secondary mortgage market – Investors who buy mortgage securities from lending institutions as investments.

Self-management – Managing a building without the help of professional building managers.

Service contract – A contract with a service company for maintaining the equipment in a building. Most co-ops and condos have service contracts for major building components such as boilers, elevators and so on.

Setback – An open space between the property line and the face of a building, often occupied by a plaza or roof terraces.

Shareholder – A holder of shares and legal voter in a corporation. In a cooperative, a shareholder also holds a proprietary lease allowing him or her to live in an apartment in the building.

Sidewalk vault – A hollow area beneath the sidewalk.

Sponsor – The initiator of a co-op or condo conversion. The sponsor may already own a rental building and convert it to a co-op or condo or may buy the building from the landlord for that purpose. Because New York City law requires that only 15 percent of the building residents must agree to buy in order to make the conversion legal, the sponsor often remains a "holder of unsold shares" for many years as a voting shareholder.

Sponsor shortfall – A negative cash flow situation that arises when a sponsor owns numerous unsold apartments and the maintenance fees or common charges he must pay to the co-op or condo exceed the rental income he is able to generate.

Sublet – The renting of an apartment to a person other than the original rental tenant or, in the case of a co-op or condo, the owner.

Sublet fee – A fee charged by many co-ops and condos to either the apartment owner or the sublettor for the right to sublet the apartment. May be a one-time fee per lease or an annual fee.

Tax abatement – A government incentive program that offers reduced taxes in return for investment in building or neighborhood upgrades.

Tax assessment – The amount of real estate taxes that will be charged to a building based on the assessed value attributed to that piece of real estate by the city of New York.

Transfer fee – A fee charged by a co-op or condo upon the sale of an apartment unit.

Underlying mortgage – The mortgage held by a co-op building, which uses the building as collateral, similarly to the way a home owner takes out a mortgage against the value of his home.

Unit owner – The owner of a condominium apartment unit.

Unsold shares – Those corporate shares remaining unsold in a co-op. Since a co-op conversion only requires that 15 percent of the building residents agree to buy their units, it is possible that at the time of conversion, 85 percent of the shares may be unsold. As units are sold, that percentage is reduced. In the meantime, the sponsor is the holder of unsold shares.

Warranty of habitability – A guarantee given by a landlord to a tenant that a rental property will be maintained in a fit condition for habitation throughout the duration of the lease. In some states such a warranty is mandated by law.

Waterproofing – Refinishing the exterior of a building to close up any cracks or areas that have become porous in order to make the building resistant to water infiltration.

Workout – A mutually agreeable financial arrangement arrived at between a defaulting property owner and the financial institution holding the mortgage.

Wrap mortgage – A secondary mortgage taken out by the sponsor against the value of a co-op building.

Industry Resources and Reference Guide

Please note: This is a list of all those professionals and agencies mentioned in the book, and is not intended to be a comprehensive list of professionals serving the co-op and condo community.

Accountants

Czarnowski & Beer
Stephen Beer, CPA
555 Madison Avenue, Suite 2500
New York, New York 10022-3301
(212) 832-3317

Jacobs & Schwartz
Marvin Schwartz, partner
100 Jericho Quadrangle
Jericho, New York 11753
(516) 822-7085

Marin & Montanye
Martin M. Marin, former partner
Richard Montanye, partner
1800 Northern Boulevard
Roslyn, New York 11576
(516) 625-3700

Prisand-Newman
Norman Prisand, principal
6851 Jericho Turnpike, Suite 225
Syosset, New York 11791-4421
(516) 364-8585

Zucker & Shernicoff
Charles Zucker, partner
Mark Shernicoff, partner
1700 Broadway
New York, New York 10019-5905
(212) 956-9700

Architects and Engineers

Braxton Engineering
Charles Marino, president
220 West 19th Street, 9th Floor
New York, New York 10011
(212) 645-2600

SUPERSTRUCTURES architects and engineers
Paul Millman, principal
853 Broadway, Suite 800
New York, NY 10003
(212) 505-1133

Attorneys

Aborn & Anesi
Robert B. Anesi, Esq.
470 Park Avenue South
New York, New York 10016
(212) 684-6111

Alvin I. Apfelberg, counsel to Jacobs & Moskowitz
19 West 44th Street, 9th Floor
New York, New York 10036
(212) 688-2666

Association of the Bar of the City of New York
42 West 44th Street
New York, New York 10036
(212) 626-7373

Attorney General's Real Estate Financing Bureau
Gary Connor, chief
Frederick K. Mehlman, former chief
New York State Department of Law
120 Broadway, 23rd Floor
New York, New York 10271
(212) 416-8170

Baer Marks & Upham
Aaron L. Danzig, Esq.
Christopher J. Lagno, Esq.
805 Third Avenue, 21st Floor
New York, New York 10022
(212) 702-5838

Law Offices of C. Jaye Berger
C. Jaye Berger, Esq.
110 East 59th Street, 27th floor
New York, New York 10022
(212) 753-2080

Brown & Wood
Daniel J. Sitomer, partner
1 World Trade Center
New York, New York 10048
(212) 839-8675

Cutler & Fish
Stuart Fish, partner
708 Third Avenue, 17th Floor
New York, New York 10017
(212) 983-1199

Deutsch Tane Waterman & Wurtzel, P.C.
Marcie Waterman, partner
120 Broadway, Suite 948
New York, NY 10271-0040
(212) 766-4000

Bruce D. Friedberg & Associates
Bruce D. Friedberg
10 East 40th Street, Penthouse-45th Floor
New York, New York 10016-0301
(212) 889-1052

Gallet Dreyer & Berkey
David Berkey, partner
Stanley Dreyer, partner
845 Third Avenue, 8th Floor
New York, New York 10022
(212) 935-3131

David A. Goldstein, Esq.
230 Park Avenue
New York, New York 10169
(212) 986-9087

Graubard Mollen Horowitz Pomeranz & Shapiro
Michael A. Salberg, partner
600 Third Avenue
New York, New York 10016
(212) 818-8800

Haas, Greenstein, Cohen, Gerstein & Starr, P.C.
Dennis Greenstein, partner
57 West 38th Street
New York, New York 10018
(212) 398-7900

Hall, Dickler, Kent, Friedman & Wood
Eric Gonchar, Esq.
909 Third Avenue
New York, NY 10022
(212) 339-5400

Helene W. Hartig, Esq.
200 West 54th Street, Suite 1J
New York, New York 10019
(212) 757-8080

Jacobs Zinns & Braff, P.C.
Jay Zinns, partner
220 Fifth Avenue
New York, New York 10001-7708
(212) 684-3800

Kera & Graubard
Martin Kera, partner
8 West 38th Street
New York, New York 10018
(212) 302-2810

Kurzman Karelsen & Frank
Phyllis Weisberg, partner
230 Park Avenue, Suite 2300
New York, New York 10169
(212) 867-9500

Loeb and Loeb
Michael Beck, Head of New York Real Estate
   Department
345 Park Avenue
New York, New York 10154
(212) 407-4000

226

Moroze Sherman Gordon & Gordon
Issac Sherman, partner
521 Fifth Avenue, 34th Floor
New York, New York 10175
(212) 867-0300

Rosen & Livingston
Bruce A. Cholst, Esq.
Peter I. Livingston, Esq., partner
Morton H. Rosen, Esq., partner
261 Madison Avenue
New York, New York 10016
(212) 687-7770

Salon, Marrow & Dyckman
Robert D. Tierman, Esq.
685 Third Avenue
New York, New York 10017
(212) 661-7100

Schechter & Brucker
Howard Schechter, partner
350 Fifth Avenue, Suite 4510
New York, New York 10118
(212) 244-6600

Schiff, Turek, Kirschenbaum, O'Connell, LLP
Allen Turek, partner
750 Lexington Avenue
New York, New York 10022
(212) 980-5577

Schiller & Associates, P.C.
Craig Schiller, Esq.
598 Madison Avenue,15th Floor
New York, New York 10022
(212) 688-4100

Snow Becker Krauss, P.C.
Marc Luxemburg, partner
605 Third Avenue
New York, New York 10158
(212) 687-3860

Stroock & Stroock & Lavan
Richard Siegler, partner
Joseph Giamboi, Esq.
Seven Hanover Square
New York, New York 10004
(212) 806-5400

Tuchman, Katz, Schwartz, Gelles & Korngold
Paul Korngold, partner
6 East 45th Street
New York, New York 10017
(212) 687-3747

Varet & Fink
David B. Buss, partner
53 Wall Street
New York, New York 10005-2815
(212) 858-5300

Wagner, Davis & Gold
Ronald Gold, partner
99 Madison Avenue,11th Floor
New York, New York 10016
(212) 481-9600

Eric S. Weiss, Esq.
271 Madison Avenue, Suite 1000
New York, New York 10016
(212) 986-6565

Wolf Haldenstein Adler Freeman & Herz, LLP
Stuart M. Saft, partner
270 Madison Avenue
New York, New York 10016
(212) 545-4600

Back Office and Training

The Back Office, Inc.
Harold Wolf, president
21 East 40th Street, Suite 1705
New York, New York 10016-0501
(212) 481-3434

B.J. Murray, computer specialists
Brian Murray, president
Glenn P. Murray, vice-president of sales
311 New Hyde Park Road
North Hills, New York 11040
(516) 365-3630

Realty Resources
Ben Braunstein, president
199 Jericho Turnpike, Suite 201
Floral Park, New York 11001
(516) 437-9100

Banks and Finance

Bankers Capital Realty Advisors
Steven M. Alevy, vice president
110 East 59th Street
New York, New York 10022
(212) 909-0580

Crossland Savings Bank
John E. Gunther, in-house counsel
211 Montague Street
Brooklyn, New York 11201
(718) 780-0400

First Funding, mortgage brokers
Patrick Niland, managing partner
90 Park Avenue, Suite 1600
New York, New York 10016
(212) 984-1865

Independence Savings Bank
Joseph Morgano, executive vice-president
195 Montague Street
Brooklyn, New York 11201
(718) 722-5300

Lehman Brothers
Three World Financial Center
New York, New York 10285
(212) 526-7000

Merrill Lynch
Gary Kokalari, financial consultant
1185 Avenue of the Americas, 19th Floor
New York, New York 10036
(212) 382-8500

Mortgage Bankers Association
Russel G. Matthews, president
Mark Iannone, past president
Patricia Niemas, past president
54 Shelter Lane
Roslyn Heights, New York 11577
(516) 626-7263

National Cooperative Bank
Paulette Bonano, vice-president
Sheldon Gartenstein, vice-president
Edward Howe, vice-president
Two Grand Central Tower
140 East 45th Street, 35th Floor
New York, New York 10017
(212) 808-0880

Somerset Investors Corp.
Jules Reich, president
10 Cutter Mill Road
Great Neck, New York 11021
(516) 829-9032

Winter & Company
Gregg Winter, president
174 Pacific Street
Brooklyn, New York 11201
(718) 834-1441

Brokerage–Real Estate

Ambrose-Mar Elia Co., Inc.
Marilyn L. Herskovitz, executive vice-president
770 Lexington Avenue
New York, New York 10021-8165
(212) 752-7789

The Corcoran Group
Barbara Corcoran, president
Esther Kaplan, vice-president
Jody LaMonte, vice-president
Anita Perrone, vice-president and director of public
    relations
645 Madison Avenue, 18th Floor
New York, New York 10022
(212) 355-3550

Fox Residential Group
Barbara S. Fox, president
1015 Madison Avenue, Suite 502
New York, New York 10021
(212) 772-2666

Greenthal Residential Sales Corp.
Joyce West, executive vice-president, director
488 Madison Avenue
New York, New York 10022
(212) 688-8900

William B. May Co.
Peter R. Marra, president
Roberta Faulstick Benzilio, executive vice-president
Christopher Thomas, vice-president and sales
    manager
575 Madison Avenue
New York, New York 10022
(212) 872-2200

150 Montague Street
Brooklyn, New York 11201
(718) 230-5500
397 Flatbush Avenue
Brooklyn, New York 11238
(718) 230-5500

The Prudential
MLBKaye International Realty
Marilyn Harra Kaye, president
555 Madison Avenue
New York, New York 10022
(212) 415-0400

City and State Agencies

Community Dispute Resolution Centers Program
Thomas Christian, state director
A.E. Smith State Office Building, 1st Floor
P.O. Box 7039
Albany, New York 12225
(518) 473-4160

Court Dispute Referral Centers
Michael E. Tarail, city-wide director
346 Broadway, Suite 400W
New York, New York 10013
(212) 374-8127

New York City Department of Environmental Protection
Marilyn Gelber, commissioner
Albert F. Appleton, former commissioner
59-17 Junction Boulevard, 19th Floor
Corona, New York 11368-5107
(718) 595-6600

New York City Department of Environmental Protection
Bureau of Water & Energy Conservation
Rick Gunthorpe, manager, residential water survey
   program
Jay Haas, deputy director
Warren Leibold, director of conservation
59-17 Junction Boulevard, 13th Floor
Corona, New York 11368-5107
(718) 595-6682/6643/6656

New York City Tax Commission
Glen Borin, counsel
One Centre Street, Room 936
New York, New York 10007
(212) 669-4410

New York State Attorney General's Office
Dennis Vacco, Attorney General
120 Broadway
New York, New York 10271
(212) 416-8000

New York State Department of Health
Childhood Lead Poisoning Prevention Program
Jim Raucci, program administrator
Nelson Rockefeller Empire State Plaza
Albany, New York 12237
(518) 473-4602

Toilet Rebate Program Office
16 East 32nd Street, 2nd Floor
New York, New York 10016
(212) 685-5575

Consulting

RLH Associates
Roberta Hendler
91 Payson Avenue
New York, New York 10034
(212) 567-1327

Rottenstein & Golowa, J-51 specialists
Meir Mishkoff, consultant
56 Willoughby Street
Brooklyn, New York 11201-5235
(718) 855-6110

Education and Lobbying

Action Committee for Reasonable Real Estate Taxes
Council of New York Cooperatives
Martin Karp, chairman
2112 Broadway, Suite 202
New York, NY 10023-2142
(212) 496-7400

The Apartment House Institute of New York City
   Technical College
Dick Koral, Director
300 Jay Street, M214
Brooklyn, New York 11201
(718) 260-5225

Associated Builders and Owners of Greater New York
Jerome Belson, president
Herbert Warshavsky, executive director
25 West 43rd Street, Suite 311
New York, New York 10036
(212) 921-3737

Council of New York Cooperatives
Mary Ann Rothman, executive director
2112 Broadway, Suite 202
New York, NY 10023-2142
(212) 496-7400

Federation of New York Housing Cooperatives
Charles Rappaport, president
138-10 Franklin Avenue
Flushing, New York 11355
(718) 353-5080

Institute of Real Estate Management
Nicholas Stolatis, president
Hillary Becker, past president
40 Wall Street, Room 2124
New York, New York 10005
(212) 944-9445

National Association of Home Builders
James Irvine, president
1201 15th Street, N.W.
Washington, D.C. 20005
(202) 822-0200
(800) 368-5242

National Association of Housing Cooperatives
Herb Levy, executive director
1614 King Street
Alexandria, Virginia 22314
(703) 549-5201

New York Association of Realty Managers
P. Leonard Jones, president
98 Sideview Avenue
Staten Island, New York 10314
(718) 983-6331

Queens Co-op/Condo Coalition
Chandra Jain, president
Jimmy Lanza, past president
P.O. Box 150153
Kew Gardens, New York 11415
(718) 847-0413

Rent Stabilization Association
John Gilbert, past president
Joseph Strasburg, current president
1500 Broadway, 3rd Floor
New York, New York 10036
(212) 944-4700

Elected Officials

Kemp Hannon
New York State Senator
Chairman Health Committee for New York State
Legislative Office Building, Room 707
Albany, New York 12247
(518) 455-2200

Charles Millard
New York City Councilman
City Hall
New York, New York 10007
(212) 788-7286 (City Hall)
(212) 535-5554 (District Office)

Catherine Nolan
New York State Assemblywoman
879 Woodward Avenue
Ridgewood, New York 11385
(718) 456-9492

Claire Shulman
Queens Borough president
120-55 Queens Boulevard
Kew Gardens, New York 11424
(718) 286-3000

Peter Vallone, speaker
New York City Council
City Hall
New York, New York 10007
(212) 788-7210 (City Hall)

Insurance

Distinguished Properties Associates
Division of Douglas Elliman
909 Third Avenue, 11th Floor
New York, New York 10022
(212) 350-2300

Gallagher-Newman
Nancy Gelardi, vice-president
199 Main Street
White Plains, New York 10601-3200
(914) 997-9208

Hanover Insurance Company
Joni Stern, underwriting specialist
860 Centennial Avenue
Piscataway, New Jersey 08855
(908) 457-0577

Kaye Insurance Associates, L.P.
Tod C. Powers
122 East 42nd Street
New York, New York 10168
(212) 210-9200

Mackoul & Associates
Robert E. Mackoul, president
156 Scranton Avenue
Lynbrook, New York 11563
(516) 596-0202

The Owens Group
Barbara Strauss, vice-president
619 Palisade Avenue
Englewood Cliffs, New Jersey 07632
(201) 568-2300

Seaman Ross & Weiner
Alex Seaman, president
6851 Jericho Turnpike
P.O. Box 468
Syosset, New York 11791-4421
(516) 496-7600

Versatile Insurance Programs Corp.
Steven Brenner, president and chief executive officer
1800 Northern Boulevard, Suite 216
Roslyn, New York 11576
(516) 625-4040

Maintenance

Allied Renovation Corp.
Vana Post, president
3630 37th Street
Long Island City, New York 11101
(718) 729-2480

ATC Environmental, lead consulting
Vincent Coluccio, vice-president
104 East 25th Street
New York, New York 10010
(212) 353-8280

Atlas Welding & Boiler Repair
Richard Blaser, president
2960 Webster Avenue
Bronx, New York 10458
(718) 293-3300

Compusave Fuel Systems, heat computers
Larry Zucker, president
136-61 72nd Avenue
Flushing, New York 11367-2327
(718) 268-5900

Con Edison
Bob Peterson, energy conservation specialist
Chrysler Building Conservation Center
405 Lexington Avenue
New York, New York 10017
(212) 599-3435

Ecker Manufacturing
Robert Ecker, vice-president
Sally Karpen, sales/marketing representative
1981 Marcus Avenue, Suite C116
Lake Success, New York 11042
(516) 358-1400

Ecker Window Corp.
Sally Karpen, account executive
928 Mclean Avenue
Yonkers, New York 10704
(914) 776-0000

Empire Mechanical Air Conditioning
Roy Antonoff, vice-president
111 Eighth Avenue
New York, New York 10011
(212) 924-7903

Energy Investment Systems, energy audits
Alan Tabachnikov, vice-president of construction
  management
45 West 21st Street
New York, New York 10010-6865
(212) 366-6661

M. Farbman & Sons
Fred Weintraub, licensed plumber
502 West 126th Street
New York, New York 10027
(212) 749-6000

Haven Technical Associates, Inc.
Mark Klein, project engineer
98 Sideview Avenue
Staten Island, New York 10314-3253
(718) 983-6331

Knudson Elevator
Lou Ballato, director of operations
22-05 43rd Avenue
Long Island City, New York 11101-5099
(718) 937-3780

Metrosolar, Storm Windows & Window Film
Richard Peritz, president
17 Hicks Street
Lindenhurst, New York 11757
(516) 957-9727

Optimum Applied Systems, Heat Computers
Herbert Vitel, vice-president
145 Palisade Street
Dobbs Ferry, New York 10522
(914) 693-9001

Sentry Contracting
Linda Peters, sales and marketing
202 Caton Avenue
Brooklyn, New York 11218
(718) 633-8445

Skyline Windows
Steven Kraus, current president
Richard C. Apfel, vice-president of large-volume
  sales
Vincent Rua, past president
625 West 130th Street
New York, New York 10027
(212) 491-3000

The Trane Company, HVAC specialists
333 Seventh Avenue
New York, New York 10001-5083
(212) 868-0066

U.S. Energy Controls, energy systems
Gerald Pindus, president
7840 164th Street
Flushing, New York 11366
(718) 380-1004

Management

ABR Management
Andrea Bunis, president
554 Fifth Avenue
New York, New York 10036
(212) 302-5544

AKAM Associates
Leslie Kaminoff, president and chief executive officer
Jill Smith, CPA, vice-president of finance
302 Fifth Avenue, 9th Floor
New York, New York 10001
(212) 643-2100

American Landmark Management Corp.
Oskar Brecher, managing director
555 Madison Avenue, 8th Floor
New York, New York 10022
(212) 207-8000

The Argo Corporation
Mark Moskowitz, president
Marina Higgins, vice-president
Jeff Levy, director of management
10 Columbus Circle, Suite 1400
New York, New York 10019-1301
(212) 757-5830

Bellmarc-Regal Management
Marc Broxmeyer, principal
1501 Broadway, Suite 3201
New York, New York 10036
(212) 944-5240

Bren Management Corp.
Martin Kera, president
8 West 38th Street
New York, New York 10018
(212) 302-1524

Castle Management Corp.
Greg Carlson, director of management services
111 Brook Street
Scarsdale, New York 10583
(914) 472-3434

Century Operating Corp.
Richard Barry, chief executive officer
Robert Harwood, corporate treasurer and CPA
Seven Penn Plaza, 14th Floor
New York, New York 10001
(212) 239-8800

Cooper Square Realty, Inc.
David Kuperberg, president
6 East 43rd Street
New York, New York 10017
(212) 682-7373

Elm Management
Arnold Zabinsky, president
Vincent Occhipinti, vice-president of management
1983 Marcus Avenue, Suite C-136
Lake Success, New York 11042
(516) 358-3600

Carol Ferrara Associates, Inc.
Carol Ferrara, president
80 East 11th Street, Room 405
New York, New York 10003
(212) 475-8811

Marvin Gold Management
Jeffrey Gold, vice-president
2940 Avenue X
Brooklyn, New York 11235
(718) 332-0777

The Greenthal Group
Timothy J. Fine, executive vice-president and
   managing director
4 Park Avenue, 3rd Floor
New York, New York 10016
(212) 340-9300

Heron Management
Ronni Arougheti, executive vice-president and general
   counsel
909 Third Avenue
New York, New York 10022
(212) 753-3210

J.C. Klein
Joseph Cusenza, president
Three Hanover Square, Suite 15G
New York, New York 10004
(212) 425-3001

Kreisel Management
Neil Kreisel, president
Michael Samuel, managing agent
331 Madison Avenue
New York, New York 10017
(212) 370-9200

Lawrence Properties
Asher Bernstein, president
David Zweig, director of marketing
855 Avenue of the Americas
New York, New York 10019
(212) 868-8320

Maxwell-Kates
Robert Freedman, president
9 East 38th Street, 6th Floor
New York, New York 10016
(212) 684-8282

Merlon Management
Lori Fields, director of co-op management
491/2 First Avenue
New York, New York 10003
(212) 473-6359

NRK Management
Andrea Scheff, president
1110 Second Avenue
New York, New York 10022
(212) 421-8400

Orsid Realty
Neil Davidowitz, vice-president
156 West 56th Street, 5th floor
New York, New York 10019
(212) 247-2603

PRC Management
Michael Abeloff, managing director
19 East 92nd Street
New York, New York 10028
(212) 628-9300

Pride Property Management
Glenn Kuffel, president
708 Third Avenue
New York, New York 10017
(212) 690-0800
600 Palisade Avenue
Englewood Cliffs, New Jersey 07632
(201) 567-2150

Wallack Management
Burton Wallack, president
18 East 64th Street
New York, New York 10021
(212) 753-3381

Walter & Samuels
Matthew Newman, managing agent
419 Park Avenue South, 15th Floor
New York, New York 10016
(212) 696-7123

Real Estate Research

Bold Property Information Systems
Ben Morgan, director of operations
149 Fifth Avenue, 16th Floor
New York, New York 10010-6801
(212) 673-7700

Corporate Loss Prevention Associates
Joseph V. Clabby, president
39-50 Crescent Street
Long Island City, New York 11101
(718) 786-2700

Diversified Evaluation Group
real estate appraisals
Dominic Pompeo (formerly of Pompeo and Mulle)
1801 86th Street
Brooklyn, New York 11214
(718) 234-1012

Pickman Realty Corp.
Greg Carlson, former vice-president
118-21 Queens Boulevard, Suite 316
Forest Hills, New York 11375
(718) 575-0045

Voting

Co-op Election Company
Alex Miller, president of shareholders
Joyce Miller, president of co-op communications
17 State Street, 27th Floor
New York, New York 10004
(212) 805-7000

Honest Ballot Assocation
Maralin Falik
272-30 Grand Central Parkway
Floral Park, New York 11005
(718) 279-8683

234

I N D E X

A

Abrams, Robert, 179
Accountants
    apartment evaluation and, 13, 14
    budget plans and, 66
    financial reports and, 64-65
    mortgages and, 89
Accounts payable list, 58
Accredited management organizations (AMOs), 47, 49
Accredited residential manager (ARM), 49
Accrual basis accounting, 58, 64, 68
Action Committee for Reasonable Real Estate Taxes, 190-91, 193
Adler, Sam, 33-36, 143-46, 181-85
Advisory Committee on Lead Poisoning, 185
Air-conditioning, 109, 122-23
Air quality, 211
AKAM Associates, 64
Alevy, Steven M., 87-88
Alterations, 163, 171
Amenities, 16-20. See also specific amenities
    use restrictions on, 169
    value of, 17-18
American Institute of Certified Public Accountants (AICPA), 60, 67, 72-73, 82, 84
Anesi, Robert B., 53-55
Annual audit report, 64
Annual shareholders' meeting, 29, 31.
    proprietary lease amendments and, 4
Antonoff, Roy, 109
Apfel, Richard C., 126
Apfelberg, Alvin I., 28, 35, 149-50, 156
Appleton, Albert F., 140
Appraisals
    amenities and, 17-18
    insurance and, 202
    refinancing and, 95
Arbitration, 139, 177
Architects, 135-38
Architectural amenities, 16-17
Arougheti, Ronni, 65, 66, 147, 148-49
Arrearages, 11, 69
Asbestos, 95, 211
Associated Builders and Owners of Greater New York (ABO), 48
Association of Home Appliance Manufacturers, 123
Attorney general, 145, 150
Auditor's report, 59-60
Audits, 61, 68, 132

B

Back Office, The, 52
Balconies, 19
Ballato, Lou, 110-11
Bankruptcy, 146-49
Barocas, Joseph, 121
Barry, Richard, 46, 47
Beck, Michael, 146, 149
Becker, Hillary, 47
Beer, Stephen, 11, 66, 67-69, 83, 85, 202
Belson, Jerome, 48
Bentley, John, 126

Benzilio, Roberta Faulstick, 13-16
Berger, C. Jaye, 123-25, 138-39
Berkey, David, 144, 145
Bidding process, 137-38
Blake, Dick, 111, 112
Blaser, Richard, 109, 110
Board of directors, 57-59. See also specific topics
    buying an apartment and approval of, 15-16
    collection problems and, 69
    committees of, 26, 28, 73, 103, 105
    elections, 4, 28-33
    late fees and, 162-63
    litigation and, 35-36
    meetings, 36-39
        calling of special, 35, 158
        minutes of, 11-12, 27
        preparation for, 37-38
    members
        carried away with power, 35
        communication and, 12, 39-41
        limiting liability of, 164
        roles of, 25-28
        self-dealing and sweetheart deals of, 34-36
        terms for, 4, 28
    operations of, 25-41
    quorums, 29, 33, 34, 163
    rule-making and, 158-62
    shareholders relationship with, 3, 33-36, 155
    sponsors and, 149-50
    subletting and, 172-75
    treasurer, 26-27, 63, 64, 73
Boilers, 111-14
    cathodic protection of, 111, 112
    CIRA report and, 84-85
    cleaning, 113-14, 118
    corrosion, 111
    pollution liability coverage for, 210-11
    separating hot water from, 116-17
    service contracts for, 109-10
    time controllers and, 119-20
    use of checklist for, 107, 108
    water treatments for, 111-13
Bold Property Information Systems, 10, 12
Bonnano, Paulette, 78, 79
Borin, Glen, 197
Brangham, William, 65-67, 78-80, 84-86, 108-11
Braunstein, Ben, 50, 52-53, 53
Brecher, Oskar, 70-72, 84, 85, 139, 201, 203
Bribes, 53-55, 131-32
Brodnitz, Louise, 95-97
Brown, Elizabeth Whitcomb, 109, 110
Broxmeyer, Marc, 39-41
Budgets, 65-67, 70-72. See also Reserve funds
    capital and operating, 59, 60
    capital improvements, 70
    income and, 67-69
    maintenance and operation, 68, 103-4
    managing agents role in, 65, 66
    monitoring of, 66-67

projections for the future, 65, 67
reserve planning and, 70-72
reviews of, 66
Building and grounds committee, 103, 105
Buildings, New York City Department of (DOB), 12, 109, 137
Bulous, Elizabeth, 152, 153-54
Bunis, Andrea, 206
Business Corporation Law, 3, 6, 25-27, 29
"Business judgment rule," 160-62
Buss, David, 153
Buying an apartment, 5, 9-20
    amenities as consideration of, 16-20
    bidding process and, 16
    board approval and, 15-16
    financial statements and, 10-11
    giving the building a physical and, 11-12
    postwar versus prewar, 20
    what can you afford, 13-14
By-laws, 3
    amendments to, 4, 156, 160, 162, 163-64
    board elections and, 28
    house rules and, 155
    personal coverage and, 206
    rights of inspection and, 167
    role of board members as defined by, 25, 27, 28
    rule-making and, 158-59
    subletting and, 159, 160

C

Capital budgets, 59-60
Capital expenditures, 67, 75
Capital improvements, 133-35
    budgeting and, 65, 70
    change orders, 132
    CIRA guidelines and, 84
    contract disputes, 138-39
    energy-saving, 140-41
    financing of, 62, 139-42
    reserve funds and, 73
    seeking bids for, 134-35
    supervision of, 135
Carlson, Greg, 190-91
Carter, Bill, 48
Century Operating Corp., 63-64, 78
Certificate of occupancy, 96
Certified property manager (CPM), 47, 49
"Certiorari" attorneys, 197, 198
Checklist system for preventive maintenance, 105-8
Chesler, Vicki, 1-7, 48-50
Chodkiewicz, Ken, 201-3
Cholst, Bruce, 32, 33, 158-72
Christian, Thomas, 176
CIRA guidelines, 82-86
    budgeting and, 66, 67, 89
    reserve planning and, 72-73, 75
City franchise tax, 189-90
Clabby, Joseph V., 53-55
Class I properties, 188, 190, 191, 194
Class II properties, 187-88, 190-91, 194, 196
Class IV properties (commercial real estate), 194
Collection of maintenance fees, 64, 68, 69, 172
Coluccio, Vincent, 183
Common charges, 7, 14, 17, 54, 162, 179
Common Interest Realty Associations (CIRA), 65

Community Associations Institute, 71, 98
Compactors, 104, 107, 110
Computers
    for apartment heating, 119-22
    for financial reports, 63
Condominiums, 2-3, 6-7
    cooperatives differentiated from, 6-7
    foreclosure of, 7
    governing documents of, 3-4, 158-59
    lien priority in event of foreclosure of, 6
    mortgages and, 74
    unit owners' rights, 167
Connor, Gary, 98, 99-100, 180
Conrad, Andrea, 191-95
Consumer Affairs, New York City Department of, 54
Consumer's Advantage, 130
Contracting projects, 131-42
    awarding and customizing the contract, 132-33
    change orders, 132
    contract disputes, 138-39
    evaluating bids for, 131-32
    seeking bids for, 134-35
    seeking professional advice for, 135-38
    sources of funding, 139-42
    specification book for, 134
    supervision of, 135
Contractor financing, 62
Contracts. See Service contracts
Co-op and Condo Abuse Relief Act, 34
Co-op and Condo Task Force, 178
Co-op Election Company, 32
Cooperatives, 2, 3
    business corporations compared to, 3, 5
    condominiums differentiated from, 6-7
    finances of, 59-62
    governing documents and, 158-59
    maintenance and late fees, 13-14, 67-69
    mortgages and, 74
    shareholders' rights and, 165-67
Corcoran, Barbara, 97
Corruption, 53-55, 131-32
Council of New York Cooperatives, 46, 62, 67, 72, 85, 98
CPA (certified public accountant)
    apartment evaluation and, 13, 14
    budget plans and, 66
    financial reports and, 64-65
    mortgages and, 89
CrossLand Savings, 147-48
Cursio, Andrew, 63, 67, 72-77

D

Danzig, Aaron, 13, 198-200
Davidow, Robert, 51
Davidowitz, Neil, 46-47
De Kleinman, Karen, 35-36
Delinquent payments, 70
Dershowitz, Barbara, 100-102
Dichter, William, 121
Dinkins, David, 190, 191, 192
Directors' and officers' (D & O) insurance, 204, 208-10
Direct Rental Payment Law, The, 178
Disclosure statements, 55
Domestic hot water (DHW), 105, 116-17, 118
Donohue, Antonia, 148

Dreyer, Stanley, 197
Duncraggen,The, 146-49

E

Ecker, Robert, 125
"EER" rating, 123
80/20 tax rule, 4-5, 153
Elections. *See* Board of directors, elections
Elevators, 104, 109, 123-25
Embezzlement, 58
Energy Investment Loan Program (EILP), 140-41
Engineers, 135-38
    assessments by, 11, 82-83, 89, 133-34
    bidding process and, 137-38
    fiduciary responsibility of, 136-37
    legal requirements and, 137
Engineer's report, 11, 82-83, 133-34
Environmental assessments, 211
Environmental Protection, New York City Department of (DEP), 140
Escrow Services of New York, 52
Esposito, Angelina, 50-53, 125-27
Essex, Andrew, 62-65
Evaluation of apartment, 9-13
    financial statements and, 10-11
    financing and, 13-16
    physical condition of building and, 11-12
Eviction proceedings, 156

F

Facade inspection report, 137
Falik, Maralin, 30
Falk, Ed, 44-45
Fannie Mae (Federal National Mortgage Association), 61, 97, 98, 99
Fass, Suzanne, 192
Federal Deposit Insurance Corporation (FDIC), 147
Federal Home Loan Mortgage Corporation, 87, 97, 98
Federal National Mortgage Association, 61, 87, 97, 98, 99
Federation of New York Housing Cooperatives, 46, 62, 180
Fernandez, Gail, 10, 12
Ferrara, Carole, 38
Fidelity bonds, 58
Fields, Lori, 107-8
Finance, New York City Department of, 187, 191, 195
    The Property Division of, 195
    The Tax Information Line, 197-98
Finance committees, 26, 73
Finances (financing), 57-86. *See also* Budgets; Financial reports;
    Mortgages; *and other specific topics*
    buying an apartment, 5, 13-14, 15-16
    CIRA guidelines, 82-86
    cooperative finances, 59-62
    fiscal fitness, 78-80
    refinancing, 68, 80-82, 87-92, 94, 95-100
    selling an apartment, 22-24
Financial reports, 57-59, 62-65
Financial statements, 10-11, 59-60, 67, 68
Fine, Timothy J., 44
Finkelstein, Edward, 204
Fish, Stuart, 31, 33
Foreclosures, 7, 11, 143, 145, 146, 151
Fox, Barbara S., 20-22
Freddie Mac, 97, 98, 143
Freedman, Robert, 29

Friedberg, Bruce D., 25
Fuel oil, 210, 211
Fuel storage, 211
Fuel usage, 70, 109, 117, 119-22

G

Gaddis-Marcus, Anne, 31-33, 45-48, 97-100, 201-3
Garbage compactors, 104, 107, 110
Gartenstein, Sheldon, 89, 98-99, 148
Gelardi, Nancy, 208, 209
Gilbert, Lisa, 108
Giuliani, Rudolph, 192-93, 195
Gold, Jeffrey, 47, 48
Gold, Ronald, 148
Gold, Steven, 157-58
Goldstein, David A., 168-69
Gonchar, Erich, 11
Gordon, Albert, 33
Governing documents, 3-4, 158-59, 172-73. *See also specific*
    documents
    changing, 3-4, 159-60, 162-64
    differences between condos and co-ops, 6-7
Gratuities, check policy on, 55
Greenstein, Dennis H., 11-12, 152
Groveman, Jane, 204
Gunther, John E., 148
Gunthorpe, Rick, 140

H

Haas, Jay, 128
Haggerty, J. Henry, 12
Hallahan, Dinnene, 204
Halperin, Donald, 49
Hannon, Kemp, 180
Harrison, Wayde, 177-78
Hartig, Helene, 33
Harwood, Robert, 63, 64
Haugh, William, 121
Health, New York City Department of, 181-82
Health clubs, 17
Heat computers, 119-22
Heating and heating systems, 104-5, 108, 113-17, 118-19
Heller, James, 51
Hendler, Roberta, 79, 177-78
Henry, Edward, 37, 38-39, 110
Herskovitz, Marilyn L., 20-22
Hicks, Harry, 204
Higgins, Marina, 106
Holton, Judy, 46
Honest Ballot Association (HBA), 30
Hot water, 105, 116-17, 118
House rules, 3, 4, 155-58, 169
    changing, 157-58, 159-60
    enforcing, 156-57
    gaining legal entry and, 168-69
Housing and Community Renewal, New York State Division of
    (DHCR), 49
Housing Preservation and Development, New York City Department
    of (HPD), 49

I

Iannone, Mark, 99
Income, 67-69
    additional sources of, 68-69

Income tax, federal, 61, 62
Independence Savings Bank, 101-2
Inspections, 83, 105-6
    of boilers, 114
    of books and records, 164-67
    part of the refinancing process, 95-97
    of roof, 104
Institute of Real Estate Management (IREM), 47, 49
Insurance, 70, 201-11
    directors' and officers', 204, 208-210
    errors and omissions, 58
    liability, 163, 202, 203
Interest payments, 93-94
Interest rates, 91, 92
Internal Revenue Code (IRC)
    qualified personal residence trust, 199-200
    Section 216, 4-5, 60-61
    Section 277, 61-62, 188-89
    Section 421a tax-abatement program, 189
Internal Revenue Service (IRS), 4-5
    estate taxes and, 198-200
Investments, 27, 67
    reserve funds and, 73, 75-77
    selecting the right kind, 76

J, K

Johnson, Christina, 195-98
Jones, Otis, 49
Judd, Peter H., 121
Kaminoff, Leslie, 47-48, 57-59, 101
Karp, Martin, 191, 193-94, 195
Karpen, Sally, 125
Kaye, Marilyn Harra, 9, 12
Kelman, Andrew, 181, 193
Kera, Martin, 29, 34, 35
Kesten, Audrey, 157
Kickbacks, 53-55, 131-32
Klein, Mark, 113-16
Knolls Co-op Section 1, 51
Kokalari, Gary Q., 78-79, 92-93
Kopp, Larry, 66
Koral, Dick, 103-5, 107, 111, 116-17, 118-19, 122-23, 125, 126
Kovner, Stephanie, 10, 13
Kozera, Thomas R., 205
Kreisel, Neil, 155, 157
Kuffel, Glenn, 37
Kuperberg, David, 131-32

L

Ladd, Alex, 36-39
Lagno, Christopher J., 198-200
LaGoff, Mazie, 37-38
LaMonte, Jody, 10, 12-13
Langsner, Alan, 206
Lanza, Jimmy, 145, 180-81
Late fee provisions, 68, 162-63
Law and governance, 155-88
    board control, 164-71
    legislation, 178-81
    rule-making, 158-62
    shareholders' rights, 155-62
Lead exposure, 182-83
Lead Poisoning Prevention Act, 181-85
Leaks, 105, 111, 128

Leases, proprietary, 3, 4, 155, 156, 158, 159, 160, 162, 163, 164, 167, 169-72. *See also* Sublets
Legal entry, gaining, 168-69
Legislation, 178-81
Levandusky, Ronald, 160-62
Levandusky vs. One Fifth Avenue Apartment Corp., 33-34, 158, 160-62
Levine, JoAnn, 145
Levine, Mitchel, 26, 27, 28, 50-51
Levy, Jeff, 106
Liability insurance, 163, 202, 203
Liberman, Mark, 147
Liebold, Warren, 129, 130
Lien priority, in event of foreclosure of condo, 7
Livingston, Peter I., 164-68
Loans. *See also* Mortgages
    apartment evaluation and, 10-11
    difference between condos and co-ops and, 5
Local Law 10, 137
Long-term fixed-rate financing, 92-93
Low-flow/low-flush plumbing fixtures, 105
Low-interest-rate loans, 140-41
Luongo, Chris, 105-8, 139-42, 175-81, 191-95
Lurie, Brett, 149
Luxemburg, Marc, 29-30, 34

M

Mackoul, Robert E., 204-5, 206-7
Maintenance, 65, 95, 96, 103-30
    central air-conditioning system, 123
    elevators, 123-25
    engineer's report and, 11
    preventive, 105-8, 110
    timetable for, 104-5
Maintenance contracts, 70, 83, 108-11, 123-25
Maintenance fees, 14, 57, 67-68, 91
    apartment evaluation and, 11
    collection of, 64, 68, 69, 172
    difference between condos and co-ops and, 6
    increases, 67-68
    late charges and, 68
Management firms, 6, 43-45
    board relationship with, 43
    budget plans and, 66
    choosing, 43-50
    contracts for, 5-6
    establishing priorities, 43-44
    fees and services, 45
    financial reports and, 57-59
    speaking to other clients, 44-45
Managing agents, 5-6, 89, 103
    board elections and, 29, 31-32, 34
    board meetings and, 38
    board operations and, 26, 27
    bribes and kickbacks and, 54-55
    budget plans and, 65, 66
    certification of, 48-50
    choosing, 45-48
    collection problems and, 69
    financial reports and, 57, 58
    reserve fund planning and, 71
    self-managing or, 50-51
    services to expect from, 47-48
Marra, Peter R., 16-20

Marin, Martin M., 83-84
Marino, Charles, 82-83
Martin, Allyson, 209
Martin Act, 145
Mediation, 175-78
Mehlman, Frederick K., 143, 145
Metro Group, The, 111
Milano, John A., 169
Millard, Charles, 192, 194
Miller, Joyce, 32
Millman, Paul, 135-38
Minutes of board meetings, 11-12, 27
Mishkoff, Meir, 141
Monthly statements of receipts and disbursements, 58-59
Morgano, Joseph, 101-2
Mortgage Bankers Association (MBA), 98, 99
Mortgage rates, 70
Mortgage recording tax, 81
Mortgages, 14, 15, 62, 80, 81, 87-102
    apartment evaluation and, 10
    difference between condos and co-ops, 5, 6
    floating rate, 93-94
Moskowitz, Mark, 43, 45
Murray, Francis J., 140-41
Murray, Glenn P., 53

N

Nardi, Richard, 143, 144
National Association of Homebuilders (NAHB), 48
National Association of Housing Cooperatives, 62
National Association of Realtors, 49
Neutro-Chem Company, 112
Newman, Matthew, 84-86
New York Association of Realty Managers (NYARM), 47, 49-50
New York City Council, 190-93
Niemas, Patricia, 99
Niland, Patrick, 88-92, 95
Nolan, Catherine, 194

O

O'Brien, James J., 111-13
Occhipinti, Vincent, 105-6, 139, 140
O'Cleireacain, Carol, 191
Office of Thrift Supervision (OTS), 147
Oil, Fuel, 210, 211
Oil tank cleaning, 118-19
Open accounts payable report, 64
Operating budget, 59-60
Operating expenses, 67
Osnato, John, Jr., 26
Outdoor space. See also Gardens; Roofs; Terraces
    as amenity, 18-19
    board control of, 169-72
Ownership, 1-7. See also Condominiums; Cooperatives

P

Parking, 18-19
Payroll, 66, 70
Peritz, Richard, 127
Perrone, Anita, 12, 13
Peters, Linda, 141-42
Peterson, Bob, 125, 127
Pets, 15
Pindus, Gerald, 119-20, 121

Pollution liability insurance, 210-11
Poppiti, Albert J., 50
Post, Vana, 142
Powers, Tod C., 210-11
Preventive maintenance, 105, 110
Prisand, Norman, 72
Property risk report, 10
Property tax rates, 70
Proprietary leases, 3, 155, 156, 158, 159, 160, 162, 163, 164, 167, 169-72
    amendments to, 4
    gaining legal entry and, 168-69
Prospectus, 3-4, 11, 28. See also Engineer's report
Prout, Mark, 108
Proxies, 28, 29, 16

R

Rakos, John, 128, 129, 130
Rappaport, Charles, 46, 47, 180
Ratliff, Duke, 43-45
Real estate taxes, 14, 61, 65, 70, 190-95
Real Property Tax Reform Commission, New York City, 192-93
Real property transfer (RPT) tax audit, 152
Realty Resources, 52-53
REDI reference books, 10
Refinancing, 68, 80-82, 87-92, 94, 95-100
    checklist for, 90
Refrigeration coolants, 122-23
Registered apartment manager (RAM), 48-49
Reich, Jules, 152, 153-54
Reports. See also Financial reports
    engineer's, 11, 82-83, 133-34
    facade inspection, 137
    year-to-date, 63-64
Reserve funds, 5, 57, 67, 89, 98
    apartment evaluation and, 11
    managing, 72-73
    planning and, 70-77
    strategies for, 70
Resolution Trust Corporation (RTC), 151-53
Richwerger, Kurt, 193
Roofs, 104, 117
    board control of, 169-72
    gardens on, 18, 169-70
Rosen, Morton H., 33, 36
Rothman, Mary Ann, 98
Rothschild, Walter, III, 87
Rowley, Laura, 25-30, 146-49, 187-90
Rua, Vincent, 126

S

Saft, Stuart M., 22-24, 36
Salberg, Michael, 45
Samuel, Michael, 142
Scheff, Andrea, 31, 32-33
Schiff, Samuel, 208-10
Schiller, Craig, 133-35
Schreyer, Paul, 131-32
Schumer, Charles E., 99
Schwab House, 50-51
Schwartz, Marvin, 82, 83
Seaman, Alex, 202
Self-management, 50-53
Selling an apartment, 20-24

board approval and, 6, 24
contract process and, 22-24
expediting the sale process, 100-102
ten don'ts, 21-22
ten do's, 20-21
Serken, Ed, 9-13
Service contracts, 70, 83, 108-11, 123-25
Service logs, 106
Shamburg, Robin, 119-22
Shernicoff, Mark B., 59-62, 202, 203
Shogi, Kate, 82-84, 127-30
Shuchman, Hedvah, 44
Shulman, Claire, 98, 99, 100, 145, 178-80, 181
Siegler, Richard, 189-90
Sitomer, Daniel J., 182-83
Small, Larry, 99
Smith, Jill, 57-59, 64
Somerset Investors Corporation, 152-54
Spaet, Arthur, 103
Special meeting, 4, 158
Sponsors
    bankruptcy and, 146-49
    default, 65, 143-54
    keeping an eye on, 149-50
    -owned apartments, 10-11
    subletting and, 175
Squire, Andy, 44
Stark, Martha, 191
Starr, Randy, 152
State Board of Equalization and Assessment (SBEA), New York, 190
Steam traps, 115-16
Stern, Joni, 206
"Stop-gap" strategies, 67-68
Storm windows, 19, 127
Strauss, Barbara, 208, 209
Sublets (subletting), 79, 98, 155, 157, 159-60, 172-75
    condos and co-ops and, 6
    establishing a reasonable policy on, 174
    fees, 69, 174-75
    risks of, 173-74
Sunnyside Towers Owners Corp. v. John A. O'Sullivan and Margaret O'Sullivan, 168-69
Superintendents, 103, 108
    maintenance checklists and, 107
Suthergreen, David, 120
Swimming pools, 17

T

Tabachnikov, Alan, 120-21
Tank gauge (petrometer) check, 119
Tarail, Mike, 177
Tax abatements, 61, 141.
    apartment evaluation and, 11
    421a, 189
    J-51, 11, 61, 94, 141, 188
Tax assessments, 11, 61-62, 187-88
    buying an apartment and, 15
    challenging, 197
    how property is assessed, 195-96
    information sources for, 197-98
Taxation issues, 4-5, 60-61, 187-200
Tax Commission, New York City, 187-88, 195, 197-198
Tax exemptions, 141

Tax Information Line, The, 197-98
Taxes. See also Internal Revenue
    corporate, 62, 189
    estate, 198-200
    gift, 198-199
Taxpayers for an Affordable New York, 190
Tax reform, 187-98
Terraces, 18-19, 20
    board control of, 169-72
Thomas, Christopher, 9, 11, 18, 19, 20
Tierman, Robert D., 172-75
Toilet rebate program, DEP, 140
Toilets, 128-29
    controlling the amount of water, 129
    leaks, 128
Transfers, 58
Trusts, 199-200
Turek, Allen M., 147-48, 151-54

U, V

Uniform Commercial Code (UCC) sale, 144
Universal Metering Program, 127-28
U.S. Energy Controls, 119-20
Vallone, Peter, 193, 195
Vantage Group, 130
Variable union contracts, 65
Vari Vac subatmospheric heating systems, 114-15
Vendors, 54-55
Views, as adding value to apartment, 19
Vista Window Film, 127
Voss, William, 52, 53
Voting process. See Board of directors

W-Z

Wagner, Hilory, 203-5
Waldon, Tim, 110
Wallack, Burton, 108-9
Walter, Michael, 63, 64
Warshavsky, Herb, 48, 49
Washing machines, 130
Water, 105, 116-17, 118
Water conservation, 105, 127-30
    survey, 140
Waterman, Marcie, 29
Water meters, 128
Weatherproofing, 104
Weatherstripping, 126
Weintraub, Fred, 128
Weisberg, Phyllis, 30, 36
Weiss, Eric, 196
Wesner, Robert, 37, 38
West, Joyce, 9-10, 11
Williams, Bruce, 148
Windows, 17, 19, 104, 117, 125-27
    adding value to apartment, 19
    heat loss and, 125-26
    installation of new, 125-26
    repairs and upgrades of, 126-27
Winter, Gregg, 80-82, 93-95
Wolf, Harold, 50, 52
Workouts, 144
Work permit, 137
Zasloff, Adele, 100-101, 102
Zinns, Jay, 31
Zucker, Larry, 120

Who are Vicki Chesler and Matt Kovner?

Vicki Chesler, executive editor, and Matt Kovner, publisher of  *The New York Cooperator*, have been involved in the New York City publishing scene since the 1970s and the co-op and condo community since 1980. Both are well known in the New York real estate industry as experts in the field of cooperative and condominium ownership, and have appeared on numerous radio and television shows across the country including Good Day New York on Fox Television and NY1 television news. They have been quoted in *The New York Times, The London Times, Newsday, The New York Post* and other prominent publications. They are the founders and producers of the annual Co-op & Condo Expo, a trade show and educational event held each May in Manhattan, and founders of *The New York Cooperator*, a 15-year-old monthly magazine for co-op and condo owners.

Mr. Kovner, in addition to being publisher of *The New York Cooperator,* teaches a continuing education course on co-ops and condos at New York University's Real Estate Institute and has lectured extensively on all aspects of apartment ownership. He is president of the board of his Manhattan condominium, a member of the board of directors of the Executives Association of Greater New York and a member of Associated Builders & Owners of Greater New York. He also owns a house in upstate New York.

Ms. Chesler, in addition to her role as executive editor of *The New York Cooperator,* is editor of *Co-op & Condo Ownership: The Complete Guide for Apartment Buyers, Owners and Boards,* a 250-page book covering all aspects of apartment ownership. She has spoken extensively on the subject of co-op and condo ownership as a lecturer and in the media. She is a member of the Real Estate Board of New York and lives in a condominium in Manhattan and a house in upstate New York.

What is *The New York Cooperator*?

The New York Cooperator was founded in 1980 by Vicki Chesler and Matt Kovner, currently the executive editor and publisher of this monthly magazine. *The Cooperator* was created to help co-op and condo owners, buyers and board members understand the rules and regulations governing co-ops and condos, what their rights and responsibilities are and how to effectively and efficiently run their buildings. With a readership of 60,000 in the New York metropolitan area and beyond, *The Cooperator* has kept the co-op and condo community informed on a monthly basis for the past 15 years. Articles cover topics ranging from buying and selling to management concerns to building maintenance to finance and law. *The Cooperator* is available to readers free of charge by calling 1-800-COOP404 or writing to *The New York Cooperator,* 301 East 45th Street, New York, NY 10017.

The Cooperator also produces ongoing educational seminars and an annual trade show called the Co-op & Condo Expo. Held each spring in Manhattan, the Expo features dozens of exhibition booths offering information on a wide variety of products and services for co-ops and condos, plus a series of educational seminars. The Expo is free of charge. For more information on *The Cooperator* or any of its educational offerings, call 1-800-COOP404. Information is also available on the Internet at http://www.cooperator.com.

Book and Subscription Order Form

For fifteen years, *The New York Cooperator* has been recognized as a leading source of information for board members, managing agents and apartment owners throughout the metropolitan area. Every month, the magazine features articles covering management, maintenance, finance, law, interior design and more. Join more than 60,000 people who receive *The Cooperator* free every month by returning the form below!

Free Subscription Form

Name: _____

Address: _____

City/State/Zip: _____

Phone Number: _____

I live in a Co-op: _____ Condo: _____ Rental: _____ Units in building: _____

Our Board President is: _____

Our Managing Agent is: _____

Mail or fax to: The New York Cooperator, 301 East 45th Street, NY, NY 10017
phone 1-800-COOP-404• fax (212) 682-7369

For additional copies of *Co-op & Condo Ownership: The Complete Guide for Apartment Buyers, Owners and Boards,* fill out the order form below and include $19.95 plus $3 shipping & handling and $1.89 for tax ($24.84 total). Prices for orders of more than one book can be obtained by calling 1-800-COOP-404.

Book Order Form

Name: _____

Company: _____

Address: _____

City/State/Zip: _____

Phone Number: _____

Quantity: _____ $ _____

Payment Method: Check _____

American Express: Name: _____

Account #: _____

Expiration Date: _____

Mail to: The New York Cooperator, 301 East 45th Street, NY, NY 10017